The Electronic
Superhighway

The Electronic Superhighway

The Shape of Technology and Law to Come

Ejan Mackaay, Daniel Poulin and Pierre Trudel (eds.)

Contributors:
G. Basque
K. Benyekhlef
T. R. Bruce
A. H. Caron
R. Gérin-Lajoie
J.-C. Guédon
E. Mackaay
D. Poulin
L. Press
R. S. Rosenberg
P. Samuelson
P. Trudel

Computer / Law Series 18

1995
Kluwer Law International
The Hague / London / Boston

A C.I.P. Catalogue record for this book is available from the Library of Congress.

ISBN 90-411-0135-7

Published by Kluwer Law International,
P.O. Box 85889, 2508 CN The Hague, The Netherlands.

Sold and distributed in the U.S.A. and Canada
by Kluwer Law International,
675 Massachusetts Avenue, Cambridge, MA 02139, U.S.A.

In all other countries, sold and distributed
by Kluwer Law International,
P.O. Box 85889, 2508 CN The Hague, The Netherlands.

Cover design: Bert Arts

Published in French by
Les Editions Yvon Blais (Cowansville, Quebec, 1995)
under the title
Les autoroutes électroniques - usages, droit et promesses.

Printed on acid-free paper

02-0896-200 ts

Kluwer Law International incorporates the publishing programmes of
Graham & Trotman Ltd, Kluwer Law and Taxation Publishers,
and Martinus Nijhoff Publishers.

Printed in the Netherlands

Acknowledgements

This book presents the Proceedings of a one-day conference held in Montreal on the 13th of May 1994, on the subject of *The electronic superhighway—the shape of technology and law to come*. The conference was organised by the Centre de recherche en droit public of the Université de Montréal, with the co-operation and financial support of several organisations to whom we wish to record our debt of gratitude:

- Les Éditions Yvon Blais Inc.
- *f*ONOROLA
- the Association québécoise de développement de l'informatique juridique (AQDIJ)
- the Centre de recherche informatique de Montréal (CRIM)
- The Department of Justice of Quebec
- The Department of Industry, Commerce and Technology of Quebec

In preparing the book we have incurred other debts. Mrs Mary Baker translated various papers originally presented in French. Her English translations match the elegance of the original French. We thank Professor Egbert J. Dommering and Dr P. Bernt Hugenholtz for their most helpful suggestions during the editing process. Putting the papers into a uniform camera ready format, even with computer help, turned out to be a more formidable enterprise than we anticipated. Mrs Sylvie Thériault took charge of this task with competence and equanimity.

We are very pleased to see these proceedings published in Kluwer's prestigious *Computer/Law Series* and thus presented to a world-wide public, while the French version is simultaneously published under the title *Les autoroutes électroniques - usages, droit et promesses*, by Les Éditions Yvon Blais (Cowansville, Quebec, 1995).

Ejan Mackaay
Daniel Poulin
Pierre Trudel

Montreal, July 1995

About the Authors

Guy Basque is Assistant Director of the Université de Montréal's computer services. He first studied mathematical physics and came to computer science by way of scientific calculus, before taking an active interest in the technical infrastructure. Since 1989, he has been closely associated with the different stages of development of the institutional network and with the introduction of Internet at the Université de Montréal. He is in close contact with thousands of regular users and has accumulated over the years a wide experience in the use of Internet in the university environment, particularly in matters of security, access policies as well as technical and material resources.

Karim Benyekhlef is a member of the Québec Bar since 1985. He worked as a lawyer at the Department of Justice of Canada from 1986 to 1989 and was appointed professor at the Faculty of Law of the Université de Montréal in 1989. His expertise lies in the fields of public liberties and law pertaining to information technologies. He is the author of many publications on the latter subject, including his recent *La protection de la vie privée dans les échanges internationaux d'informations*, Éd. Thémis, 1993.

Thomas R. Bruce served for several years as Director of Educational Technologies at the Cornell Law School. Two years ago he was appointed to the faculty at Cornell as Research Associate and Co-Director of the Legal Information Institute, an apparatus for pursuing electronic-publishing ventures which he co-founded with Professor Peter Martin. He is the author of Cello, an Internet browser for Microsoft Windows, which has been widely distributed and used on the Internet. An earlier project, a video documentary on the three-hundred year history of the Supreme Judicial Court of Massachusetts, was recently released throughout the public schools in the state. He holds a Master of Fine Arts degree from Yale School of Drama. He is, so far as he knows, the first faculty member at the Cornell Law School to have misplaced his JD degree somewhere along the way.

André H. Caron holds an undergraduate degree from the University of Montreal, a Master's Degree (Communication Sciences) from Boston University (1971) and a Doctorate in Education from Harvard University (1976). He is past Chairman of the Department of Communications and Founding Director of the *Centre for Youth and Media Studies*, and the *New Technologies Research Laboratory*, Université de Montréal. Research interests: programming policy; political and cultural aspects of media; children and television; the impact of new technologies on society. Recent publications: *Le défi des télévisions nationales à l'ère de la mondialisation* (edited with P. Juneau, 1992), *Analysis of the adoption of a new technology,* *the Vidéoway system* (1992); *Use of Vidéoway in 1992: Becoming part of subscriber's lifestyle* (1993); a series of studies entitled *An analysis of Canadian children's programming and preferences* (1989-1993).

Robert-Gérin Lajoie is Head of Laboratories at the Computer Science and Operational Research Department of the Université de Montréal, since 1986. He holds a Master's degree (Computer science, 1981) from the same university. Mr Gérin-Lajoie has more than 15 years of experience in computer science at the leading edge of progress, as a technical expert responsible for computer projects and team manager. Professional interests: the administration of large Unix and multi-platform networks; modern tools for distribution and access to information; implementation of multi-platform networks of Unix systems and Macintosh personal computers or Intel-MSDOS workstations; planning of TCP/IP and Appleshare networks, *routers* and cabling.

Jean-Claude Guédon (Ph.D in History of Sciences, Wisconsin-Madison University) has been professor at the Université de Montréal since 1973, initially at the *Institut d'histoire et de sociopolitique des sciences*, from 1987 on both at the programme of comparative literature and at the Department of comparative literature. Since 1987, Professor Guédon has taken an active interest in videotex (Minitel et Alex), the Internet. In 1988, he started working on an intelligent electronic magazine which was published for first time in 1991, with support from Apple Canada, the SSHRC, Université de Montréal and from the *Ministère de l'Enseignement supérieur et de la science du Québec*. Since 1993, Dr Guédon is a member of the Electronic Committee of the Canadian Human Sciences Federation/Fédération canadienne des études humaines and is in charge of its electronic server.

Ejan Mackaay has been Professor at the Faculty of Law, University of Montreal, since 1972, and is a member of the *Centre de recherche en droit public* . He has been a correspondent of the Royal Netherlands Academy of Sciences since 1986. Research interests: new technologies and law; economic analysis of law. He is a member of the Editorial Board of several journals including *Artificial Intelligence and Law*, *Cahiers de propriété intellectuelle*, *Computerrecht*, *Droit de l'informatique et des télécoms*, *Computer Law & Practice*. Recent publications: *Législation canadienne en propriété intellectuelle/ Canadian Legislation on Intellectual Property 1995*, E. Mackaay and Y. Gendreau, Carswell, 2nd ed., 1994; *Nouvelles technologies et propriété,* (E. Mackaay ed.), Éd. Thémis, Montréal, 1991.

Daniel Poulin was appointed Professor at the Faculty of law of the Université de Montréal in 1993. He holds graduate degrees both in law and in computer science. He is a member of Board of Directors of the *Association québécoise pour le développement de l'informatique juridique* since 1992. Professor Poulin is the author of many scientific publications and papers on the use of artificial intelligence and information retrieval techniques in law. His *Interpretation and legal expert systems* is soon to be published in Kluwer's Computer/Law Series. Interest in the use of large-scale networks in law has led Daniel Poulin to take charge of developing the electronic environments at the *Centre de recherche en droit public*. He has co-ordinated the creation of the first Canadian Gopher server in law, which now gives access to recent decisions of the Supreme Court of Canada.

Laurence I. Press, after working with IBM in Santa Monica, CA, and at the UCLA Western Data Processing Center, earned a Ph.D. at UCLA (in AI). He worked at the System Development Corporation Research Directorate, the University of Southern California, and the University of Lund, and as a consultant to personal computer manufacturers and software companies. He is Professor of Computer Information Systems at California State University at Dominguez Hills since 1986 and contributing editor at the CACM. Publications: two books and 160 articles, reports, and papers. Recipient of the Meritorious Performance and Professional Promise, Outstanding Professor, and Lyle Gibson Distinguished Teacher awards. Current interests: networking in less-developed nations; planning information processing technology and curriculum at a globally-oriented, hi-tech campus.

Richard S. Rosenberg (B.A.Sc. (Engineering Physics) and M.A.Sc. (Electrical Engineering), both University of Toronto) earned a Ph.D. (Computer Science) from the University of Michigan, where he taught, before joining, in 1968, the University of British Colombia, where he is now associate professor at the Department of Computer Science. Research interests: artificial intelligence, natural language understanding, discourse, natural language interfaces to databases, social impact of computers, privacy, work, information networks and intellectual property. Recent publications: *Free speech, pornography, sexual harassment, and electronic networks* (1993), *Parsing with principles* (1993), *Artificial intelligence in the real world: a critical perspective* (1992), *A data management strategy for transportable natural language interfaces* (1992).

Pamela Samuelson is currently Professor of Law at the University of Pittsburgh Law School, where she specializes in intellectual property issues raised by new technologies. Professor Samuelson is the author of numerous publications and a contributing editor of the computing professionals journal, *Communications of the ACM*, for which she writes a regular "Legally Speaking" column. She is chair of the Computers & Law Section of the Association of American Law Schools and a member of the Board of Directors for the Center for Computer-Aided Legal Instruction. She is also past chair of the Intellectual Property Section of AALS.

Pierre Trudel is Professor of Law at the Université de Montréal, and was director of the *Centre de recherche en droit public*, from 1989 till 1994. Research and teaching interests: civil law, legal theory, legal epistemology, civil rights, fundamental information rights, intellectual property and information, media and communication law. Recent publications: *Accès aux documents des organismes publics et protection des renseignements personnels*, Wilson & Lafleur, 1989; *Droit de la radio et de la télévision*, (with France Abran, and with the collaboration of Lucie Guilbault) Éditions Thémis, 1991, winner of the Prize of the Quebec Bar Foundation, 1993; *La carte à mémoire : ses aspects juridiques et technologiques* (1992) and *La preuve et la signature dans l'échange de documents informatisés* (1993) both at Les Publications du Québec.

Table of Contents

Introduction

Ejan Mackaay, Daniel Poulin and Pierre Trudel

The electronic superhighway is a world-wide information and communications structure gradually emerging as the direct descendant of telephone, cablevision and the Internet. Precisely what form the structure will take is not yet clear. Even the proper term is in dispute: *National Information Infrastructure* (NII) is the term used in the United States to designate a commission studying the phenomenon; the government of Canada created in 1994 the *Information Highway* Advisory Council.

Henry H. Perritt Jr sees the national information structure emerging from the convergence of five cultures and three conceptual models.[1] Each of the five cultures has its own traditions and outlook. The first culture is that of broadcasters, entertainment producers and cable carriers; the second is the telephone companies; the third, the world of text publishers, librarians, government information enterprises; the fourth is Internet users, and the fifth computer hardware and software producers. All of these cultures will contribute to the emerging communications structure. A moment's reflection makes one realise how different in outlook they are, be it on regulated vs unregulated markets, on innovation and its rewards, on universal service at affordable prices versus letting the chips fall where they may, on interoperability of thc products and services of different providers.

Three different conceptual models present themselves concurrently, in Perritt's view, on the information highway. Broadcasting, that is, one-to-many one-way communication, generally open but not interactive; messaging or one-to-one to many-to-many communications of material ranging from text to video and audio signals, generally open and interactive; finally, databases, that is, many-to-one communication, generally proprietary and closed, but interactive.

The blending, merger or rivalry and displacement of these cultures and models is unlikely to be a smooth and easy process. The contrasts are too stark. The Internet, perhaps the dominant force in the emerging superhighway, is an anarchic society in the noble sense of the term: a society without rules imposed from above. It is the new frontier, a community in which traditional rules do not exist or are open to question. The computing industry is fiercely innovative and competitive. The broadcasting and

1 Paper presented to the Conference on Business and Legal Aspects of the Internet and Online Services, New York, 30 September 1994. The text may be found at the following WWW address http://ming.law.vill.edu/chron/articles/regulation_and_public_access.html.

E. Mackaay et al. (eds.), The Electronic Superhighway, 1–3.

telephone industries, by contrast, were, until recently, heavily regulated, with a predominant emphasis on public and universally accessible service. Text publishers, librarians, government information enterprises are somewhere in between these polar opposites.

The emergence of the electronic superhighway will force the convergence, adaptation or even disappearance of "cultures" that could hitherto develop in their separate ways. The "clients" of these cultures will inevitably be affected, and not necessarily in ways of their choosing or liking. Most citizens will want or feel compelled to change some of their work and play habits as the information highway takes shape. The process may entail acrimony for some and golden opportunities for others. The freedom of expression defended by some will be decried by others as abuse or excess, with concomitant calls for regulation or other norms and standards. Altogether, the emergence of the electronic superhighway will not be a marginal phenomenon passing most citizens by; rather it will strike at the heart of their work or play environment. It will entail, to use a fashionable term, a "*débat de société*", a debate on the society we want to live in.

The papers in this volume are an attempt to capture the flavour of this debate in midstream. Part I deals with the environment of the electronic superhighways. The first paper, by Guy Basque, gives a brief history and overview of the Internet, which is likely to be the main source of inspiration for the form the electronic superhighway will eventually take. Larry Press, in the second paper, contrasts Internet with the other major source of inspiration, that is interactive television. He shows how quickly both have grown and continue to grow, with the attendant "culture shock". Interactive television is also the topic of the third paper, by André Caron. This paper reports a detailed empirical study of user reactions to the Vidéoway system in the Montreal area. In its conclusion, the paper stresses that Vidéoway is not truly interactive. In that sense it lags behind the image of total interactivity that the media project of the information highway proposes and that Internet actually offers, and may create disappointments as a result.

Part II presents two developments in which the Internet opens possibilities that were not viable before. Tom Bruce shows how easy communication, massive storage and hypertext linking (Web technology) change the perspectives for law teaching and legal research. One significant question here is the role of for-pay versus for-free services. The paper gives examples of sponsoring and altruism in the development of Web services for the legal community. Jean-Claude Guédon, in the second paper of this Part, examines the viability of electronic publishing for academia. The problem here is that traditional paper-based journals are in a conundrum. Specialisation and pressure to publish lead to more journals, but limited or decreasing budgets lead to fewer subscriptions. This in turn pushes the price per subscription up and further reduces the number of subscribers: a perfect recipe for constriction. Does electronic publishing offer a way out? The paper looks at that question as well as the repercussions of such publishing for the sense of community within academe.

Part III focuses on the legal questions raised by the electronic superhighway, in particular as it takes shape in Internet. The point here is not so much to tell the net community what they can and cannot do by current legal rules, but to take stock of what that community consider it can legitimately do and not do and then to formulate rules they can live with. This is law in the making. Karim Benykhlef, in the first paper, gives an overview of legal issues of electronic commerce: evidence, liability, consumer protection, privacy and conflict resolution. Pamela Samuelson, in the second paper, looks at intellectual property rights issues. Digital information is infinitely malleable; any use of it, even for browsing, entails copying and falls within the purview of copyright. This gives copyright a reach and a bite well beyond the original intent and makes it look maladjusted to digital data. Is copyright dying or merely in need of explicit, broad "user rights"? Richard Rosenberg, in a substantial paper, looks at the question of freedom of expression on the information highway. The availability of pornography and incidents of sexual harassment have led some to call for restriction of the benign anarchy which so far has characterised the Internet. Others have denounced this as a call for censorship and consider the remedy worse than the ill. Rosenberg's paper examines arguments and practices on all sides of this debate and concludes against a priori controls. Pierre Trudel and Robert Gérin-Lajoie examine the question of how we come by those norms to govern the conduct of Internet participants: awareness campaign, self-regulation, broad principles with details left to enforcement agencies, regulation, criminal law or common law. They examine different communication contexts (media, private and public, local and general networks) and types of questionable behaviour (threats to privacy, obscenity and hate propaganda, harassment, copyright piracy) to conclude that fundamental rights and human dignity should be protected on the information highway as much as elsewhere. In conclusion they call for study of how self-generated norms emerge.

Part I

Electronic Superhighways - Environment

Introduction to the Internet

Two Cultures, The Internet and Interactive TV

The Domestication of a New Communication Technology : The Videoway System

Introduction to the Internet

Guy Basque

The invitation to open this seminar on law and the Internet with a general presentation of this network has provided an interesting but difficult challenge, because the Internet is a vast subject worthy of hours of discussion. I will therefore attempt to keep to the essential and I apologize to those well-acquainted with the Internet for the relative superficiality of my talk.

Before we begin, let us note that the Internet is above all an exciting technological, political and social adventure which began in American university circles about fifteen years ago, and continues now in a great many countries throughout the world. From a few tens of thousands of users in 1984, the Internet has developed at a phenomenal rate, to the point that there is now no precise count of the number of users. According to various studies, the number of users is estimated at about 15 million, give or take 30%, taking into account errors inherent in the sampling process.

In spite of the importance the Internet has acquired in university institutions and the high media visibility it currently enjoys, the technical side of the Internet remains astonishingly simple. Briefly, this super network is based on rather modest telecommunications infrastructures, a minimal set of data-exchange protocols and an address space which allows Internet member bodies to communicate with each other. All of this is topped by an information centre (NIC: Network Information Center). The major financial investment is in the computer environment situated on the periphery of the network, in other words in the member organizations.

Operating costs are relatively low compared to those of similar services offered by commercial telecommunications firms. In fact, the Internet is based in very large part on circuits rented from telecommunications firms, on regional, national or international scale. Since these are dedicated circuits, they are not subject to duration or volume-use fees as are the services offered to residential or commercial users. Seen from this angle, the Internet is a non-profit telecommunications enterprise indirectly subsidized by its partners.

In fact, the Internet's importance lies essentially in the contributions made by its members. This is the seat of the wealth and dynamism of this network. A wealth made up of what the members of different organizations bring to it, of the enormous "connectivity" it permits, and of the numerous

E. Mackaay et al. (eds.), The Electronic Superhighway, 7–19.

types of interactions it allows to be created and which inevitably pose all sorts of unforeseeable new problems.

1. A brief history of the Internet

1.1 THE ARPANET NETWORK

In the mid-sixties, the RAND Corporation published a report on the security of telecommunications networks and their vulnerability in case of armed conflict. Among the weaknesses pointed out in the RAND report were the excessive centralization of certain networks and the fact that intermediary communication nodes were dependent on major coordination centres and had practically no operational freedom in case of a break in communication with the control centres.

At about the same time, a project of the Advanced Research Project Agency (ARPA), a United States Defense Department organization responsible for coordinating military research activities, was to set up a computer telecommunications network to allow university researchers and military suppliers working on defence contracts to exchange data and coordinate their research activities. Rather than mandating existing firms to develop a custom network to answer the researchers' needs, ARPA asked the researchers themselves to develop an experimental network which would respond to the needs expressed in the RAND report. This is how the ARPANET network was born.

The main goals of the ARPANET project were the following:

- The network was to be constructed using proven technology and equipment available on the market: conventional communication links, modems, computers, etc.
- The network was to have no critical dependency on real-time supervision by a control centre.
- The network was to be designed so that operating costs could be spread among different partners.
- The architecture of the network was to be sufficiently extendable and permit practically unlimited growth.

The decentralization of the control centres also implied large savings regarding the mode of financing research centres. Extreme decentralization meant development financing could be ensured largely by different partners and ARPA was not obliged to maintain expensive central support infrastructures.

ARPANET's initial decentralization goals still apply and can be found in the present development philosophy of the Internet.

1.2 THE ARRIVAL OF THE NATIONAL SCIENCE FOUNDATION

From 1970 to 1980, ARPANET spread its tentacles into most major American universities with large defence contracts. However, many institutions did not have access to it, either because they did not have the justification of military contracts, or because they simply did not have the professional resources necessary to support such technology.

That institutions in other countries might connect to ARPANET was unthinkable, except through closely watched links which let a little electronic mail filter through.

Thus, around 1984, the National Science Foundation (NSF) was invited by the major research agencies of the American government to take over from ARPA and pursue the expansion of the network to include all university institutions and research organizations, and eventually develop the international aspect.

NSF's first action was to set up a national network (NSFNET) permitting the main regions of the United States to be interconnected and to finance the establishment of regional networks in order to allow universities to reach the national interconnection centres. Once the regional networks were established, all universities had to do was to invest in inexpensive equipment to link up to it.

From 1984 to 1988, the NSFNET network experienced phenomenal growth. From a few hundred computers in 1984, the network included over 100,000 systems in 1989. This is when the need began to be felt elsewhere, especially in Canada, due to the proximity to the American border. Organizations similar to the NSF in other countries began to negotiate the installation of links on an international scale.

1.3 INTERNATIONALIZATION OF THE INTERNET

In 1988, with international tension diminished, the NSF began to open links between the Internet and other countries. In Canada, research centres and universities obtained large numbers of IP (Internet Protocol) addresses. For example, most Canadian universities have class-B network status. A class-B Internet network can have 256 class-C networks, and each class-C network can serve 256 systems. In all, that comes out to 65,536 Internet addresses for each university.

Results were immediate. In record time, the national network CA*Net (the Canadian equivalent of NSFNET) was set up. Meanwhile, regional networks began operating. In Quebec, the regional network is called RISQ (*Réseau inter-ordinateurs scientifiques québécois*). It was established thanks to the initiative of the *Centre de recherche informatique de Montréal* (CRIM) and the universities. Similar developments occurred in the other provinces: Ontario, Nova Scotia, British Columbia, etc.

At present, the RISQ network includes 22 main members, who communicate over high-output lines and over fifty affiliated members, who communicate on lower-output lines. For now, the affiliated members of the RISQ network are mostly non-profit organizations. Commercial enterprises mainly use the network to exchange non-commercial information.

1.4 COMMERCIALIZATION OF THE INTERNET

Until 1992, most long-distance communications in the United States were done through the NSFNET and commercial use was limited by the policy set out in the AUP (Acceptable Use Policy) of the NSF. In order to meet the swiftly growing demand of enterprises wanting to offer their commercial departments the same services as their research and development divisions, a second national network was established. This network is operated by a consortium called the ANS, which is composed of IBM, MCI and Merit Inc.

Parallel to the beginning of the commercialization of the Internet, in 1993, negotiations took place at the political level in view of transferring the NSFNET network to private enterprise. As of April 1995 the NSFNET will have to pay for itself. Provisions have been made for universities to receive subsidies directly from the NSF in order to pay the cost of using infrastructures formerly offered free of charge by the NSF.

A similar movement can be expected in Canada during the next years, and over time this could alter the face of the Internet considerably. Furthermore, it should be noted that since the last presidential elections in the United States, there has been more and more talk of an electronic superhighway project which would encompass the other traditional forms of communication, such as voice and image, and which would involve telephone and cable television companies. Discussion of this is in full swing in Canada and alliances are in the making between the government and industrial partners.

It is still too early to say what the future electronic highway will be. It will probably take decades to accomplish. Until then, the Internet is, and will be for some time, the one and only operating prototype electronic highway.

2. Users and suppliers of services

When speaking of the Internet, the notion of "user" is ambiguous. To be precise, the real Internet users are not individuals but the organizations which operate the networks and provide the services. Only at the level of service suppliers does the notion of "user", in the ordinary sense of the term, take on concrete meaning.

In effect, the Internet is organized as a federation of networks and takes physical form as a set of communication links permitting client computers to communicate with each other directly. The Internet does not exist as an autonomous corporative entity. In reality, interface with the Internet occurs at the level of the networks of the members. This, the periphery, is where services are offered to users.

The vast majority of Internet users must pass through the intermediary of a service supplier to gain access to the Internet. In turn, the service suppliers must belong to corporative or regional networks, which are connected to national networks at a higher hierarchical level. It is only really at the level of national networks that the administrative aspects of the Internet come into play.

This said, the intermediate networks at the various levels and the server suppliers have a margin of manoeuvre which allows them to increase their clientele without always having to ask for supplementary resources from their superiors in the hierarchy. As we said at the beginning, the Internet can operate and develop without constant intervention from a central organization.

For example, a relatively long time can pass before a client of a telephone network receives a telephone, and before anyone can reach them by consulting the directory assistance service, given the extreme centralization of this service. In the Internet, workstations can be added in a local network, their coordinates can be registered in a local Domain Name Server (DNS), and as soon as this is done, the workstations can be reached from anywhere in the Internet. There is no need to wait for the workstations to be registered in some kind of central registry.

3. Internet Services

The average Internet user can use the Internet without knowing its internal workings. Only knowledge of the main services and mastery of a set of basic commands are necessary. The largest and most widely used services are the following:

- TELNET: a protocol permitting interactive communication to be performed with another Internet site. Briefly, this protocol allows long-distance telephone communication, charged by the minute, to be bypassed.
- FTP: a protocol allowing files to be transferred from another computer (in the Internet there are thousands of sites offering free anonymous FTP access). Essentially, it is a system which allows files to be moved more rapidly and more directly than with TELNET.
- E-Mail: thanks to the SMTP (Simple Mail Transfer Protocol), users can exchange electronic mail. Various services are associated with electronic mail, such as mail list managers (LISTSERV) and many connected services.

- News: the Internet includes a sub-network of services called UseNet. This network is made up of a system of electronic bulletin boards where users can discuss various subjects. Presently, UseNet includes about 2700 conferences on all subjects. Each day about 100 000 articles are published, which represents about 100 million octets of information.
- Gopher: a distributed system of hierarchically organized information which can contain cross-references between the various levels. Developed at the University of Minnesota, this system began to be used in 1992 and there are now over 1700 servers registered in the world. For each approved central server in the central registries, there are probably 5 to 10 secondary servers.
- WAIS: the acronym for Wide Area Information System. The WAIS is based on a network of documentation sources which can be accessed through key-word searches. This system was originally developed by the ThinkCom and APPLE companies.
- WWW: the acronym for Wide World Web. This is a distributed information system which can be accessed in "hypertext" mode. This system was originally developed by the CERN (*Centre européen de recherche nucléaire*) in order to allow its 3500 researchers to have rapid, efficient access to research results.

As this list clearly shows, each system favours a certain form of communication. A well-informed Internet user must be familiar with the different services available.

Let us outline the characteristics of the various services:

3.1 THE TELNET SERVICE

The TELNET service permits interactive telecommunications services between a user sitting in front of a terminal or workstation, and computers offering all sorts of services all over the world, without having to use the long-distance telephone service, the cost of which would be prohibitive for very long-distance communication.

Among the most popular services available through TELNET are access to university and research-centre library catalogues, and access to central information systems of various government and university organizations. This means of communication strongly advanced the development of CWISs (Campus Wide Information Systems) throughout the world.

3.2 THE FTP SERVICE

The FTP service is used to transfer files between the local system, where the user possesses an account, and other computers in the Internet. The Internet's arrival has lead most organizations to operate systems called

"Anonymous FTP servers", which store data the organization wishes to make available to the public. People can consult this data freely, and have the possibility of importing many kinds of information.

Worldwide, there are at present thousands of servers accessible to the public. In order to facilitate searches, for software for example, there are servers called ARCHIE, which can be consulted for lists of sites in the world where what one is looking for is available. In passing, let us mention that the Archie system was developed at McGill University and that the Archie server for Eastern Canada is now operated by UQAM.

3.3 ELECTRONIC MAIL

Electronic mail is undoubtably the most frequently used Internet option. Internet electronic mail addresses have become status symbols. Increasing numbers of people simply refuse to communicate except by electronic mail. In many circles, not to have an electronic mail address means frankly to be excluded from certain discussions.

Many auxiliary services, increasing the advantages of this mode of communication, have grown up around electronic mail:

LISTSERV: these are servers which allow messages to be transmitted to lists of users and discussion forums to be held on all sorts of subjects. There are now about 3500 major discussion lists in the Internet, and to have access to these lists, one can consult the central lists in the UseNet news groups, in various anonymous FTP sites, or else do key-word searches on various WAIS servers.

NETFIND: these are information systems which can be accessed through the TELNET service, and which allow users to look for electronic mail addresses. This service is an inestimable aid because, due to the completely decentralized nature of Internet, there is no central directory. In passing, let us note that the absence of a central directory of Internet users is the most surprising aspect for new users, who believe that the Internet operates like the telephone system.

3.4 THE USENET NETWORK

Strictly speaking, USENET is not a network but a bulletin-board service which allows all Internet users to publish articles in approximately 2,700 discussions on a wide variety of subjects. In USENET terminology, these discussions are called "Newsgroups". An article published in a major newsgroup may allow its author to be read by many tens of thousands of people.

Every day around 100 000 articles are published in the newsgroups transmitted by USENET. In terms of disk space, this represents over 100 mega-bytes of information.

On average, three new newsgroups are created each day. Often their creation is triggered by major international events such as the Gulf War, the latest earthquake in California, UN intervention in Somalia, etc.

Articles published in USENET allow users to get information on the Internet and keep themselves uptodate on developments.

3.5 GOPHER SERVICES

GOPHER, developed at the University of Minnesota, is a completely original system which permits information structured in hierarchical directories to be spread over the whole Internet. What is special about this system is that it allows links to other hierarchical structures available in Gopher servers elsewhere to be added to the hierarchical structures. Through links existing between the various systems, a global information space is created in which one can travel for hours.

The term "Gopher Space" is used to designate the computer space accessible through Gopher. This space can be navigated by reading the information available in the directories and jumping from one Gopher server to another. When useful information is found, it can be saved in local files on one's workstation, or the place where the information is found can be marked using markers kept in a personal file. Later, the information desired can be directly accessed from the markers: the path initially used need not be followed again.

Like the anonymous FTP service and electronic mail, the GOPHER service has many auxiliary information-research services, in particular the VERONICA system. This system plays a role analogous to that of ARCHIE, but its operation is limited to Gopher servers. There are now over 1700 Gopher servers on the central register maintained by the University of Minnesota.

3.6 WAIS SERVERS

WAIS servers mainly specialize in documentation research. Based on the ISO Z39.50 norm, an international norm conceived to access documentation resources, these servers allow key-word searches. During a search, one obtains a list of titles of documents in order of relevance. From this list one can see the contents of documents, import them into one's computer and store them locally for future consultation.

Increasingly, WAIS servers can be accessed though Gopher systems.

3.7 WWW SERVERS

WWW (World Wide Web) servers are a recent innovation in the Internet, but they are currently experiencing a boom. The WWW concept goes further than that of Gopher or WAIS. It allows the incorporation of the functions offered by these systems, but it also permits the introduction of hypertext references within the text. One can thus obtain clarifications of certain words or expressions by "clicking" or by directly choosing the words in question. Information searches are no longer done according to a rigid hierarchical model, but according to a linked network model.

Since WWW systems are more recent than Gopher and WAIS systems, the functions of the other systems have been integrated into them. WWW systems present information in a more sophisticated way because they can diffuse multi-media information. WWW servers contain much greater graphic information than the other systems, but this can lead to rather serious overload in certain networks.

WWW servers are ideal applications for future electronic highways, which could provide high-speed transportation of multi-media data.

3.8 IN SUMMARY...

As this list shows, the Internet is first and foremost a means of communication and information exchange. Originally created to allow researchers and university professors to exchange data in the United States, the Internet has been present in most research centres and universities in industrialized countries since 1990.

These means of communication, through their speed and through the large number of people who can be reached, give birth to new types of interaction on which there is not yet well-established agreement. At this level, we are starting from scratch and the Internet is a laboratory.

Many rules are adopted in the various newsgroups, for example concerning etiquette in network exchanges, but no one is legally bound to respect them. In fact, many users do not respect them or contest them openly.

4. The major results of the Internet

Given the Internet's origins and limited initial goals, the development of this network is likely to be the most important innovation in communications of the end of the twentieth century. Its development and dazzling explosion have shown beyond any reasonable doubt that a certain form of global village is possible in communications.

Furthermore, the development of the Internet has shown that there is no need to set up highly centralized, extremely hierarchical organizations in order to achieve large-scale effects. It suffices to establish relatively homogenous infrastructures, to institute minimal information exchange norms from the beginning, and then to let the *milieu* do the rest. The results are now there to prove it.

Among Internet's major achievements, let us note the following:

- Any one can now access most catalogues of the majority of the world's universities, as well as the catalogue of the Library of Congress in Washington. It is reasonable to think that in coming years, municipal libraries will also be linked. This development alone could justify the existence of the Internet.
- As well as references to traditional publications, an increasing number of people can access public interest information which was previously difficult to obtain. One need only think of the major museums which have begun to transmit images of their works of art over the Internet, of NASA which transmits images gathered by various space probes, and of meteorological services, of weather pictures transmitted by satellite, etc.
- Through servers like FTP, Gopher, WAIS and WWW, any institution situated in the Internet can transmit its publications, data, software, etc. worldwide. For example, the Faculty of Law, which organized this seminar, now uses a Gopher server to disseminate all sorts of legal information, including decisions of the Supreme Court of Canada.
- Regarding community groups, Internet has been the inspiration and model for the creation of community networks called Freenet which are beginning to be developed in major cities. There are now two Freenets operating in Canada, one in Victoria and one in Ottawa, but dozens of others are being developed, including one in Montréal, which could go into operation in the Fall.
- Along other lines, the Internet's importance should not be measured merely by the quantity of information it allows to be carried and transmitted. The Internet's most important long-term effect, and which will be cited in the future, is that it brings people together and facilitates discussion on many different sorts of subjects which it would not have been possible to address with traditional means of communication.

4.1 INTERNET'S GROWING PAINS

The Internet is not merely a new communications tool, it is also a laboratory which allows new forms of communication to be tested, their limitations to be noted and new approaches to solving problems to be researched and developed.

4.2 PRESENT AND FUTURE INTERNET USERS

In order to understand the Internet and the economic, political, legal and social problems it entails, the various aspects linked to its history and development, and to the *milieu* in which it grew must be considered. These various factors have helped to project an image, in the minds of users, which is different from the traditional image of commercial telecommunications companies. The image of the Internet which has developed over time risks having considerable influence over the development of communications infrastructures in the future and over coming policies on electronic highways.

First, for the historical reasons mentioned above, the Internet initially developed in university circles and, since it is based on dedicated communications infrastructures, in other words since there is no direct cost for use once the infrastructure is set up, services are overwhelmingly offered free of charge. In fact, most organizations which offer their members access to the Internet do not even have the infrastructure to count the number of times it is used, let alone to "bill" for them.

Second, since the services appear to be cost-free, people use them extensively, and not just for professional reasons, but increasingly for personal or private motives. Over time, users have appropriated this new medium and many have come to consider it public property like libraries and highways. Thus they scorn the rights and obligations of the organizations offering these services. Since in many places there are no suppliers offering commercial access to the Internet, the users taking advantage of these services through the institutions to which they belong are regarded as pariahs by the rest of the population.

As Freenets come to major American cities, community groups are beginning to get deeply involved and there is increasing talk of free access to the Internet. If this movement takes off, the means of financing national infrastructures, which risk rapid saturation, must be examined.

4.3 SECURITY

The security and confidentiality of the Internet is the subject of heated debate in various circles. Security questions do not concern the Internet itself so much as the systems of users. In effect, the Internet allows total "connectivity", but it is incumbent upon users to protect their systems against various types of intrusion. Yet most systems were not designed to operate in hostile environments and intrusions are frequent. Every month there are reports of breaches of security involving different systems. There is a volunteer organization which investigates these questions, the CERT, but it has no coercive power over users or manufacturers to prevent the former from intruding illegally or to oblige the latter to mend the known holes in the defences of their systems.

At the level of the host computers through which users pass to access the Internet, security is far from absolute. It is well-known that password files on most UNIX systems with access to the Internet, though encoded and in principle indecipherable, are available to users and can thus be read by unscrupulous individuals. Users whose passwords are dictionary words or personal information which can be known by third parties leave themselves open to having their accounts pirated. Once the password is known, pirates can then undertake more consequential intrusion and thus cause serious damage.

There is even specialized software called "password cracker", which allows the security of passwords in a system to be tested, using a set of dictionaries containing hundreds of thousands of words. In order to allow systems managers to test the vulnerability of passwords chosen by users, this software is publicly available. This surprises many people; yet this approach is very revealing of the philosophy which reigns in the Internet. Rather than hide the instruments which could prove destructive if they fell into the wrong hands, the solution is to spread them and make them easily available, so that every one knows they exist and can use them to protect him- or herself.

Regarding confidentiality, the security of data is very relative and, in general, not guaranteed. First, in most systems of operation, the user accounts are the property of the system administrator and the password of the person responsible (the ROOT user in UNIX systems) is all that is needed to read the data and mail of users. As a professional, the system administrator is held to respect the confidentiality of the data of users, but this provides no protection against pressure from his or her employer and, moreover, his or her password can be pirated in the same way as the passwords of users.

4.4 ENCRYPTING DATA

As a means of warding off the inevitable intrusion into the network, encrypting increasingly seems to be the only viable long-term answer. However, this solution raises numerous problems. In order to be efficient and to permit users to exchange data without having first to negotiate encryption modalities, the algorithm must be governed by a norm. Furthermore, to protect users from possible abuses and to be able to identify wrongdoers, legal authorities must, if so required, be able to decrypt the messages. How can we be assured that this right will be used correctly and that it will not create an opportunity for other types of abuse?

The American government has promoted a technology called Clipper Chip, which should allow users to encrypt their data according to an algorithm governed by a norm. This norm ensures relatively good confidentiality while allowing control organizations to decrypt messages in case of serious problems. In order to prevent officers of the law from arbitrarily decrypting any message, two independent organizations will be in charge of delivering the special keys required to decrypt messages and of verifying authorization mandates obtained from competent authorities in order to permit the decrypting.

The problem then rests largely on the political autonomy of the control organizations and on their independence with respect to political power. Many people doubt that this will be possible and a good number would like to see unregulated encrypting. In short, they would prefer to let market forces and competition determine the best solutions.

To summarize, with its beginnings in a relatively modest initiative by an organization subsidizing research in the United States, the Internet has become, over the years, the prototype of the communications network of the global village. This network is increasingly used as a model of reference for the electronic highway, and since the latter will take a long time to build, the Internet will remain for many years to come a living laboratory for all sorts of experiments with fascinating implications for the future.

This evolution concerns all organizations as well as citizens. It is thus of utmost importance that people take an interest in it and participate as actively as possible.

References

Ed. Krol, *The Whole Internet - User's Guide & Catalog*, 2nd edition, O'Reilly & Associates, Inc., 1994.(20) *"Status Report on Two-Way Testbeds"*, Cable Television Information Center, Washington, D. C., May, 1973.

Carrol, Jim and Rick Broadhead, *Canadian Internet Handbook*, Prentice Hall Canada, 1993.(20) —, *"Status Report on Two-Way Testbeds"*, Cable Television Information Center, Washington, D. C., May, 1973.

Two Cultures, The Internet and Interactive TV

Larry Press

The Clinton adminstration has set ambitious goals for a national and global information infrastructure (NII and GII). The administration plan for the NII was articulated by Vice President Gore in a speech in Los Angeles.[1] He stated the administration would:

1. encourage private investment in the NII
2. provide and protect competition
3. provide open access to the network
4. act to avoid creating a society of information "haves" and "have nots"
5. encourage flexible and responsive government action.

In another speech, the Vice President called for a GII. He called upon "legislators, regulators, and business people" to build and operate a GII, which would "circle the globe with information superhighways on which all people can travel", and he pledged "vigorous, continued participation in achieving this goal".[2]

In the U.S., both the Internet and interactive TV communities are working toward this infrastructure. While they use some of the same terms and have both received the administration's attention, these groups seem to be pursuing independent courses — they work in different industries, attend different conferences, and have different cultures. This paper summarizes the current state of each effort, then it discusses some of the key differences between the two.

1. Internet Update

There are several discernible Internet trends — it is growing rapidly, becoming increasingly commercial, becoming increasingly global, and new ways of accessing the Internet, new "on-ramps", are developing.

1 Gore, Al, *"Remarks at Royce Hall, UCLA"*, Los Angeles, January 11, 1994. Anonymous ftp, sunsite.unc.edu, pub/academic/political-science/internet-related/VP-Speech-at- UCLA.

2 Gore, Al, *"Remarks Prepared for Delivery, International Telecommunications Union"*, Buenos Aires, March 21, 1994. Anonymous ftp, sunsite.unc.edu, pub/academic/political-science/ internet-related/Gore's-Delivered-Remarks-on-NII-12- 21-93.

E. Mackaay et al. (eds.), The Electronic Superhighway, 21–35.

The Internet is large and growing rapidly. Between January 1993 and January 1994, the number of hosts grew from 1,313,000 to 2,217,000, a 69% increase,[3] and monthly traffic on the US NSF backbone alone is about 10 terabytes.[4] With an estimated 20 million users, the Internet is larger than many nations, and has a highly educated, mostly professional population.

There are many signs of increased commercialization. Most organizations which build IP internets (small i), register them with the Network Information Center, regardless of whether they connect to the Internet or not. Registrations are growing at 12% per month, and roughly 75% of those are from business enterprises. The Internet is positioned to provide the backbone which glues enterprise-wide and inter-enterprise networks together. Many businesses have been worried about the lack of security on the Internet, but we know how to install firewall computers in front of corporate networks and encryption and signature authentication are being designed and deployed. Facilities for billing are also being tested, and there are a number of experimental Internet-based "malls" and "markets". Another indicator of commercial interest is the fact that at least 4 business-related Internet newsletters began publication during the second half of 1993. Note that the U.S. government is funding development of new technology and standards, not enterprises, though there has been some controversy over the line between them.

The Internet is becoming more global. Sixty two political units are directly connected, and the international growth rate is 9% per month (in numbers of networks).[5] At current rates, international connectivity will exceed U.S. connectivity around October, 1994. Table 1 summarizes global connectivity and recent trends.

---

3 Lottor, Mark, Report-9401, directory pub/zone, ftp.nisc.sri.com, January, 1994.

4 Aupperle, E. "NSF backbone trends", *Internet Society News*, 2, 4 (Winter 1994), 13. (1).

5 —, "Internet global statistics: 1993", *Internet Society News*, 2, 4 (Winter 1994), 7.

Table 1 : Global Connectivity

Global connectivity is growing steadily, but it is concentrated in developed nations.[6]

	August 1, 93	February 15, 94
Full IP	57	61
Email	137	146
None	99	91
Total	236	237

Source : These figures are from: Landweber, Larry, *"The Connectivity Table"*, Version 10, February 15, 1994, anonymous ftp, ftp.cs.wisc.edu, connectivity table directory.

There are also new ways to get onto the Internet. Performance Systems International (PSI) is test-offering Internet connectivity via cable TV. Marty Schoffstall, PSI's chief technical officer, predicts a rosy future for Cable TV access to the Internet. He feels the Internet and cable company cultures are compatible — both are "cowboys".

Wireless Internet e-mail has been available since 1992 from RadioMail, and several vendors are introducing cellular packet- switched data services. Networking pioneer Paul Baran is developing a system for wireless connectivity over CATV. Even ISDN has been resurrected as a viable path to the office LAN from home or the road. Forrester Research interviewed 50 Fortune-500 companies, and after considering six alternatives, concluded that "[by 1995, ISDN] will be the first option to provide affordable, nationwide, near-ubiquitous, switched digital connectivity for low volume access".[7] Around the turn of the century, we may see satellite-based access. Perhaps the most promising satellite venture is Teledesic, which plans a network of 840 low-earth orbiting ATM switches.

There is even a new Internet "off-ramp". Carl Malamud and Marshall Rose have developed software which lets Internet hosts receive e-mail messages (text or graphic), and automatically forward them to a specified fax phone number. The message forwarder could do this as a free service (perhaps within a corporation or at a public library). Alternatively, they could obtain revenue by charging a fee or by printing a paid ad at the bottom

6 Goodman, S, Press, L., Ruth, S. and Rutkowski, A., "The Global Diffusion of the Internet: Patterns and Problems", *Communications of the ACM*, in press; Press, L., "The net: progress and opportunity", *Communications of the ACM*, 35/12 (December 1992), 21-25.

7 Batson, J. and Hyland, J. L., "Don't Laugh, It's ISDN," *The Network Strategy Report*, vol. 7, no 7, pp 2-13, Forrester Research, Cambridge, MA, June, 1993.

of the fax cover sheet. There are already servers in several cities, and several companies are buying ads[8].

Finally, bulletin board systems (BBS), which began with hobbyists and community information providers, are becoming commercial, and connecting to the Internet. Boardwatch Magazine, which covers BBS, has a regular Internet section, and their annual conference has an Internet track. In a reader survey, they chose 100 top BBS, and 21 of them offer Internet connectivity or e-mail.[9] These are not toy systems. Several have over 10 Gbytes on line, and they average 25 dial-in lines. The largest has 35 Gbytes, and receives 5,000 calls daily on 280 lines. Many BBS specialize, with topics from community information, software, Christian values, pornography, and senior citizens to Batman.

Jack Rickard, Boardwatch Editor and Publisher, estimates that there are 53,000 publicly-accessible BBS in North America and 92,000 world wide.[10] This includes 22,000 Fidonet BBS, which have store-and-forward communications between them. When asked about the Internet, Rickard says, "when somebody can put an ftp- server/BBS on the Internet for a couple thousand dollars, it will certainly change the network". It will also be interesting to see how being networked changes the BBS.

2. Interactive TV

For years, there was discussion of an NII by the year 2015 or 2020. The phone companies would extend fiber from the center out — first inter-city, then to local exchanges, and finally to the curb or home. In the interim, we could connect to our digital networks using modems or ISDN. Judging by the rate of ISDN deployment, the phone companies were not in a big rush.

The Cable TV industry has accelerated the process. Cable TV began as a means of getting signals to outlying areas. Programming came to a head-end, where it was broadcast over coaxial cable in trunk lines to feeder lines to drops to homes. Amplifiers were located at quarter-mile intervals along this network. By 1992 cable ran by 97% of U.S. households and connected 61% of them (see Table 2).[11]

---

8 For information on the Internet-fax gateway, send a request to tpc-faq@town.hall.org.

9 —, "Boardwatch-100, Readers' Choice BBS Contest Results", *Boardwatch Magazine*, September 1993, pp 68-80.

10 Rickard, Jack and Funk, Gary, "The International FidoNet — 22067 Bulletin Boards with an Attitude", *Boardwatch Magazine*, August 1993, pp 66-80.

11 Green, R. R., Testimony before the Subcommittee on Technology, Environment, and Aviation, Committee on Science, Space, and Technology, U.S. House of Representatives, March 23, 1993.

Table 2 : Cable TV Deployment

Cable TV is growing rapidly, and converting trunk lines to optical fiber. This network may be used for movies, shopping, and other services.[12]

	1975	1980	1985	1990	1992
TV households (millions)	70	78	86	93	93
Percent of TV households served	13	23	46	59	61
Homes passed (millions)	23	35	65	86	91
Percent of TV households passed	33	45	76	92	97

To increase capacity, reliability, and picture quality, the cable companies have been converting trunks from coaxial cable to optical fiber. It costs only about $50 per subscriber to run fiber to neighborhood nodes of about 1,500-2,000 homes. The next step will be the extension of fiber to nodes serving 200-500 homes. The industry estimates that the cost of converting the U.S. cable plant in this manner is about $20 billion, compared to $200-400 billion for a comparable rebuilding of the telephone plant. The major cause of these savings is that coaxial cable running to the homes would not be replaced[13].

At some point, entertainment and cable companies realized this hybrid network, coupled with improved computing and compression technology, would be capable of delivering digital movies. If they could provide movies on demand from the safety and convenience of the home, they could take over the estimated $12 billion[14] annual video-rental business[15], justifying much of the needed investment. Throw in a share of the $70 billion catalog shopping and $4 billion video game markets[16] and the $2 billion already sold through TV shopping,[17] and the "interactive TV" community was born.

2.1 VIDEO ON DEMAND

During the last year, dozens of interactive TV alliances have been formed between entertainment, cable, phone, and computer companies. They speak of many applications, but focus first on video on demand. There have been

12 Green, R. R., *ibid.*

13 The statistics and estimates in this section were taken from [7].

14 Zoglin, Richard, "The Info Highway", *Time*, April 12, 1993, pp 56-61.

15 Twenty percent of this revenue is from late charges on overdue rentals, which would not occur with video on demand.

16 Zoglin, Richard, "The Info Highway", *Time*, April 12, 1993, pp 56-61.

17 Zinn, L, De George, G., Shoretz, R., Yang, D. J. and Forest, S. A., "Retailing will never Be the Same", *Business Week*, July 26, 1993, p. 54-60.

several market tests in which a digital system is simulated using operators who manually mount tapes on VCRs, but automatic, digital testbeds are now under development. As an example, let's look at the 4,000-customer trial set for Orlando Florida[18].

Silicon Graphics (SGI) is designing the video-on-demand hardware and software, and Jim Barton, Vice President of their Media Systems Division, described the project. The head-end hardware will be a cluster of 14 SGI servers on an FDDI ring. Two of the machines in the cluster will function primarily as session managers and transaction processors, and the others will deliver MPEG-compressed video. The video servers have 1.2 Gbit/s backplanes, and can have up to 24 processors, 12 Gbyte memory, and several hundred Gbytes of disk. The FDDI ring will be used for control and coordination within the cluster. Perhaps 50 popular movies will be on-line at all times, with the top 10 or so on multiple servers. Another 5-10,000 movies will be available on robot-accessed tape, with a few minutes lead time for mounting. Small video segments will be transferred from the video servers to an AT&T ATM switch, and sent over 1.5 mb/s, full-duplex lines to homes.

The network will terminate in TV set-top boxes designed by SGI. The design is foreshadowed in a SIGGRAPH paper by Jim Clark, the Chairman of SGI.[19] Clark speculates on a $200 (mid 1990s) box with MPEG decompression, encryption, display-device independence, and built-in graphics and image processing capability. The initial prototype will be a modified SGI Indy workstation with a 100 mhz MIPS R4000 processor and a Scientific- Atlanta add-in board for decompression and analog signal processing. There will be no storage, and relatively little memory. Bootup and client software management will be handled at the head-end, reducing system cost. For those who wish to go beyond the basic box, there will be PCMCIA slots.

There are other interesting video prototypes under way. For example, Oracle is assuming a less intelligent set-top box, and designing a video server using an nCube multiprocessor system. According to John Kish, Oracle's Senior Vice President, Business Development, they will test it in Omaha with U.S. West as a partner. Kish says Oracle plans to port their video-server software to many machines, including SGI's, but they have decided on a 512-processor nCube machine for this test. (Oracle president Larry Ellison is a major investor in nCube, but Kish insists the selection was made independently). Kish expects the 512-processor machine to serve 3,000 video streams, and says the technology scales well. He envisions serving 100,000 video streams in a few years, and says the cost of capital

18 Two-way analog tests date back to the early 1970s. One of the earliest was also in Orlando, conducted by Orange Cablevision [20].

19 Clark, J., "A Tele-Computer", *Proceedings of SIGGRAPH '92*, pp 19-23, Addison-Wesley, Reading, MA, 1992.

equipment must be around $200 per stream for movies to pay off. Oracle and SGI have very different architectures — isn't competition nice?

2.2 SHOPPING — THE OTHER APPLICATION

Shopping has also caught the attention of the interactive TV community. It is highlighted in popular press accounts, and when executives discuss financial justification.[20] Many of the interactive TV alliances have prepared short, insipid, concept- demo videotapes showing hypothetical interactive shopping. They portray virtual travel through malls — scanning the shelves till you find something you like, then zooming in to rotate the object, try different colors, bicker about the purchase with your spouse (a la Ricky and Lucy), and buy it. The products demonstrated are things like vases or dresses, never tractors or staple goods.

If that is what home shopping becomes, I won't spend much time browsing in the video mall. But, if the NII were to increase the efficiency of the market for a variety of goods and services, it would have significant economic impact (as it already has in capital markets).

Theoretically, an efficient market provides information about goods and services, and rational, well-informed consumers make optimal decisions. However, Herbert Simon received a Nobel Prize in economics for demonstrating that such perfection does not exist in the real world. Information is not perfect, and it costs. Furthermore, shoppers have finite cognitive skills and time, so they do not optimize, they merely "satisfice", making decisions which satisfy their constraints. The NII could increase market efficiency by providing both better information and analysis tools.

Let us consider relatively large purchases first, for example an auto, an appliance, or some office or industrial equipment. (Items you might screen on-line, and eventually purchase in person). One could imagine a comparative shopping service (more like a database than virtual travel) with information on product specifications, prices, delivery times, and guarantee terms. There could be video presentations by manufacturers, independent product reviews, comments by satisfied and dissatisfied customers (with their e-mail address), and discussion groups among consumers and producers. There could also be information to allow comparison of local distributors or service providers. Such information would ease Simon's first market limitation. The second constraint, the consumer's finite rationality, could be relaxed with tools for discovery, analysis and presentation — agents, models, and expert systems.

The NII also has the potential to increase market efficiency for staple goods. I am more curious about the effect of the NII on supermarkets than

---

20 Zinn, L, De George, G., Shoretz, R., Yang, D. J. and Forest, S. A., "Retailing will never be the same", *Business Week*, July 26, 1993, p. 54-60.

on boutiques in malls. It would be convenient to ask "what will it cost me to purchase the following grocery list from various stores near me this week". Or to see current prices for a specific computer or program. This sort of purchase will be concluded on line, and the line between retailing and distribution may shift. I really want to know what it will cost to get the items on the grocery list to my home, not which store or stores to buy it from. Of course information products like news, software, and music can be both browsed and distributed on line.

While the interactive TV community has the publicity lead on shopping, shopping might be a better fit with the Internet. Interactive TV people envision mass markets with relatively few vendors. The temperament of the Internet community points more toward a bazaar than a mass market, with easy entry and many vendors. The Internet community also has experience with the information retrieval and analysis tools which will underlie the electronic market.

All of this is a bit glib. The interactive TV community is starting trials, but widespread rollout will take many years. Technical innovation and standards are needed, and these will be followed by a long rollout period, which will begin in affluent areas. The non-technical questions are more difficult. For example, will there be alternative comparison shopping services for a class of item? Will comparison shopping services charge consumers, be funded by vendors, or be provided as a common good. The latter possibilities raise questions of regulation of goods markets, analogous to present regulation of security markets. What steps would be taken to insure accuracy? What would be the legal liabilities and procedures? Who would be able to list products?

3. Two Cultures

With apology to C. P. Snow, the Internet and interactive TV communities have different cultures, and like Snow's scientific and liberal arts cultures, they communicate poorly. They do not attend each other's conferences or, in many cases, even seem aware of what the other is doing. Still, in the long run, they will converge or at least be linked via gateways. This section outlines some differences between these communities.

3.1 Applications

The Interactive TV community is justifying its investment with plans for movies and home shopping. Those are the applications featured in their demonstration video tapes and in discussions with technologists. They also promise to bring us single and multi-player games, and education is invariably mentioned as a possibility, though one has the feeling that it is a poor cousin, perhaps because the players do not have experience in that sector.

Much of the initial vision and funding for the Internet was due to J. C. R. Licklider, the first head of the Information Processing Techniques Office at ARPA (the Advanced Projects Research Agency of the Department of Defense). Licklider sketched an outline for what he called an "intergalactic" network, and was influential in providing funding for the ARPAnet, which evolved into the Internet. The application Licklider envisioned was support for a community of scholars:

What will on-line interactive communities be like? In most fields they will consist of geographically separated members, sometimes grouped in small clusters and sometimes working individually. They will be communities not of common location, but of common *interest*.[21]

The first applications were remote login and file transfer. Electronic mail was soon added.[22] These are still the basic Internet services, but an extra level of tools to integrate distributed servers, e. g., Gopher, Wide Area Information Servers (WAIS), and World Wide Web (WWW), have increased efficiency and ease of use.

Internet and interactive TV applications are different, because they serve different users. Interactive TV is targeting the consumer at home, and (in the U.S.) the Internet has broadened in focus from scholars and computer scientists to include students at all levels and business people. This diversification seems likely to continue in light of the U.S. government having called for connectivity for all classrooms, libraries and clinics.[23]

3.2 Data Types

While interactive TV is being designed for video from the start, and the phone companies control audio communication, the Internet deals primarily with text and programs. There are several Internet image archives, and experiments have begun with audio and motion video, but they are still limited to a few hundred sites and very crude. The Mosaic browsing and retrieval client for WWW allows for an extensible library of data types. Mosaic is achieving wide circulation, and is being adopted in several commercial packages, but it still requires IP connectivity and higher data rates than the majority of Internet users have today. A packet-switched

---

21 Licklider, J. C. R. and Taylor, Robert W, "The Computer as a Communication Device", *Science and Technology*, April, 1968, 21-31, at 30.

22 Marill, Thomas and Roberts, Lawrence G., "Toward a Cooperative Network of Time-Shared Computers", *Proceedings of the 1966 Fall Joint Computer Conference*, 425-431.

23 Gore, Al, *"Remarks at Royce Hall, UCLA"*, Los Angeles, January 11, 1994. Anonymous ftp, sunsite.unc.edu, pub/academic/political-science/internet-related/VP-Speech-at- UCLA.

network like the Internet is also poorly suited to isochronous transmission needed for smooth, interactive audio and motion-video communication.

3.3 TERMINAL DEVICE

Interactive TV is being designed around low-resolution television sets which are viewed from a distance and controlled using a remote channel-selector, a configuration which is poorly suited to the volumes of text common on the Internet. It is well suited to pointing and selecting, games, and relatively infrequent interaction, such as the "VCR" controls on movies. It may also work well with some forms of browsing and shopping, but much comparison shopping and analysis involves text and numeric data presentation and analysis.

The Internet began with Teletypes, but has really been built around desktop computers. As connectivity bandwidth increases, and the cost of digital electronics declines, it will be possible to use one terminal device on the desktop or from the couch. The hardware differences between TV sets and computers may eventually disappear, but the attitude and viewing positions are quite different.[24]

3.4 GEOGRAPHIC SCOPE

The US Administration has called for a GII as well as an NII, and the Internet is more global in outlook. While there is some activity in Europe, the bulk of investment in Interactive TV trials is planned for relatively affluent areas in North America. On the other hand, the Internet has been expanding globally for many years. Over half of the Internet networks are in the US, but, as we have noted, the growth rate outside the US is greater, and 146 political entities have at least e-mail connectivity (91 do not).

In spite of the impressive global spread of the Internet, there are some sobering concerns.[25] About one fifth of the world's population has access to far more capability than the rest. There is a direct correlation between measures of national development and the quality of network services available to advanced industrial and less developed countries (LDCs).[26] The connectivity to an LDC may be as little as a Fidonet link to a few PCs with a handful of regular users. Even within the most advanced, well connected countries the majority of the populations have little or no participation. For

24 Press, L., "Compuvision or Teleputer?", *Communications of the ACM*, 36 (September 1993), pp. 66-80.

25 Goodman, S, Press, L, Ruth, S. and Rutkowski, A., "The Global Diffusion of the Internet: Patterns and Problems", *Communications of the ACM*, in press; Press, L., "The net: progress and opportunity", *Communications of the ACM*, 35/12 (December 1992), 21-25.

26 Ruth, S., Goet, R., "Must invisible colleges be invisible? An approach to examining large communities of network users", *Internet Research*, 3, 1 (Spring 1993), 47.

example, despite the much proclaimed connectivity of U.S. universities, where access is almost a free good, Internet utilization is generally confined to a minority of faculty and students. Going beyond universities, U.S. connectivity is concentrated in urban areas and is relatively sparse in regions such as the Midwest and in poor regions and neighborhoods. These discrepancies are probably greater in developing nations.

3.5 MEDIA

Historically, the Internet has used telephone company facilities, with the U.S. backbone growing from 56 kb/s to T3 speeds. Connected networks typically use telephone company facilities, running from these speeds down to switched connections using analog modems. Only now are we seeing the beginning of low-speed wireless and cable TV-based access.

The interactive TV community originally thought of using an augmented telephone network, but is now also heavily involved with cable TV. The differences between telephone and cable TV companies may, in the long run, become blurred as they begin offering competing services, but for now, they have a different experience.

The telephone companies have a tradition of providing a highly-reliable, automatically transaction-billed service, and seamless global interoperability. By contrast cable companies typically do flat monthly billing, tolerate service interruption, and serve limited areas. Cable companies have a high level of penetration to U.S. homes, but do not typically serve business. The phone companies cover business and homes. (About 80% of U.S. homes fall within 18,000 feet of a switching office, and even more businesses do). The telephone companies are also used to universal access and symmetrical, two-way transmission. Finally, the telephone companies are (for now) profitable and wealthy. AT&T is diversified, selling ATM switches and video servers, buying related companies, and talking about linking local cable providers. The phone companies are also testing "asymmetrical digital subscriber lines", a technique for delivering 1.5 mbit/sec compressed video (VCR quality) over copper wire, though many feel this is at best an interim solution.

3.6 ACCESS ETHIC

In terms of the administration's NII goals, this may be the most profound difference between the Internet and interactive TV communities. Whether for distribution via cable, video rental, or theater, the interactive TV community centrally produces and broadcasts programming. This is also the case with TV-shopping and catalog sales companies, where there are few information providers and many consumers.

Open access is one of the U.S. administration's goals for the NII, and low-cost access, with every user a potential publisher, is a basic tenet of the Internet. The motivating applications were file transfer and remote login, and any host on the original ARPANET could provide either service. These are reflected in the FTP and Telnet services offered by IP-connected Internet hosts today. Even the design and implementation of the Internet protocols is done using the open, democratic mechanism of published Requests For Comment, which may originate with anyone in the community.

While Internet information providers began with FTP archives, the rapid acceptance of WAIS, Gopher, and World Wide Web attests to the ongoing assumption that everyone on the Internet is a potential publisher. I would imagine that nearly every U.S. university publishes gopher or FTP archives and sponsors discussion lists. (I personally maintain two archives and have initiated many listservers). Many of these publications are of relatively local interest, but the Internet-wide "New List" and "Net Happenings" lists include well over 100 announcements per week.

We have been speaking of access by publishers, but access by users is also an issue. As we have seen, the U.S. administration hopes to avoid a gap between those who have and do not have network access[27]. Regulatory and funding pressure will probably make this an issue for both the Internet and interactive TV communities.

3.7 ECONOMIC ORIENTATION

While the interactive TV community speaks of education and community information, potential profit is clearly their prime motivation.

The Internet began in the education and research community. When the National Science Foundation (NSF) began providing backbone connectivity in the U.S., acceptable use policies prohibited commercial activity; however, it was planned that NSF would eventually withdraw, and there would be a transition to commercial use. As we saw above, this is occurring. Still, the growing appearance of commercial activity on the Internet is relatively new, and there remains a large constituency focusing on education and community service. The Internet community debates the issue of usage-based charges; the interactive TV community assumes them.

This difference in economic orientation also grows from the attitudes of the two communities toward the price of information. The Interactive TV

---

27 This possibility was foreseen from the start. Licklider and Taylor wrote:

> "Will 'to be on line' be a privilege or a right? If only a favored segment of the population gets a chance to enjoy the advantage of 'intelligence amplification', the network may exaggerate the discontinuity in the spectrum of intellectual opportunity".
>
> [Licklider, J. C. R. and Taylor, Robert W, "The Computer as a Communication Device", *Science and Technology*, April, 1968, 21-31, at 31].

culture is based on the sale of copywritten information for royalties, while the Internet grew from the academic community which values information sharing. (Though both reward early publication).

3.8 ROLLOUT SCHEDULE

While there were some early trials using manual simulation of Interactive TV, two-way digital trials have yet to begin. If they are successful, broader rollout in affluent parts of North America will begin in the latter half of the decade. It will be many years until a significant number of households and businesses have interactive connectivity.

If we extrapolate current trends, we can expect that by that time, the Internet will have grown significantly, will have a higher percentage of commercial utilization, and will support a wider variety of data types and users. On the other hand, it may still be poorly suited for the distribution of movies and other connection-oriented communication.

3.9 METHOD OF CAPITAL FORMATION

The method of capital formation on the Internet is in keeping with its democratic access ethic. While the original technology was developed (and is being extended) by the U.S. government, and backbone services were subsidized during the startup period, the bulk of the capitalization has come from users. Each user is responsible for their own computer or host as the case may be. User-supplied hardware, software, communication links, and staff account for nearly all of the investment in the Internet. The interactive TV community, like the on-line services industry, follows the more traditional model of a controlling entrepreneur raising capital to finance necessary investment. While the Internet is often criticized as being government funded, both communities seem committed to the adminstration goal of private investment. The difference is not government vs. private, but centralized vs. decentralized funding.

I must admit to a degree of discomfort with the interactive TV community. After all, it is headed by the folks who bring us "Cops", reruns of "Gilligan's Island", and commercials for 1-900 numbers and "workman's compensation" lawyers. Do we want them in control of the deployment and application of a technology that may have as much impact on society and our worldview as the clock or electric light?

Regardless of who is in charge and what their motivation is, NII technology will have profound effects — good and bad, foreseen and unanticipated. I already see this in my own work, where daily collaboration with remote colleagues would be impossible without the Internet. On the other hand, my time is finite, so I have significantly reduced professional collaboration and social interaction with people at my physical workplace. My productivity has been enhanced markedly, but my daily working relationships and organizational loyalty have shifted. The shift from local to remote is more pronounced when we consider the mass media. We know Johnny Carson better than we know our neighbors, and we are touched more deeply by televised events than those on our own blocks.

Working and playing in cyberspace will change our relationship to time, abstraction, and people. It will change our values, perception, and addictions. Regardless of who builds the NII, let's keep our eyes open.

References

(1) Aupperle, E. "NSF backbone trends", *Internet Society News*, 2, 4 (Winter 1994), 13. (1).

(2) Batson, J. and Hyland, J. L., "Don't Laugh, It's ISDN," *The Network Strategy Report*, vol. 7, no 7, pp 2-13, Forrester Research, Cambridge, MA, June, 1993.

(3) Clark, J., "A Tele-Computer", *Proceedings of SIGGRAPH '92*, pp 19-23, Addison-Wesley, Reading, MA, 1992.

(4) Goodman, S, Press, L, Ruth, S. and Rutkowski, A., "The Global Diffusion of the Internet: Patterns and Problems", *Communications of the ACM*, in press.

(5) Gore, Al, "Remarks at Royce Hall, UCLA", Los Angeles, January 11, 1994. Anonymous ftp, sunsite.unc.edu, pub/academic/political-science/internet-related/VP-Speech-at- UCLA.

(6) _______, *"Remarks Prepared for Delivery, International Telecommunications Union"*, Buenos Aires, March 21, 1994. Anonymous ftp, sunsite.unc.edu, pub/academic/political-science/internet-related/ Gore's-Delivered-Remarks-on-NII-12- 21-93.

(7) Green, R. R., Testimony before the Subcommittee on Technology, Environment, and Aviation, Committee on Science, Space, and Technology, U.S. House of Representatives, March 23, 1993.

(8) Landweber, Larry, "The Connectivity Table", Version 10, February 15, 1994, anonymous ftp, ftp.cs.wisc.edu, connectivity table directory.

(9) Licklider, J. C. R. and Taylor, Robert W, "The Computer as a Communication Device", *Science and Technology*, April, 1968, 21-31.

(10) Lottor, Mark, Report-9401, directory pub/zone, ftp.nisc.sri.com, January, 1994.

(11) Marill, Thomas and Roberts, Lawrence G., "Toward a Cooperative Network of Time-Shared Computers", *Proceedings of the 1966 Fall Joint Computer Conference*, 425-431.

(12) Press, L., "Compuvision or Teleputer?", *Communications of the ACM*, 36 (September 1993), pp. 66- 80.

(13) _______, "The net: progress and opportunity", *Communications of the ACM*, 35/12 (December 1992), 21-25.

(14) Rickard, Jack and Funk, Gary, "The International FidoNet - 22067 Bulletin Boards with an Attitude", *Boardwatch Magazine*, August 1993, pp 66-80.

(15) Ruth, S., Goet, R., "Must invisible colleges be invisible? An approach to examining large communities of network users", *Internet Research*, 3, 1 (Spring 1993), 47.

(16) Zinn, L, De George, G., Shoretz, R., Yang, D. J. and Forest, S. A., "Retailing will never Be the Same", *Business Week*, July 26, 1993, p. 54-60.

(17) Zoglin, Richard, "The Info Highway", *Time*, April 12, 1993, pp 56-61.

(18) _______, "Internet global statistics: 1993", *Internet Society News*, 2, 4 (Winter 1994), 7.

(19) _______, "Boardwatch-100, Readers' Choice BBS Contest Results", *Boardwatch Magazine*, September 1993, pp 68-80.

(20) _______, *"Status Report on Two-Way Testbeds"*, Cable Television Information Center, Washington, D. C., May, 1973.

The Domestication of a New Communication Technology : The Vidéoway System

André H. Caron

Looking back over the twentieth century, the arrival of the new communication technologies is considered by many to have been a major watershed. Whether we condemn them as the worst or glorify them as the best of the many changes that have since occurred, these technologies have slowly but surely invaded our everyday existence.

Some would say that the technologies merely reflect society's values. Others make the case that they are the determinants and main impetus of social change; that they remove from the individual the option of controlling their effects. In any case, whether we agree or not with the technology driven paradigm, all of us recognize that new media have a strong potential for transformation.

The most significant characteristic of many of these new communication technologies is that they are used in the home. They have become important tools for the entertainment of household members and, particularly when associated with mass media consumption, increasingly affect how adults' and children's leisure time is organized and managed.

The adoption of a new technology in a household can be visualized as a sort of passage through several phases[1]. In the medium term, it brings about changes in daily habits. During the first couple of months, some of these changes may be linked to the technology's novelty. As different family members adapt to it in what is termed the "domestication phase", however, its use becomes integrated in the ongoing patterns of household activity.

The adoption process will naturally vary from one individual to another, as well as by sex and age or generation, and in terms of how the technology itself progresses and evolves.We have seen a number of false starts or outright failures in this area of new technologies. The importance of users' perceptions about the "friendliness" of a technology or its potential usefulness (factors that directly influence whether or not they will decide to invest time and money in it) has often been underestimated as well.

---

1 Rogers, E. (1983). Elements of Diffusion. In E. Rogers (Eds.), *Diffusion of innovations*, New York: Free Press.

E. Mackaay et al. (eds.), The Electronic Superhighway, 37–53.

The adoption of a technological system is, in summary, a process: something active that fluctuates, develops and organizes itself over time. These attributes characterize not only user attitudes and behaviour but also apply to the technology itself. The Vidéoway system, for example, is a technology in evolution. Its content and form are the subject of continuing trial and development. Adoption of a technological innovation thus comprises two systems, one technological and the other human, that constantly interact, and where changes in one element of the system may bring about changes in different elements of the other system as well.

The Vidéoway technology was first introduced in January of 1990 in Montreal, Canada. It encompasses many elements, from closed-captioning for the hearing-impaired and a Pay-TV decoder, to videotext and interactive television, the two principal components of the system. Videotext incorporates a multitude of services (weather reports, lottery results, road conditions, education, news, TV listings, financial information, and others) as well as video games, (including games of skill, puzzles and parlour games). Subscribers also have access to interactive television, either in the form of programmes designed specifically for the interactive mode, which include entertainment, educational programming and drama for young people, or conventional programming in an enhanced interactive form, such as newscasts, game shows, sports, and variety shows. In the latter, viewers can select content and camera angles or obtain answers to questions.

When, only two years after its commercial introduction, Vidéoway had attracted 150,000 subscribers, researchers at the New Technologies Research Laboratory at the Université de Montréal's Communication department were asked in 1992 to design an in-depth study on the diffusion of this new interactive technology[2] in order to *identify the principal characteristics of the average Vidéoway user.* Based on a representative sample of the subscribers, the results which are presented in this paper are to our knowledge the first set of data collected on such a large scale concerning the diffusion of an interactive technology and its adoption by the general public.

The specific purpose of the study was to learn more about Vidéoway subscribers and to capture their perceptions and level of use of certain components such as videotext services and interactive television. We considered, moreover, that any study on the adoption of a new technology would have to take into account not only the principal adopter in any given household, but also the family members and social context in which the technology was being used, particularly in the case of technologies involving the mass media.

---

2 Although we are aware that Vidéoway is technically not yet a fully interactive system, given it is perceived by the public as such, we shall continue referring to it, in this paper, as an interactive medium.

1. Methodology

The findings we describe were collected during the fall and early winter of 1992 by means of two surveys of a random sample of subscribers to the Vidéoway system. An initial telephone survey of the households in the sample was followed by the completion of a written questionnaire which was mailed to each respondent.

In order to make the survey as representative of Vidéoway subscribers as possible, we respected the proportions of the two groups of subscribers, those who subscribed to Pay-TV (VW+PTV) as well as to Vidéoway and those who suscribed to Vidéoway (VW) only. Our data showed that in 1992 four respondents in five were Pay-TV subscribers and one in five was not. No households who were benefiting from a free trial period or any other promotion when the data was collected were included in the sample.

The purpose of the telephone survey was to gather basic information such as family make-up of subscriber households and preliminary data on the use of the Vidéoway system. After this first contact, we used a mailing to inform respondents that they would be receiving a *written questionnaire* from us within the next few days.

The several sections of the written questionnaire[3] were grouped in three general categories: first, general and socio-demographic questions; second, questions related specifically to the Vidéoway system, such as reasons for subscribing, perceptions about the user-friendliness of the system, and so forth; and, third, questions about the extent and frequency of use of the various Vidéoway features and users' opinions about the technology. The questions were designed to elicit both quantitative and qualitative information.

In order to be able to take into account the perceptions and uses of the various services to which the respondents had access and to determine the detailed user profile of *each member of the family*, four versions of this questionnaire were developed. Each corresponded to a probable category of household members, i.e. principal respondent, spouse (or other adult in the household), teenager and child. No household received more than four questionnaires, however.

The final sample consisted of 1,326 households with a total of nearly 3,000 respondents. The rate of participation in our study was more than 70%. which is remarkably high, given the requests for survey information that members of the public receive from many sources.

---

3 The questionnaire was developed with the collaboration of resource persons at Vidéotron, Vidéoway Plus, TVI, etc.

Because of the time frame, the data reported below are based on 1,276 households, comprising 1,276 principal respondents, 960 spouses, 278 teenagers and 364 children[4].

Table 1 : Distribution of Respondents According to Questionnaire Categories

Questionnaire Categories	Total
Principal respondents	1276
Spouses	960
Teenagers	278
Children	364
TOTAL	2878

Unlike television ratings, which by means of viewer diaries and "people meters" can manage to give a relatively accurate evaluation of the popularity of a particular broadcast, our results concerning time allocation should rather be considered as *general trends*. They are based on respondents' perceptions of the amount of time they believed they were spending on the various aspects of Vidéoway.

2. Results

2.1 RESPONDENTS' PROFILE

The sample consisted of almost equal numbers of men and women. According to the information provided by the persons to whom the questionnaire was addressed, principal respondents were, on average, 42 years of age, their spouses or partners, 39, teenagers, 15, and children, 9 years of age.

The average Vidéoway subscriber household consisted of slightly more than three people and had an annual family income of about $46,000, which is slightly above the national average. With respect to level of education, almost a quarter of the adult respondents had finished elementary school or attended high school, nearly half had graduated from high school or attended CEGEP (colleges in Quebec offering preuniversity and technical courses) or

4 The results of the analyses were weighted according to the actual family makeup of the households.

the equivalent, and one in five had completed CEGEP or the equivalent or had had some university study, which is also above the national average.

With respect to employment, respondents included in almost equal proportions of about 20% in each case, skilled workers, unskilled workers, and people who were retired or at home. The office worker category was also strongly represented in the sample.

On average, subscribers said they had had the Vidéoway system for a year and a half (18.8 months).

2.2 HOME TECHNOLOGIES

Vidéoway subscribers use a number of other "domestic" technologies. We identified three areas in which such services and equipment were used: (1) telephone services, (2) audio-visual equipment and (3) microcomputers .

Table 2 : Home Technologies

Home Technologies	%
1- Telephone services	
- Touchtone	80%
- New specialized services	27%
2- Audiovisual Equipment	
- VCR	87%
- Video Game Units	52%
- CD player	43%
3- Microcomputers	
Microcomputer	27%

Telephone is now inevitably linked to the new technologies. One of the most popular services reported by respondents was Bell Canada's Touchtone service; eight out of ten respondents have access to a Touchtone line. More than a quarter use new Bell Canada specialized services such as Ident-a-call, which identifies the calling number.

The VCR remains the most popular audio-visual technology; almost nine out of ten respondents have access to one. A little over half of the respondents own a video game unit, and more than four in ten own a CD player.

More than one quarter of the respondents have a microcomputer at home.

2.3 SUBSCRIBING TO VIDÉOWAY

Of all the sources of information liable to influence the decision to subscribe to Vidéoway, more than one person in three felt that the most important was the one-month trial period; this impression was particularly strong among the Vidéoway subscribers who did not already have Pay-TV. The social environment was also a strong influence; relatives and friends were mentioned as the second most important source of information in the decision to subscribe.

Since technology of this sort is adopted first and foremost for its content, it is not surprising that Pay-TV subscribers cited movies as the major factor motivating them to subscribe to Vidéoway. It is interesting to note, however, that for respondents overall, even for Pay-TV subscribers, it was the availability of videotext games that influenced their selection of the Vidéoway system. Other videotext services, interactive television, and the broadcast of certain special events in interactive mode were also identified as factors underlying the decision to opt for this technology.

2.4 USER-FRIENDLINESS OF THE VIDÉOWAY SYSTEM

Overall, it seems clear that newcomers to the Vidéoway system did not feel they had been confronted with an impenetrable technology. A great majority of respondents felt that learning the various Vidéoway functions was fairly easy or very easy (80%). This observation does not hide the fact that respondents nonetheless raised certain technical problems they considered were preventing them from making full use of the different features of the Vidéoway terminal. This is an issue that was the subject of a number of spontaneous comments, and will be dealt with in greater detail later in the report.

A vast majority of respondents (85%) indicated that once the learning period was over, they *felt fairly or very comfortable* with the operation of the Vidéoway terminal.

2.5 USE OF VIDÉOWAY

The total amount of time people devote to using a medium is a strong indicator of how valuable they find it and to what extent it has become part of their daily existence. Similarly, frequency of use, i.e. the number of times a week Vidéoway users consult a service, play a game or watch an interactive programme provides additional information on viewing habits.

Our results are reported under three headings: patronage[5], in other words the number of respondents who used the service in the past two weeks; frequency of use, the number of times a service was used within a given week; and weekly viewing time, or the time devoted to an activity from Monday to Sunday for each Vidéoway category.

Videotext Games

In terms of patronage of videotext games, a majority of respondents (70%) indicated that they had accessed that aspect of the technology during the two weeks prior to the survey. Young people were the largest age group to state that they had played videotext games during the previous two weeks.

With respect to frequency of use, considering only users, i.e. respondents who indicated that they had played videotext games during the weeks preceding the study, three out of four (73%) said they had used them twice a week or more. Surprisingly, for those who assume that only teenagers would be avid players , it was the Vidéoway respondents of 50 years and over who were the most frequent users

Figure 1 : Frequency of Use of Videotext Games

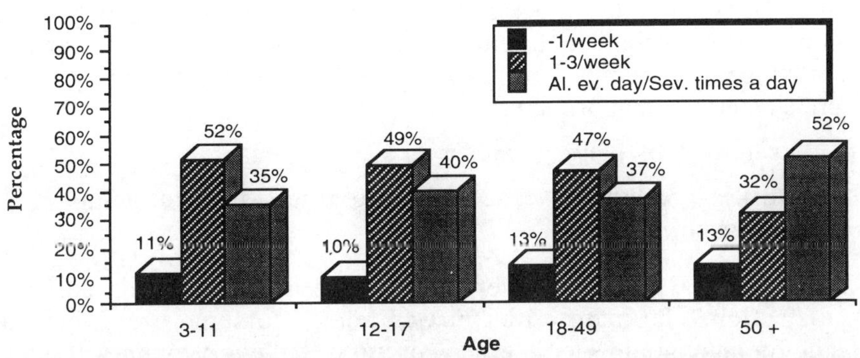

Per capita (that is, all subscribers, users or not), *nearly four hours* from Monday to Sunday were spent on videotext games. Users' weekly playing time averaged five and a half hours per week.

5 For lack of a better word, the term patronage is used to refer to the percentage of a given population which reports having used a service over a certain period of time.

Asked about their favourite games, the top five mentioned by respondents overall were Quilles (bowling), Styx, Patiences (solitaire), Dé-Plus (dice) and Poker. While there were some differences in the order of preference depending on the age and sex of the respondents, in general, the same games recurred for each category of respondents.

One of the most interesting phenomena we observed was the respondents' tendency to play Vidéoway videotext games in company with other people. More than half the users (56%) reported playing games very or fairly often as a group activity. Younger people, more than any other age group, were apt to do so.

We shall digress briefly here on the topic of educational games for children . In terms of use, more than one child in two between the ages of 3 and 11 (54%) indicated that he or she had accessed children's games during the two weeks prior to the study. If we consider use by children 3 to 6 years only, however, we note that nearly three out of four accessed the service during the two-week period. As for frequency of use, over half the children 3 to 11 years of age (55%) played these games twice a week or more. The younger children (3-6 years) tended to access the games an average of four times a week, more often than the older children (7-11 years), who used them about twice a week.

Spontaneous Comments on Videotext Games

A series of open-ended questions encouraged respondents to give their spontaneous views on different aspects of Vidéoway. With regard to videotext games, subscribers expressed interest based largely on this feature's entertainment or recreational value:

> "I can relax by playing cards with VW." (spouse)
>
> "I. like everything, especially the questionnaire games." (teenager)

It is important as well, however, to draw attention to certain sources of dissatisfaction. The main criticism was related to some users' insatiable appetite for an ongoing supply of new or more challenging games. Technical drawbacks such as the waiting time for downloading and the inadequacy of the remote control as a high performance game tool were also mentioned:

> "Games like presto are updated only once a month; that's not enough." (principal respondent)
>
> "If we use games like super-Hangman often, the words should change more often." (spouse)
>
> "More educational features for young people on math, history" (principal respondent)

"Not enough war, aviation and auto racing games; action games." (principal respondent)

"Waiting time too long during downloading." (spouse)

"Remote control not very functional for some games. A special remote control with a joystick would be appreciated." (spouse)

Videotext Services other than Games

In terms of patronage, slightly more than two out of three repondents (69%) indicated that they had accessed videotext services other than games (such as weather, astrology, lottery, information) during the two weeks prior to the survey.

With respect to frequency of use, over seven out of ten said they had accessed other videotext services at least twice a week, and the weekly average was four times.

As for weekly viewing time, respondents overall reported spending slightly more than *an hour and a half a week* on videotext services other than games. Among users, weekly viewing time averaged nearly two and a half hours per week, with an average of 20 minutes a day. As was the case for videotext games, respondents 50 years old and over tended to spend more time on videotext services than other groups of respondents.

We should emphasize that nearly three users in five (58%) said they turned on the television set twice a week or, more specifically, to obtain information in videotext mode; this tendency was more marked among women than among men.

A variety of information that is available through the traditional media of radio and television is also offered to subscribers by videotext services. It is interesting to note that there seems to be some indication of new habits in the making; viewers seeking information are moving away from these more traditional media toward Vidéoway's videotext mode. *Over a third of the respondents, for example, reported that they now prefer to consult Vidéoway, for the horoscopes, lottery results and weather forecasts, that until recently they customarily accessed in the traditional media.* They nonetheless, clearly indicated their loyalty to the traditional media for such information as the news or TV schedules.

Table 3 : Obtaining Specific Information on Vidéoway vs. in the Traditional Media (Radio, Newspapers, Television)[6]

Information	Prefer Videoway	Prefer Traditional Media	Both	Not Interested
Weather	47%	13%	36%	2%
Lottery	64%	6%	20%	8%
Horoscope	33%	7%	21%	36%

Spontaneous Comments on Videotext Services

From the spontaneous comments expressed in the data, we can see that videotext services are appreciated for a number of reasons:

> "Extraordinary discovery — great menu variety — freedom of action." (principal respondent)
>
> "Videotext for relaxing."
>
> "Greetings we can send." (spouse)
>
> Nonetheless, respondents also indicated some dissatisfaction with the slowness of downloading or about the excessive number of services that they did not find useful or interesting:
>
> "Several services I never use, for example horoscope, lottery..." (principal respondent)
>
> "Videotext services: entertainment, maintenance, things I don't watch." (principal respondent)

Two observations should be made at this point. First, although the quantity of types of available content available on videotext services was considered ample in terms of sheer numbers, respondents did not always perceive it as providing greater diversity. Second, different tastes must be taken into account. Features that are very popular with some people may not appeal to others.

Interactive Television

With respect to patronage three respondents out of five (59%) indicated that they had tuned in to TVI, Vidéoway's interactive television service, during the two-week period prior to the survey.

6 This evaluation was reported by principal respondents and spouses only.

The frequency of use, i.e. the number of times TVI viewers tuned into TVI, amounted to an average of three times a week. Just over two-thirds of them (67%) watched interactive television twice a week or more.

The per capita weekly viewing time of TVI, for survey respondents overall, averaged about *three hours,* while for viewers only, average viewing hours amounted to about five from Monday to Sunday. We should explain that interactive television broadcasts both traditional programmes in interactive mode (e.g. Jeopardy, Hockey, TVA newscast) and programmes designed exclusively for interactive television (e.g. L'Ascenseur, Safari).

As for their preferences, the programmes L'Ascenseur (game show), Jeopardy, Black Jack 21, Miroir Miroir (humor), and À vous l'enquête (mystery show) were identified by the largest number of viewers as being their favourites. While preferences varied somewhat according to the viewers' age and gender, these five programmes appeared on the lists of all groups of respondents.

Part of the TVI broadcasting is available simultaneously in traditional and interactive modes (e.g. Jeopardy, Hockey, TVA newscast). It is interesting to note that nearly half of the viewers (48%) said they frequently chose the interactive version of the programme, and one in four (25%) said they always selected it. This tendency was even stronger among subscribers who do not have Pay-TV.

Figure 2 : Choice of the Interactive over the Traditional Version

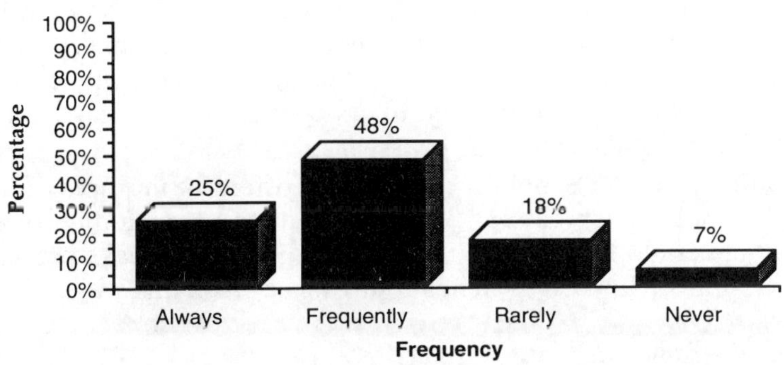

The popularity of the program Watatatow (a soap opera for young people) is of interest. This show, which was first broadcast in 1991 in both traditional and interactive modes, has been very successful with its target audience, 70% of whom have said they tune in to it at least once a week; this is the highest rate of success for any interactive programme. L'Addition S.V.P., an educational math programme, is also particularly popular among teenagers.

Spontaneous Comments on Interactive Television
Respondents were enthusiastic about the participatory format provided by TVI, as shown in the following spontaneous comments:

> "Interactive programmes that are just what I asked for." (spouse)
>
> "I like the interactive programmes very much because you can be part of the action." (spouse)
>
> "I like the interactive programmes: hockey, jeopardy." (spouse)

They also mentioned the scarcity of new programming, however:

> "I can't wait to get some new interactive programmes." (principal respondent)
>
> "Reruns of Miroir-Miroir for the past year." (teenager)

Television viewing habits

Vidéoway also provides the viewer with access to various television channels available on cable. Vidéoway subscribers have, in general, more than two television sets in their homes. On average, Vidéoway subscribers[7] estimated spending some 16 hours a week watching traditional television, a figure lower than the national weekly average of approximately 24 hours a week.

Four out of five respondents in the survey were subscribers to Pay-TV. A vast majority of these (92%) indicated they had exposure to Pay-TV during the two-week period prior to the survey. Overall, respondents devoted slightly more than thirteen hours to this fare of television content between Monday and Sunday.

One of the Pay-TV options Vidéoway offers is multiplexing on it's movie channel Super Ecran. Viewers can choose among three film selections at certain times of the week. During the two weeks preceding the survey, viewers on average watched four films a week this way.

Spontaneous Comments on Pay-TV
Many respondents appreciated the multiple choice options on Pay-TV, but also stressed content (as is the case with many movie channels) as their main source of dissatisfaction:

> "Too many violent films and not enough comedies." (spouse)

---

7 These results should be considered only as general indications. Assessment of time spent on television viewing habits could be more accurately measured if obtained from a TV viewing log or an electronic measuring device.

> "Too frequent repetition of films — it's like always eating leftovers." (principal respondent)

2.6 GENERAL REACTIONS TO THE VIDÉOWAY SYSTEM

In the last part of the questionnaire, a series of open-ended questions encouraged respondents to give their spontaneous reactions. They were asked to comment in particular on the features of Vidéoway that gave them the least and the most satisfaction. In addition, they were invited to add any other remarks that they wished. The very large response to this invitation proved to be an invaluable qualitative addition to our analysis.

Table 4 : Vidéoway Features Respondents Find Most Satisfying

Games
Pay-TV
Interactive television

Respondents' comments indicated that they appreciate Vidéoway overall, and, in particular, games (the diversity), pay television (the absence of commercials) and interactive television (téléparticipation), as well as the general variety of the content.

> "Knowing that there are several options 'my TV has no limits'". (spouse)
>
> "Having several things available when I want: weather forecasts, games, finance..." (spouse)
>
> "Customized TV." (spouse)
>
> "When the children come over to visit, they enjoy the games." (principal respondent)
>
> "The educational aspect that VW brings to the children." (spouse)
>
> "VW will be more attractive when we can carry out transactions from the home." (principal respondent)

Some respondents mentioned the survey itself and seemed pleased to have the opportunity to express their opinions.

> "Interesting survey, and I encourage you to continue to consult us." (principal respondent)

> "I would like to know whether filling out the questionnaire serves a useful purpose and whether it will be taken into consideration." (principal respondent)

While the vast majority of respondents had a relatively favourable opinion of Vidéoway, a number expressed reservations. When they were asked to indicate spontaneously what they found least satisfying about the terminal or to provide their personal comments on Vidéoway, respondents mainly focused on technical aspects, TVI and cost.

Table 5 : Vidéoway Features Respondents Find Least Satisfying

Technical aspects
Interactive television (content)
Cost

There were a number of comments about the remote control, its fragility, and its performance in some games. Moreover, with respect to the technical aspects of the technology, there are problems related to connecting the system to other kinds of technology in the home and to using a VCR. Pricing and a need for more frequent updating were raised by game and interactive TV fans, as the following comments illustrate:

> "Improve the technical aspect of the Vidéoway terminal to make it compatible with audio/video/Hi-Fi components." (principal respondent)

> "Please consider request for a better remote control with children's games they're always using the remote, and it's not sturdy enough." (principal respondent)

> "The system for obtaining programme information: too many steps, too slow." (principal respondent)

> "In general, I like Vidéoway and intend to keep it, but it is absolutely essential for you to continue to offer us new games and services to hold our interest." (principal respondent)

3. Conclusion

By 1992, after two years of diffusion, the Vidéoway technology appears to have become part of family life and everyday use for many subscribers and their families, albeit in a very gradual way. The respondents were more familiar than in previous studies with the existence of the various types of content that Vidéoway offers, including games, videotext services and interactive television programmes.

Interpersonal networks appeared to have played an important role in the technology's diffusion. Recommendations from family and friends who already had the Vidéoway system, and demonstrations of its capabilities when friends and family visit their homes have influenced the decision to adopt of many.

A difference in viewing was noted between those subscribing to Pay-TV and non-Pay-TV subscribers. Asked to estimate the average amount of time generally spent[8] on TV viewing, Vidéoway subscribers, those not subscribing to Pay-TV, perceived they now spend approximately 70% of their time on regular television and some 30% of their time on Vidéoway services (16% on games, 5% on videotext services and 8% on interactive television). It should, however, be noted that an important part of interactive television viewing is interwoven with traditional television viewing, since some interactive programmes are simultaneously broadcast in the linear mode. Vidéoway Pay-TV subscribers on the other hand, reported spending about 80% of their time on regular and Pay-TV channels and 20% on such features as games (9%) Vidéoway services (4%) and TVI (8%). Quite obviously, some traditional TV viewing time is now shifting towards these new services, but some of this time is also transferred from other leisure activities. This echoes the findings of earlier studies of the adoption of home computers where the introduction of a new technology driven activity into the home, usually causes an important displacement of the time formerly allocated to regular television. Even if people reported in our study a certain overestimation, time spent on this new technology is still sizable.

Video Games were cited as a major motivation for subscribing. Contrary to what we might think, the biggest fans of video games were people over 50, in terms of both frequency and usage time. Although it may be the case that they have more free time to spend on such services, interest is most certainly also part of the explanation.

As for interactive television, it appears that teenagers and people over 50 are the major viewers. Of these, men tend to prefer sportscasts, women are more apt to access a game show.

Another important observation in the 1992 study was related to the degree to which the technology becomes a part of the everyday habits of respondents. On the one hand, we note that nearly three people in five said they turn on the television set twice a week or more to consult a specific videotext service, a tendency more pronounced among women than among men. On the other hand, we note that respondents have developed certain information seeking habits: they prefer Vidéoway to the traditional media

---

8 These results should be considered only as general indications. They remain the individual's perception of time spent on the various aspects of Vidéoway.

for such features as lottery results and weather forecasts. Furthermore, when respondents have a choice between an interactive and a traditional version of a television programme, nearly three in four will always or frequently choose the interactive mode.

In general, if people are large-scale users or fans of a service, a game or an interactive broadcast, they will be proportionately more demanding, and their potential disappointment in the long term can be that much greater. For Vidéoway to become rooted in the everyday habits of households, it is imperative that they establish a unified strategy that takes into account the need for novelty and provides solutions to technical problems.

At the present time we are gathering additional data on a number of related issues. Although we have not completed the analysis, the comparative data we are collecting in other markets and countries, will provide us with an even better understanding of the issues involved. As an update, we know today that subscribers to Vidéoway now number over 210,000 in the greater Montreal and Quebec city areas, 25,000 in western Canada and 65,000 in the United Kingdom. We also know that in the Montreal market that the mix of Vidéoway as a stand alone and Vidéoway with Pay-TV is now at 35/65 compared to the 20/80 mix we had in 1992.

The direct competition from television that Vidéoway faces is definitely based on content. If television of the traditional type is strong on content, Vidéoway services will be more vulnerable; they will not disappear but their use will vary. In the upcoming results, we expect to find a certain adjustment or correction occurring in the percentages for usage of the various services, although we anticipate that eight people out of ten in Vidéoway subscriber households will still report having used one service or more on a regular basis.

We know at this point that the initial technical problems with the VCR hookup have been addressed, and a new remote control prototype is being tested. Because consumer adoption of this technology is more content than technology based, we can also claim that a technology such as Vidéoway must renew its services and content on a fairly regular basis to retain its momentum.

The strength of the internet highway lies in the informatic links and networks created between people. The users provide the content. With Vidéoway, the content is more television based. Thus, for Vidéoway, the next important challenge lies in its transition towards UBI, that is, becoming completely bidirectional and transactional.

Unlike many other attempts, when the original Vidéoway was launched five years ago, it did not falter at the outset. Through a combination of technological modification and user feedback it moved through and beyond the initial adoption stage to a much wider utility and audience.

Yet it is necessary to proceed with caution. Although, technically, Vidéoway is not yet truly interactive, people perceive it as such. This is important to keep in mind when we think of the potential shape of the electronic highway to be. If people continue to perceive the highway as it is presented in the media, we will soon be approaching a point where false hopes and false securities predominate. For this reason it is imperative that important issues such as privacy rights, copyrights and regulatory aspects on content be addressed before the electronic superhighway, so touted in the media, actually comes into being.

Part II

Electronic Superhighways - Uses

The Internet and Legal Information : Projects and Prospects

The Communication Highway and Academic Publishing

The Internet and Legal Information : Projects and Prospects

Tom R. Bruce

1. Man draws dogs, bites Net: a coming of age

The *New Yorker* magazine held a cartoon depicting two dogs at the keyboard of a personal computer. One animal is saying to the other, "On the Internet, nobody knows you're a dog"[1].

For the Internet community, the *New Yorker* cartoon marked a passage into adolescence. The Internet had risen far enough into the popular consciousness to be laughed at by sophisticates, a mark of wider public awareness. Many now divide the Internet's history (informally, of course; informality is an Internet hallmark) into "before the dogs" and "after the dogs" epochs; the Net-savvy mutts were just the beginning. By Christmas, eight new trade paperbacks purporting to be guides to the Internet appeared on the shelves of massmarket booksellers. By New Year's Day they were out of date.

All in all, literally thousands of Internet-related stories appeared in the non-technical press in 1993 and early 1994. Many of them made liberal use of the word "cyberspace". Most of them prominently featured the phrases "information superhighway" and "interactive television". Virtually all of them were variations on a theme: five hundred channels of interactive mud-wrestling will be coming to your home soon, courtesy of an unholy alliance of the telephone, cable television, and computer industries. The reaction from most people who had actually been working with Internet-based technologies was one of cautious approval; they liked the attention, but they didn't know whether a future in which all the bandwidth is consumed by Arnold Schwarzenegger movies was exactly what they'd been working toward. Like an adolescent with growing pains, the Internet community is not at all sure whether it wants to be an adult on someone else's terms, or if it might just be wiser to remain a child long enough for the whole thing to blow over. Like other adolescents, it is already well out of childhood with no way back.

1 *New Yorker* magazine, July 5, 1993, 61.

E. Mackaay et al. (eds.), The Electronic Superhighway, 57–67.

2. Legal information and the Net

The high-bandwidth media hype of the past several months neglects the utility of existing Internet technology. The last few years have seen substantial experiment and growth in the legal-information sphere. Four years ago (with the possible exception of a few acceptable-use policies and law-of-computing documents scattered across FTP sites) there was no legal information on the Net. Three years ago, there was one law-specific Gopher server, the one operated by the Legal Information Institute at Cornell. Two years ago, there was one law-specific WorldWideWeb server, again at Cornell. There was almost no information being mounted by government agencies at that time, and only one commercial publisher who was using Gopher as a means of vending legal information.

The situation today is quite different. Many Federal agencies are now making information available through the Net; perhaps the largest single example is the EDGAR database of securities filings. A dozen or more law schools are mounting information in one format or another; many others have plans to do so. Uniform stylistic standards are the subject of recurrent discussion in the academic legal-technology community, and it seems likely that a "legal hypertext style book" will emerge sooner rather than later. Practitioners have been slower to act; relatively few firms have direct Internet connectivity, and most are worried about security issues which were solved to the satisfaction of the defence industry years ago. Nonetheless, the first WorldWideWeb server operated by a law firm came on-line for test purposes a few hours before this sentence was written, bearing information designed to showcase the intellectual inventory of the firm. There will be many, many more.

These youthful accomplishments invite speculative comparisons with established and presumably more mature commercial legal data services. The comparisons are sometimes fuelled by enthusiasm (the "Wow! we could start our own LEXIS!" response) or skepticism ("Why should we do this at all when we have WESTLAW?"). Those two giants themselves use the Internet as a pipe through which to ship their data inventory. But looking at Internet infrastructure merely as a better or worse way of delivering the same old services to the same old markets is a profound mistake. It is equally wrongheaded to assume that the methods historically used by the computerised legal information industry to exchange money for information are the only ones available to us. To do so ignores the fact that the Internet is a very different medium, and it ignores a long history of software and hardware development in which quantitative improvements in technology, accompanied by reduction in cost, lead to enormous qualitative change.

We are witnessing a revolution of scale and of scope which in many respects will parallel the personal computer's overthrow of the mainframe, and which will occur for many of the same reasons. Perhaps that sweeping statement is simply the legal technologists' transliteration of the media hype mentioned a moment ago; I suppose you could call it the "500 channels of interactive legal information" story. If it is a fantasy, it is one firmly rooted in the reality of present-day production systems, and a look at those roots is in order.

3. What is the WorldWideWeb?

The balance of this essay will use WorldWideWeb technology as its point of departure. The Web is actually composed of three parts: a client-server protocol (HTTP) by which software running on a workstation can request data from a remote computer over the Internet; a markup language (HTML) which permits typographic information, hypertext links, images, digitised audio clips, animations, and interactive forms to be embedded in ordinary ASCII documents; and a Uniform Resource Locator scheme (URL standard) which provides a common syntax for describing the means of access to and location of virtually all data resources on the Internet. The URL notation is the basis not only of a syntactic scheme for embedding hypermedia links into Web documents, but of a kind of "protocol transparency", in which the user of Web client software need not be concerned with the actual mechanics used to deliver data to her machine.

Complete descriptions of the Web standards are outside the scope of this paper, as is detailed explanation of hypertext and what it does. I will instead concentrate on a few critical aspects and implications of the technology, with examples taken largely from our ongoing work at the Legal Information Institute. It seems only logical to begin with the hardware and software needed to support the effort.

4. Hardware and software platforms

Web server software exists for all hardware platforms commonly in use today, including all varieties of personal computers and UNIX workstations, as well as VAX minicomputers and IBM mainframes. Typically, the systems used for high-traffic servers are workstations running some variant of UNIX. This may be more a matter of affection than performance; some experimenters report that PC clones of modest capabilities (486-33's) running commercial flavors of UNIX for IBM PC's have outperformed dedicated RS-6000 workstations costing ten times as much. The unifying characteristic of the machines commonly in use as Web servers is that they are inexpensive, well under $10,000 (US) for a very capable machine with two gigabytes of disk storage, and quite possibly half that.

Connectivity costs for a Web server vary greatly depending on the type of institution running it. At most university-based sites, the cost of Internet connection for a particular machine is subsumed in some overall budget and is inexpensive on a per-machine basis; ours costs in the vicinity of $36 (US) per month. Costs for a dedicated 14.4K phone link serviced by a commercial Internet access provider, such as the one used by Venable, Baetjer, Howard, & Civiletti to provide access to their Web server, might run $2000 annually. Finally, all the software used at the server is freely distributed and costs nothing. To put these numbers in perspective, the LII's hardware, software, and connectivity cost for startup of their Web, Gopher, and listserv operations, plus one year's operating cost, was less than half the amount of money saved each year by a move to electronic proof generation at the school's two student-edited law journals.

5. Distributed hypertext

These are not, of course, the only costs involved. Hardware and software expenses are in fact a rather small part of the overall cost of electronically publishing a collection of texts, though they have a disproportionate chilling effect when an organization contemplates Internet distribution for the first time. The lifetime cost of such a system is almost entirely in the mounting and more significantly the maintenance of the collection. The fact is that if an organization wishes to provide value-added legal information, then someone or something is going to have to add the value. That value-adding process will have costs associated with it in both the near and long terms. Distributed hypertext permits organizations in different sectors to share those costs in new and interesting ways.

Earlier hypertext systems allowed the user to navigate among documents maintained on standalone computers and on local area networks; they were, in effect, confined to environments where the workstation could be fooled into believing that the disk used to store hypertext documents was physically attached to it. This was and is a serviceable technology, and its utility in the organization and retrieval of legal text has been widely recognized and acted upon. Web technology goes beyond these earlier systems in its ability to provide hypertext links across machines on the Internet, for the most part without regard to specific delivery protocols. It is easy for a Web client to access information made available through the Web itself, through Gopher servers, WAIS databases, anonymous FTP, and essentially any other access system for which gateway software can be written (examples include the HyTelnet, Hyper-G, and TechInfo formats). In cultural and administrative terms, this means that hypertext links can tie together bodies of text which are related in substance but unrelated in sponsorship, text which is mounted and maintained by different organizations, without regard for geographical or institutional proximity. The editorial and maintenance costs of a collection can be spread across many cooperating "sub-providers", each one mounting and maintaining a portion, perhaps one in which the provider has substantial expertise or interest.

The collection of US Supreme Court opinions offered by the Legal Information Institute illustrates this proposition well. The actual opinions are mounted for anonymous FTP retrieval at Case Western Reserve University under Project Hermes, an effort begun by the Court in 1990 to make decisions available electronically to public and private-sector entities. Case Western decided to use anonymous FTP — the most widely available technology at the time — as the means of distribution, dividing each text from the court into syllabus, opinion, dissents, concurrences, and so forth, and assigning each portion a unique file name based on the docket number of the case. The user of CWRU's anonymous FTP site is confronted with a directory structure full of files with names like "92-1168.ZS.filt", which is in fact the syllabus of the decision in the *Harris v. Forklift Systems* sexual-harassment case. CWRU is, of course, adding considerable value by filtering out word-processing codes, dividing the opinions into reasonably-sized chunks, and providing a publicly-accessible distribution point. For the average individual trying to obtain an opinion, however, the combination of cryptic filenames which won't pass unaltered onto a DOS-based file system and the poor navigational capabilities of most FTP clients add up to an interface best described as user-hostile.

The LII's contribution has been the construction of hypertext pages which link case names and related information to the FTP files at Case Western. This provides end users with a hypertextual, annotated table of contents from which they may select cases by actual case name and portion (e.g. syllabus, opinion, concurrence, and so forth) without needing to know or to look up the docket number. These hypertext pages are stored on Cornell's server, and the opinions remain at Case Western. CWRU bears the cost of mounting the actual opinions, and Cornell bears the cost of organizing and maintaining usable access points for the average user. We have gone on to make the collection searchable in a variety of ways, including organization by keyworded topic and full-text search. Again, only the indices and the searching software are at Cornell, with the "base text" at CWRU.

This process, which we have glibly dubbed "add-on scholarship", is much more than a workaday exercise in the librarian's or indexer's art. The same techniques can be used to unify scattered bodies of related material. We are in the early stages of a grant-funded project in which the Rules of Professional Conduct as adopted in each of the 50 states would be mounted by institutions in each of the states. Participating organizations — which might be law schools, bar associations, or law firms with a *pro bono* bent — need only mount those sections which differ from the two major variants on the Model Rules of Professional Conduct. The remainder of the corpus for each state would be drawn from a central pool, accessed section by section via hypertext links. Thus, the table of contents for any given state would contain a mixture of pointers to generic and localized sections, minimizing the work needed from any one of the participating institutions and, correspondingly, its expense.

6. Law teaching and add-on scholarship.

Two years ago, we undertook a collaboration with the Fletcher School of Law and Diplomacy at Tufts University. Fletcher personnel provided us with digital versions of a large collection of multilateral treaties; we provided a distribution point with full-text search capability on our Gopher server. One of many treaties so treated was the Berne Convention for the Protection of Literary and Artistic works, which now does double duty as an item in the Fletcher multilaterals collection and as one piece of a much more extensive collection of intellectual property materials put together by the LII. The collection includes all relevant US copyright, patent, and trademark statutes and regulations. It is, in fact, the Internet extension of a project begun a few years ago using Folio Views on a local area network. My colleague Peter Martin has used that environment to do another kind of "add-on" hypertext linking : he mounts his outline for each class presentation in his intellectual property course in hypertext form with links to the relevant portions of the core statutory material. It is not difficult to imagine that a law teacher or group of law teachers working in the same substantive area might well do the same across the Net, creating a much more seamless, electronic equivalent of the Xeroxed anthologies-cum-textbooks which have become popular in recent years. (Indeed, in the week which elapsed between the first drafting of this paragraph and the transmission of my text to the conference organizers, someone did so. A teacher of contract law at Ohio Northern University built links between a Web version of the review outline he prepares for his students and the relevant sections of the Uniform Commercial Code as mounted at Cornell.) Each teacher could retain her unique perspective, while offering those of others. No individual need bear the full brunt of mounting and organizing large chunks of core material which will be used by all. The addition of personalized annotation capability, already an experimental reality in the Web research community, would allow such resources to be highly individualized and extended by students and teachers.

7. Other channels

Though I earlier offered to confine myself to Web technology, the availability of other communications technologies and channels across the Internet begs at least a nod here, and for two reasons. First, the array of technologies available permits electronic publishers to offer additional services built on their investment in mounting electronic text. Second, the availability of electronic mail in particular means that every text placed on the Net can exist at the center of many channels of communication, some of them especially useful to an author/publisher.

The first idea is illustrated by LIIBULLETIN, a service offered by the LII shortly after we began automatically constructing pointers to new Supreme Court opinions as they were delivered to CWRU by the Court. The same software which discovered the existence of new opinions to be indexed and added to our hypertext pages could, with only minor modifications, send notice by e-mail to persons who wished to know the existence of a new opinion from the Court, in a message which also contains the syllabus of the opinion and instructions for retrieving its full text by mail. This offers a service to those who have only mail connectivity to the Net, as well as adding value through its timeliness and through its narrowcast characteristics: the alert is transmitted directly to a mailbox which the user presumably scrutinizes frequently, rather than through a broadcast or bulletin-board apparatus.

The second idea takes its power from the idea that a publicly-mounted text on the Net is visible to large numbers of other experts who presumably have access to mail and can address responses more or less directly to the author. On several occasions — though I should perhaps blush to mention it — errata or omissions in an online text have been brought to our attention very quickly by others on the Net. There is an interactive power working in the author's favor here; one need not be trapped for a year or more in an error which has been typeset and distributed to who knows where. Our experience is that the most perceptive and expert readers are the most likely to provide feedback. One anticipates a certain amount of annoyance from non-expert readers, or readers with axes to grind, but in fact this kind of communcation has in our case been very rare by contrast with a much greater volume of genuinely useful feedback received from our peers.

Of course, conversations need not be limited to errata and other problems. Substantive discussion of online works can take place, be captured, and then perhaps incorporated into the work. The capture and subsequent public offering of electronic conversation about electronic texts offers the possibility of symposia and colloquia which take place in virtual space. Because of their specific relationship with an electronically published work, such symposia can remain relatively both focussed and timely.

8. Who will participate?

Academic institutions are not the only inhabitants of the Net. We are continually surprised at the diversity of audience for the legal information we mount at Cornell. The LII version of the Supreme Court opinions is accessed by everyone from teachers in political-science departments to high-school students and researchers in government laboratories. While at first we imagined that our efforts would primarily be interesting to the legal academic community and a few venturesome practitioners, we find that we have a much larger audience, one that for the most part has not been served well by traditional on-line services. This audience first declared itself in a note to us from a corporate manager in Hewlett-Packard's London office, expressing his gratitude for our efforts in mounting American intellectual-property material. He needed and could not otherwise obtain daily access to copyright regulations. Many others have stepped forward via e-mail, including ham radio operators interested in FCC regulations, high-school civics teachers, and foreign legal scholars. The log files which record activity on our servers show that US law schools and legal practitioners are in fact the minority among those accessing our material.

The Net is a communications space common to the public, private, governmental, and academic sectors. Many synergistic efforts can result from this kind of cross-sector proximity. The LII works closely with a number of corporate sponsors who have an interest in legal and quasi-legal information, and examples of such projects exist at many places other than Cornell. The EDGAR securities-filing database was recently mounted on the Internet; it is a large and important example of government information from one agency (the Securities and Exchange Commission) being mounted with funding from another agency (the National Science Foundation) by a collaboration between a private sector entity (Internet Multicast, Inc.) and an academic institution (the business school at New York University). Our own more modest example is the mounting of the NASDAQ Financial Executive Journal, an outreach publication of the NASDAQ Stock Market.

The NASDAQ project is an interesting example of what one might call "corporate presence information", information mounted by a company not for sale or as advertising but as a means of offering access to corporate intellectual property as a new species of customer service. The value of Internet publication to NASDAQ is presence in front of its issuing companies, many of whom are high-tech corporations who already have considerable Internet presence themselves. Just as a law firm might open an office in a city where a major client is beginning business operations, NASDAQ has opened a kiosk in cyberspace as a way of showing solidarity with and service to its customers. As it happened, the service was a timely one; the first issue, which was largely concerned with strategies for avoiding shareholder suits when stock prices tumble, was put on the Net roughly a week before the sharp drop in the price of Apple Computer stock last summer. We logged a large number of accesses from individuals at 'apple.com' in the weeks that followed.

The timeliness of NASDAQ's first informational offering was coincidental, but it is not difficult to imagine that corporations — and even law firms — might find ways to make equally topical information available by design. Many already do exactly that with newsletters describing the effects of regulatory changes, pending legislation, and so on. Electronic information can, of course, be distributed much more quickly than paper, and can thus be even more timely. We routinely receive the text of the NASDAQ publication at the same time as the printer of the paper edition does, and generally have it on-line ten days prior to the mailing of the paper version.

9. Sponsorship, for-pay services, and altruism

Corporate presence information falls at the midpoint of a spectrum which has the traditional grant-funded altruism of the Internet community at one end and for-pay services such as LEXIS and WESTLAW at the other. That continuum is a spacious one, with room for many models. The notion of private sponsorship of public information, analogous to corporate sponsorship of public television in the US, falls nearer altruism. I believe this is a viable structure, though one which has not been used to any great degree. One can easily envision a database of occupational safety and health regulations sponsored by a safety-equipment company, or an on-line version of the *Physician's Desk Reference* sponsored by a pharmaceutical concern.

The other end of the spectrum is not yet well-populated either, primarily because there are as yet no commonly-accepted and reliable authentication mechanisms (passwording systems) which would permit "pay-by-the-drink" services to exist. Counterpoint Publishing, among others, has been experimenting with a subscription system which does seem to work well, although one imagines that the administrative overhead is high. Of course, it is actually possible for a company to make money by giving information away; West Publishing's recent offering of a national directory of lawyers via Gopher server can be seen as this kind of "loss leader", a useful and coherent data resource made freely available, with the implicit promise of much more to those who pay.

In any case, workable authentication schemes are no more than a year away; they are understandably the target of a great deal of interest in both the academic and commercial research and development communities. One should bear in mind that authentication is only the tip of an economic iceberg. Customer-service businesses of various kinds are needed. Imagine, for example, that you routinely access four hundred different information servers each month as you move around the Net; in a hypertext environment you might do this quite easily and naturally. How many invoices do you get at the end of the month? Four hundred? Or would you prefer to deal with a business organization which will consolidate those individual charges into a single itemized invoice, much as charge-card providers do? Some commercial on-line services (Delphi was perhaps the first) are clearly planning to position themselves in this way, but it is not clear that any one of them can do so effectively as a single member of a large and growing pool of access providers.

There are those in the academic community for whom any hint of commercialization is anathema, but their days are numbered. Altruism in the mounting of information at no apparent cost has served to jump-start use of the Net, but may not serve the public well in the long run unless the altruists raise their sights. Volunteers have sometimes done a terrible job of meeting information-quality standards we take for granted in print and in the commercial on-line services. In part this is because volunteers have been more interested in the delivery systems than in the content, and in part it is owed to the fact that they can't afford to maintain large collections individually. This is not to say that academic organizations should give up electronic publication in favor of existing commercial operations. Far from it. It is simply that organizations in academia need to find new ways to be compensated for their work; there is much about their labor that has real value in an information economy. Cost sharing and other cross-sector efforts will require an unprecedented degree of administrative cooperation and creativity in constructing relationships between academic, governmental, and private-sector players who do not at this point understand one another very well. The technology makes such cooperation possible but not inevitable; the next major strides to be made in electronic publishing on the Internet need to be administrative rather than technological innovations.

10. Content

The necessity which will mother this kind of cooperative invention may well arise from a new perception by the market that content is the only valid way to differentiate electronic products. It has, until now, been very much in the interest of electronic publishers to seize on comprehensiveness and user interface as the primary points of competition between products which offer the same substance. Consider, for example, yet another CD-ROM which contains the US Internal Revenue Code and related caselaw. It is a great deal less expensive to pay two software engineers to develop a flashier user interface, or maybe even a search engine, than it is to maintain an expert editorial staff to add that kind of value to an ever-expanding collection of documents. For the most part, end users have taken the bait, some of which (particularly enhanced searching interfaces) can admittedly be quite tasty. This will not be such a viable strategy as the market matures, and I believe the long term will favor those who add real editorial value. The electronic equivalent of small academic presses have considerable access to authorial and editorial expertise, and are thus well-positioned to add precisely this kind of value in narrow niches of their own choosing. The same is true of law firms with particular expertise. While authors have traditionally undervalued the efforts of publishers in adapting texts for the market and distributing them to those markets, so too have publishers undervalued the role of authorial content in selling books. It is not for nothing that the book is called *Prosser on Torts* rather than simply *Torts*. There is no question but what new, distributed, low-cost electronic publishing apparatus, with an audience far larger than that which is possible for any printed book, will tip the balance of traditional author-publisher relationships permanently.

11. A final word: collaboration

If the picture I have painted here is a blurry one, it is because traditional roles occupied by authors, publishers, and technologists are coming together in different combinations in different places, and those places are themselves mergers and cooperative efforts between the academic, private, and governmental spheres. The Legal Information Institute is the result of an intensive collaboration between a law teacher and a technologist, recently expanded to include a specialist in UNIX server systems and a law librarian. There is a sense of balance and interaction between substance and delivery systems in the minuscule staff roster of our Institute, and in the work it undertakes as both a receiver of academic grants and a contractor and consultant for various commercial entities. The LII offers substance of its own. It also offers, organizes, and provides contextual information about data resources which are only one mouse click away for the end user and very, very far apart by measures of physical distance or institutional culture. That information is offered by over one hundred academic, private, and governmental organizations, and those institutions communicate with and refer information-seekers to one another to an unprecedented degree. It is perhaps not surprising that the Internet — which is, after all, a very large communication system — should give rise to a large amount of communication. What is unprecedented is the degree to which it demands communication and collaboration across professional, institutional, economic, and cultural lines if we are to fully realize its potential.

The Communication Highway and Academic Publishing

Jean-Claude Guédon

The communication highway — and not information highway as it is improperly known in English — has recently generated a growing number of articles, conferences, seminars and conferences that all testify to its growing visibility. This trend is certainly encouraging as it begins to do justice to the scope of present developments. However, infrastructural concerns and a fascination for the hardware continue to monopolize center stage, while questions of functions and content remain largely neglected if not altogether ignored. It is as if governments and business had reached a consensus and decided to reverse McLuhan's provocative dictum that the "medium is the message" into its contrary: "the message has nothing to do with the medium". Neither McLuhan, nor governments and business are right as the truth lies closer to the following statement: "the message has *something* to do with the medium" and it is precisely the nature of this "something" that is so difficult to establish.

All this agitation about the "highway" is accompanied by promises of significant economic growth. Indeed, as the argument often goes, the impact of the new communication technologies is supposed to be so far reaching that it will revolutionize every facet of our lives while restoring the global economy to a state of durable expansion. At the same time, and somewhat paradoxically, the future that large companies, marketing specialists and politicians try to conjure up in front our eyes appears strikingly similar to our present. Content appears cloaked in futuristic hype to disguise its intellectual indigence. We are promised 500 television channels and countless movies on demand; we are offered an electronic mall. In effect we are being told that the ideal future would be one where all the present mercantilist practices will be boosted tremendously by the new technologies without being affected deeply by them. The future is fantasized as an enlarged, linear, extension of the present.

The priorities of financing echo the same naiveté: the cry for greater bandwidth reflects an understanding limited to material entities. It is a call for the only kinds of objects that politicians and industrial managers seem to understand despite all that has been said and written about the information age. They are "smoke-stack objects", as Toffler would say, like more cables, more trenches, more switches, more traditional jobs (digging holes, laying

E. Mackaay et al. (eds.), The Electronic Superhighway, 69–89.

wires, connecting circuits). Under "Stentorian[1] injunction", the CANARIE[2] program in Canada has had less than 5% of its budget so far devoted to content, and so is a good example of this vision.

When questions do reach beyond hardware problems and offers to provide more television channels, they are fueled by fears. For example, the problem of privacy recurs regularly and this shows that the new technologies may indeed radically affect our daily lives. They may adversely affect the meaning of individualism; they may threaten our civil rights and they may even undermine the democratic process.[3] On parallel tracks, questions about copyright show that a fraction of the business community is also worried.[4]

Sometimes, indignation also leads to content. Reactions to pornography and marginal forms of behavior appear with some regularity in the daily press,[5] with attendant calls for control and repression. But we must observe that demagoguery is of the essence here. Equating Internet with the Usenet list alt.sex.bondage is like reducing a good size city to the worst parts of its red light district. At the same time, it should be noted that, although devoid of external controls, Internet is remarkably free of obnoxious or distasteful documents. Those that exist are located in clearly designated areas and they

---

1 People outside Canada probably ignore the fact that the telephone companies of the country have organized a joint enterprise to promote and favor any commercial activity that is susceptible of aiding their common cause. This enterprise bears the highly significant name of "Stentor" -- a sure sign that these companies intend to make sure that their voice will be heard.

2 CANARIE is the Canadian Network for the Advancement of Research, Industry and Education. Despite its name, CANARIE has placed most of its investments into the upgrading of the Canadian network.

3 This adverse effect is not automatic, of course; more generally, the new technologies also create entirely new situations where both desirable and undesirable consequences ensue. Take the case of encryption for example. In essence, the State can no longer know, even when it wants to, what people are saying to each other. It can no longer effectively monitor what is transmitted across borders. On the one hand, this trend would seem to reinforce the possibilities of individualism very strongly while, on the other hand, it opens up undreamed possibilities for criminal elements. The debate around PGP, or Pretty Good Privacy, is a good example of the entirely new situation that is presently developing.

4 A good example of this is electronic publishing. An elegant and simple way to solve the copyright question would be to leave it where it should have remained all along -- namely in the authors' hands -- and work the economic contracts around this central point, rather than try to preserve the present system and insist that authors should divest themselves of their intellectual property. But this hypothesis would throw the publishing world topsy-turvy. On a more limited scale, this is probably the right way to go for scholarly electronic publishing. By nature and objectives, it is inherently different from standard commercial activities. On this point, see my forthcoming article, "Research Libraries and Electronic Scholarly Journals: Challenges or Opportunities?" to appear in *Serials Librarian* in 1995.

5 See for example, "Internet Sleaze" in the *Globe and Mail* that appeared in April 1994.

must be sought out. Users looking for these materials presumably know what they are doing[6].

In the end, what worries people most is not the content on the Internet, but rather the control over this content. There is the enduring suspicion that, perhaps, it cannot be controlled, and, in fact, it is difficult to see how it could be. While at the family level, it certainly means more difficult parenting, national governments are far more preoccupied with these questions. The circulation of foreign ideas and influences becomes essentially unstoppable. In some cases, this new context may spell the demise of a political system.

A brief glance at the past confirms the need to think about the advent of new communication technologies in more global terms than is usually the case nowadays. There is no need here to retrace the magisterial demonstration of Elizabeth Eisenstein as she unravels some of the truly staggering consequences of Gutenberg's invention.[7] However, it is a useful reminder. Once before, a whole civilization introduced a new tool for extremely limited aims. The printing press was essentially meant to produce cheap imitations of manuscripts, in particular cheap bibles. As we all know, it achieved a good deal more than that, most of it quite unexpected.

The new communicational tools carry a revolutionary potential at least equal to that of print. Poised as we are on the threshold of the communication highway, we shall have few excuses to offer posterity if we turn out to do little more than blindly moving ahead. Yet, as we are approaching the state of a fully digital civilization, the importance granted to technical problems seems to mesmerize us to the point that we still confuse communication with information. It appears urgent, therefore, to pay *serious* attention to this question.

In the limited compass of this paper, I will approach this complex question through a more limited topic, but one that I know well — namely scholarly electronic publishing. I hope to show that the rise of digitized documents implies profound social and cultural changes for the research communities. I also hope to show that ignoring these concerns, while focusing on technical problems, displays a potentially dangerous absence of vision.

1. Electronic publishing on the Internet

As a first approximation, electronic publishing is nothing more than the content of the electronic networks. To publish is indeed to make a document

6 The question of access by minors is more delicate. Presently, some of the more knowledgeable users of the modem-computer combination and some of the best explorers of cyberspace are teenagers.

7 Elizabeth Eisenstein, *The Printing Press as an Agent of Change* (Cambridge: Cambridge University Press, 1979).

public and, therefore, visible. It is also a way of treating a message so that some people can have access to it under certain conditions. These conditions are well known: right of access to the code, knowledge of the code, and the means to gain that access. In the case of print, the right of access is determined by the limits placed on censorship; the knowledge of the code is the ability to read; the means to gain access generally depend on economic contexts. Unceasingly, we should ask why the economics of a communication highway should be treated differently from that of a regular highway.

In electronic publishing, any digitized file is capable of carrying information (text, image, sound, etc.) and when it travels on a global network, it is already being published, unless its destination be limited to one person as in the mail protocol. This explains why Internet has spontaneously spawned a whole spectrum of publishing forms. Some of them appear like relatively faithful extensions of paper and print publishing, while others already display entirely original functions and forms. Thus the Usenet news appears like public postings on a village square, except that the village extends worldwide and may involve hundreds of thousands of people. A little like the public posting walls of China, the so-called dazibaos, anyone can come, read and leave another message, be it a new line of thought (a new thread in network parlance) or an answer to a previous one.

List servers act like a semi-public publishing system with possibilities to limit access and limit types of messages posted. A list server works more like a kind of parliament, a forum or any other discussion space where the entrance can be controlled according to some principle, and where debates may have to follow rules and be directed by a chairperson.

FTP sites[8] are different since they correspond to storage areas where all kinds of documents can be kept and classified as if on the shelves of a virtual library. There are thousands of FTP sites on the planet and, together, they house gigantic collections of resources which, luckily, can be identified and localized thanks to a clever data bank called Archie.[9] Thanks to Archie,[10] all these virtual libraries of documents are beginning to fuse into a large, world-wide collection that provides awesome amounts of information.

The fusion process has been accelerated and made far more visible with the advent of new tools on the network. I am referring in particular to

---

8 FTP stands for "file transfer protocol". It corresponds to one of the three basic tools of the Internet, along with Mail and Telnet. Together, the protocols needed to make these functions work across the whole network, independently of the machines used, form the basis for the Internet protocols generally referred to as TCP/IP.

9 Archie was designed by Peter Deutsch, then working for McGill University and now head of a private company in Montreal called Bunyip.

10 Any recent book on the Internet will give full descriptions of all these terms, as well as ways to use them and an idea of what can be found with each.

"Gopher" and the "World Wide Web" or WWW as it is most often called. In the case of WWW, the addition of powerful browsers, for example NCSA's Mosaic, and the very structuring of the documentation[11] allowed by this particular technique, permits the creation of multi-media documents made of parts that are scattered all over the world.

While all of these tools have fostered the advent of electronic publishing, the lack of standards, on the other hand, has slowed down developments in languages other than English. One of the more vexing problems faced by Internet is the lack of a consensus regarding the transmission of languages with diacritical signs or languages not written with the Latin alphabet. For a network that claims to be global, this is a serious impediment. Even limiting oneself to languages written in the Latin alphabet, we are presently faced with a somewhat paradoxical situation. We do not lack standards; in fact we have too many of them, and the result is that none is generalized enough to be reliable. For example, MIME[12] is a good way to send any kind of document we want through e-mail, including images and sound, and within MIME, various character sets can be documented so as to allow the transmission of French, Spanish or German with no loss of diacritical signs. However, as in many international settings, various questions of relative precedence and national or linguistic prerogatives make things somewhat more complicated, and negotiations are slow and difficult[13]. So far, the result has been that no solution has appeared sufficiently compelling to receive general approbation. Given that English-speaking countries can fully benefit from the present situation, there is no great incentive for them to help implementing solutions that, from their perspective, are more of a nuisance than an improvement.

In the case of languages not based on the Latin alphabet, for example Arabic, Japanese or Chinese, solutions implying the use of three or even four ASCII characters as a way to code the sign systems of these languages have been designed and are used, but, there again, ways to bring about

---

11 In the World Wide Web, documents are generically described by a markup language called HTML (Hyper Text Markup Language) which, itself, is a subset of SGML (Standard Generalized Markup Language). This allows the creation of viewers that reproduce what has been indicated in the text, such as diacritical, bold or italic fonts, the kind of font to be used, etc. In short, a text can be fully copy-edited and published in a very nice manner through WWW and images, sounds and even animation can be added to the documents. WWW allied to powerful browsing software such as Mosaic directly leads to multimedia publishing.

12 Acronym for Multipurpose Internet Mail Extensions. The specifications are available in RFC 1341, available on the Internet like all RFC's. RFC's or Requests for Comments are documents that are distributed to the Internet community to discuss the implementation of new or added protocols.

13 On this question, see section 6.1 of Marshall T. Rose, *The Internet message. Closing the Book with Electronic Mail* (Englewood Cliffs, N. J.: P. T. R. Prentice Hall, 1993).

agreement is not simple. Even in the case of a one-country language like Japanese, agreement is difficult to achieve as many private and public institutions have to come to some accord while the national computer industry has already made a number of choices that can claim the status of *de facto* standards[14]. What must be underscored, in any case, is that the problem is less technical than social, political or institutional.

2. Scholarly electronic publishing

The case of scholarly electronic publishing is useful to explore some of the processes at work when communication technologies undergo major changes. Moreover, it is attracting a higher degree of attention even as printed academic journals are facing greater economic difficulties with each passing year. This section will explore the nature of the transition presently unfolding. The next section will hint at possible changes in the research system stemming from this technical shift.

To those of us who are presently involved in the designing and running of prototypes of electronic scholarly journals, the fact that printed scholarly journals face grave economic difficulties appears as a sure sign that a major technical transition is in the offing — one, moreover that may also bring unexpected and profound changes to the research system. The deeper question is whether this transition is going to be accompanied by a series of unexpected consequences. In other words, as new technologies are being explored and some marshaled to solve a particular economic problem, attention should be paid to the possible, but more hidden, transformations of the research system. The expectation is that there will be such, largely unexpected, consequences. As a result, the example of electronic scholarly publishing can stand as a fair warning for the wider deployment of the communication highway.

To make this last point clearer, let us take an example drawn from the 18th century. The adoption of coal as fuel was undertaken reluctantly and only because the growing rarity of wood drove its price out of range. Shifting from wood to coal would seem to be a simple matter, but several obstacles had to be overcome. Differing combustion characteristics had led to some accidents due to the poor design of the stoves and coal was widely regarded as a dangerous source of heat. Stoves and furnaces had to be redesigned and even the quality of the metals involved had to be modified as coal fires tend to be hotter than wood fires. On the supply side, setting up coal mines requires quite a bit more planning than simply going into the

---

14 On the Japanese case, read the instructive piece by Jeffrey Shappard, "Islands in the (Data) Stream: Language, Character Codes, and Electronic Isolation in Japan", in *Global Networks. Computers and International Communication*, Linda Harasim, ed. (Cambridge, Mass.: M.I.T. Press, 1993), pp. 255-70.

forest and cutting wood. In effect, whole economic circuits had to be redesigned. But the end result was quite impressive as the use of coal, coupled with the steam engine and the spinning jenny, brought about the first phase of the industrial revolution. The quest to solve a supply problem — namely wood — led to a major transition in human history.

2.1 NATURE OF THE CRISIS FACED BY SCHOLARLY JOURNALS

What kind of crisis are scholarly journals facing? The answer is both well known and well documented[15]. First of all, the total number of scholars and scientists is increasing everywhere. Then, more and more pressure is being applied to do research and to publish. At the same time, present modes of evaluation of a researcher's work rest on various quantifiable data: number of publications and number of citations are elements that profoundly influence academic careers. Many research grant agencies, as well as tenure committees, make use of this quantitative criterion. The well known decree to "publish or perish" is, therefore, no exaggeration. Without publications, a scholar simply does not exist. The resulting rush to publish globally leads to a growing demand for publishing space which can only be met by multiplying the number of journals.

Other processes at work tend to reinforce these trends. For example, growing specialization translates into a growing number of domains of research that are ever narrower and/or more interdisciplinary. As a result, new journal titles appear in order to cover new research programs or orientations. Also, the sociology of science has documented the fact that publishing a scholarly journal is a way to exercise power. Concepts such as "gatekeepers" or "symbolic capital"[16] mark a growing awareness of, and preoccupation with, these institutional dimensions of scholarly publications. The stakes involved in scholarly publishing are sufficiently important to move a small learned society or even a university department to do all it can to create a journal of its own.

---

15 See for example *University Libraries and Scholarly Communication*, a study prepared for the Andrew W. Mellon Foundation by M. Cummings *et al.* (The Andrew W. Mellon Foundation, 1992). See also my own "Édition électronique, publications savantes et avenir des bibliothèques" in *Communication scientifique, nouvelles technologies et rationalisation des ressources: un défi pour les bibliothèques universitaires. Actes du Colloque organisé à l'occasion du 25ème anniversaire du Sous-comité des bibliothèques,* CREPUQ (Montréal, Bibliothèque nationale du Québec, 1993), pp. 45-52.

16 The notion of "gatekeeper" was introduced by Kurt Lewin, according to Robert K. Merton. See his *The Sociology of Science. Theoretical and Empirical Investigations* (Chicago: Chicago University Press, 1973), p. 521. It was taken up in sociology of science, in the more restricted sense of journal editors, by Alfred de Grazia and Diana Crane. Symbolic capital is a term conceptualized by Pierre Bourdieu. See his "Le marché des biens symboliques", *L'Année sociologique*, N° 22 (1971), 49-126.

From an economic viewpoint, the situation appears quite different as the financing of journals is becoming increasingly difficult. In fact, it is the factor that prevents journals from proliferating more rapidly than they presently do. For reasons too complex to detail here, the cost of producing academic periodicals generally increases faster than the general cost of living. Library budgets, on the other hand, do not grow at the same pace, if they grow at all. As a result, the number of subscriptions maintained by libraries is steadily going down, and, in fact, the decline would be steeper if funds previously allocated to the buying of monographs had not been redirected to journal subscriptions. Meanwhile, individual scholars, even though they may subscribe to a greater number of journals (although this is not sure because standards of living are also growing more slowly than the cost of journals), and even though their numbers are growing, cannot hope to pick up the slack left by libraries, particularly since three or four individual subscribers would be needed on the average to compensate for the loss of a single library subscription.

All that precedes triggers inexorable mechanisms that do not augur well for the future. To compensate for the declining numbers of subscribers, journals have been forced to rely on a number of expedients. First, they have increased subscription rates significantly and sometimes very rapidly. This is particularly true of library subscriptions, but the rule also applies to individual rates. However, this kind of response only compounds the problem on a global scale. Then, journals also try to reduce production costs by all means possible: fewer illustrations if any, streamlined forms of copy-editing, fewer pages printed and so on. Computers have been marshaled in this context to relocate some operations in house, such as page layout that used to be done by outside firms at a greater cost. Editors have also resorted to producing more double and even triple issues, so as to fulfill subscription promises formally, but with fewer printed pages given out and significant savings on postage. However, this results in lengthening publication delays that are already excessive.

In order to cut out subscriptions, libraries have used a limited number of techniques broadly based on usage statistics. However, as all institutions face the same problems and as they identify unwanted journals in similar ways, they reach about the same results within a few years of each other. The total outcome appears as a kind of "Matthew effect"[17]: journals that are in heavy use are bought by everybody while the other journals face decreasing numbers of subscriptions. A few journals remain economically viable and even profitable while the majority tend to confront growing financial problems. Powerful commercial houses may find these select publications quite attractive and may try to buy them up to profit from a

17 See Robert K. Merton, "The Matthew Effect in Science", in R. K. Merton, *op. cit.* (note 18), pp. 439-59.

captive market that can be exploited even more, thus putting even more pressure on the other journals.

The most common technique used to compensate for the decline in the number of journal subscriptions has been to rely on inter-library loans. Pretty soon, however, a service that was once viewed as exceptional, becomes entirely routine and loan budgets originally designed as stop-gap measures quickly become insufficient. The same old financial problem rears its ugly head once more, and librarians discover that they have merely played for time without solving their fundamental financial difficulties.

More recently, the advent of UnCover, a bibliographic collection organized by the Colorado Alliance of Research Libraries (CARL) has brought new ominous perspectives into sight. Yet, no malicious intent was meant as these libraries, reasonably enough, decided to take advantage of the fact that, together, they held about fourteen thousand subscriptions to various journals. They decided to build a data base out of all the articles contained in those journals, that can now be interrogated freely from anywhere on the entire Internet. This has been possible because UnCover has also found a clever way to finance its operations. Articles that are not available in the users' libraries can be ordered through the Internet and they are sent, sometimes within one hour, by fax to the person requesting it.[18]

The implications are potentially enormous. Suppose UnCover were to spawn a few similar setups distributed over the face of the globe so as to reduce fax costs, together they could become the sole repositories of issues of journals rarely used and libraries could then rely on them to save on their own subscriptions costs. However, many journals could probably not survive economically if all libraries gave up their subscriptions and were replaced by one data bank and its mirrors sites all over the globe. Very few journals, nowadays, could survive with only the subscription fees coming from real flesh-and-blood individuals, and the royalties coming from actual use of their articles. It is easy, therefore, to see the predicament that could result from an extension of UnCover or that of UnCover like systems. And as this prospect appears quite probable, the questions raised here are fairly urgent.

2.2 THE FUNCTIONS OF SCHOLARLY JOURNALS

A this junction, it is useful to examine the real role of scholarly journals. Stevan Harnad, for example, likes to underscore the following statistical tidbit: 80% of all articles are not read by more than two people on the

---

[18] Copyright fees are paid to the originating journals and are included in the price of the requested article. Payment is done by credit card number. I have analyzed this case in greater depth in my articles "Research Libraries and Electronic Scholarly Journals:..." *op. cit.* (note 3).

average and are never quoted.[19] Figures like these surprise and may even shock, but they do not mean that 80% of the scholarly literature should not be printed. If a politician or manager in search of quick fixes to financial quandaries were to reach this conclusion, he would, in effect, destroy the whole research system, for it, like a tall pyramid, needs a broad base. On the other hand, such statistics confirm a number of theses that have been repeatedly put forth concerning the role of scholarly journals, but which deserve being summarized here.[20] In summary, electronic scholarly publishing appears better than print for both communication and archival purposes. On the other hand, it remains inferior to print when it comes to ease of access and, more importantly, to legitimacy[21].

- While printed scholarly journals purport to fulfill a *communication* role, publication delays have undermined the validity of this claim. The phenomenon is gradually spreading and thus it becomes more and more visible. By contrast, electronic journals can maintain much shorter delays, limited only by the peer review process and copy editing, and so can still claim to act as a true communication channel.

- Scholarly journals are supposed to *archive* information. This means that the information stored is retrievable in some fashion, for example, through a combination of orderly storage, catalogs and bibliographic indexing. In this regard, digitized documents are much better than printed ones since they allow for full-text searching and multi-criteria modes of classification. It could be said, by contrast, that print *buries* as much as it archives information — a form of burial that is made more definitive by the simple fact that, since the middle of the nineteenth century and due to paper acidity, the tomb itself is threatened by self-annihilation. By contrast, digital

---

19 Stevan Harnad, from Princeton University, has been very active in discussions on electronic publishing, for example on vpiej-l. He has also launched an electronic journal, *Psycholoquy* that is often mentioned and he has published several articles on the topic. He mentioned this figure in a private communication.

20 See my article "Why are Electronic Publications Difficult to Classify?: The Orthogonality of Print and Digital media" *in* Ann Okerson, ed., *Directory of Electronic Journals, Newsletters and Academic Discussion Lists* (Washington, D.C.: ARL, 1994), 4th ed., pp. 17-21. See also two small articles I published on the same topic: "Périodiques scientifiques: une solution à l'accroissement vertigineux des coûts?", *Bulletin. La Fédération canadienne des études humaines* (été 1993), vol. 16 N°s 1 & 2, 3-6. "Irruption des périodiques électroniques savantes (*sic*)", *University Affairs/Affaires universitaires* (mai 1994), 12-3. Finally, see Teresa Harrison *et al.*, "Online Journals: Disciplinary Design for Electronic Scholarship", *The Public-Access Computer System Review*, vol. 2 N° 1 (1991), 26. PACS-Review is both an electronic and a paper journal. The electronic version can be found on the of the University of Houston Libraries.

21 The question of a suitable economic model for electronic academic journals is also a thorny question which I will not address here. On this point see my "Research Libraries and Electronic Scholarly Journals: Challenges or Opportunities?", *op. cit.* (note 4).

memory, despite its apparent volatility and fragility, is more resilient because it is eminently copiable and it is relatively easy to convert from one standard to another, from one level of technology to the next.[22]

- In the end, printed documents play a more fundamental role when they help to consecrate the results of research, to legitimize them and to lend them some degree of authority. It is in the deepest sense a collective form of *imprimatur* (to use this old Catholic term) which relies on judgment by peers. In other words, selecting and publishing a particular research paper is done in the name of a collective evaluation performed by individuals to whom this responsibility has been delegated in one way or another. Legitimacy ultimately rests on this latent act of delegation, however it may be performed in practice, and it is always conducted in terms of one criterion: quality and even excellence. What is interesting to note is that a whole series of very prosaic processes, including informal co-optation, old boys' networks, institutional images and the like, all add up to create the anonymous and, at the same time, formidable facade of the quest for excellence.[23]

In trying to unravel how an *imprimatur* may indeed contribute to legitimizing a document within a disciplinary community, I am not trying to criticize the peer review process. I am only trying to underscore how scholarly publishing is deeply implicated with the social construction of legitimacy and how, because of this involvement, it lies at the heart of the research system as we know it. Conversely, this point demonstrates why we should not change things carelessly and inconsiderately. Doing so would probably generate profound reactions on the part of scholars whose career depends on rules that must be as clear and as stable as possible. To neglect this dimension of scholarly publishing amounts to condemning oneself to total ineffectiveness.

---

22 We can surmise that computer museums will play an important role to help future generations retrieve documents stored in obsolete computer formats. In the present deployment of digitized technologies, policies should certainly be devised to ensure the systematic mirroring of information to minimize its possible destruction, and its systematic conversion into newer forms of storage and according to new standards as they emerge.

23 The most interesting in all of this is that excellence, rather than being a concept susceptible of being unambiguously defined by a fixed set of predicates, turns out to be the result of a complex, almost baroque social construction. What happens actually is that the ordering of all these day-to-day gestures lines them up to form something like an axis, an evaluative axis in fact, that can justify the presence of excellence. Work aiming at excellence attempts, naturally enough, to incorporate the characteristics required by the constructed concept of excellence, but, as a result, the latter, in return, sees its appearance reinforced and it thus acquires the trappings of objective existence.

2.3 MAKING ELECTRONIC SCHOLARLY JOURNALS ACCEPTABLE TO THE RESEARCH COMMUNITY

Because scholarly texts in effect obey Berkeley's thesis, "*esse est percipi aut percipere*", their legitimacy rests on their being accessible. Accessing electronic documents does require some new skills — something that a number of academics still resist. However, this is only a temporary problem. For one thing, the tools to log on services and navigate within them are becoming easier to use all the time, while basic computer skills are spreading rapidly to widening circles of users.

The true obstacles to the acceptability of electronic journals are more profound and they rest on institutional and social factors. In the last few centuries, means to gain visibility among learned peers have been carefully grown and their present form, however arbitrary it may appear to an observer sitting on Sirius, cannot be changed easily. The point here is to take all of these factors seriously into account so as to insert electronic publications into the research system as harmoniously as possible. The advent of electronic publishing will be accompanied by changes in the research system. However, the more gradual these changes will be, the less threatening they will appear. As a result, resistance and the risk of failure will be significantly decreased.

The best way to insert electronic publications into the research system is to give them something like the "look and feel" of printed scholarly journals. In this fashion, the new medium will find it easier to ensure legitimacy and to locate itself in a meaningful manner within the existing prestige hierarchy of printed journals. In other words, to fulfill this double objective, elements of the old (read print) system must be maintained inside the new (read electronic) so as to make novelty acceptable within the tradition-bound research system. More pithily, one must learn to maintain enough of the old within the new to make the new acceptable to the old.

Incidentally, this very simple theorem explains some of the mysterious problems that regularly plague the introduction of new technologies. The difficult part lies in applying it to real situations: how can we identify the element coming from the old order that must be temporarily maintained inside the new system, thus allowing it to take root without mortgaging its future deployment. Not putting enough old elements, or putting the wrong elements of the old order may well endanger the take-off phase of an electronic journal. Incorporating too many old elements may create an unwanted baggage that could slow down or even impede the grafting of the new medium onto the research system.

The solution to this problem rests on a simple rule: keep in mind the needs of the various "users" of scholarly journals. User is taken here in a wider sense than is normally the case. For example, the author can be said to make use of a scholarly journal in a particular way, and so does the editor. The reader's case is expected, of course, and is the most obvious of all.

An author fundamentally pursues two goals through publishing. She seeks visibility *and* legitimacy. The only way to ensure legitimacy is to maintain peer evaluation so as to avoid being a kind of vanity press. The quality of electronic journals is not inherently inferior to that of printed ones, but all doubts may be cast aside simply by having a transparent and stringent peer review process.

Still from the author's perspective, another, less obvious, dimension can also play a subtle role in the transition from print to electronic publishing, and that has to do with physical appearance. Physical presentation indeed plays an important role and it is not by chance that so much attention, care and skill have been devoted to the fine arts of typography and page layout across the last few centuries. The visual aspect of a document certainly improves its impact and reflects upon its author.

Speaking about physical appearance also allows us to correct a common misconception about electronic publishing. The digitized form of a document must not be confused with the document any more than paper money must be confused with a particular commodity or merchandise. Just like money, a digitized document is almost pure potentiality and its mode of materialization is not determined *a priori*. This means, in particular, that the reader does not have to face documents on screen. And if he does, it does not mean that the only available mode of presentation is the peculiar typography of ASCII texts as they appear on a VT100 terminal.[24] On the contrary, a digitized document can materialize precisely in the form that corresponds best to the usage sought. If, for example, the task at hand is to prepare a request for promotion or tenure, it is obvious that published paper, be it in an electronic journal, should be printed. At this stage in time, good page layout with nice fonts are more convincing than the ugly ASCII characters that presently crisscross the Internet without scars. On the other hand, the building of a concordance or the search for specific word occurrences is achieved much more easily on screen than with print.

Let us turn our attention now to the librarian's point of view (and also her patrons, of course). Here, questions of orderly storage and easy retrieval emerge, along with questions of citations. Classifying electronic documents according to parameters that artificially maintain categories spawned by printing (such as pages and page number, volume number, issue number, etc.) may be judged an unimaginative, and even conservative, choice, but the

24 The recent development of Mosaic browsers for the World Wide Web can be conceptualized as a major extension of publishing modes and, as such, clearly reveals all the possibilities that relate to a particular digitized document. As time goes on, we may expect the richness of these possibilities to increase enormously and, in any case, to reach well beyond what print can presently offer.

point is not to appear *avant garde* at all costs; rather, it is to facilitate the use of the electronic documents by a culture — that of research — with tightly defined and stringently enforced habits and customs, particularly when it comes to citing and organizing bibliographies.

A librarian (and also a reader) must also have ways and means to ascertain the *authenticity* of a particular document retrieved from a global network such as Internet. Subtle changes introduced to these texts, whether in jest or out of malicious intent, can ruin an author's reputation. Any fear in this regard will perpetuate a cautious wait-and-see attitude and can raise significant obstacles on the way to developing electronic, scholarly journals.

A quick response to this worry is that one should always go back to the original storage site to retrieve a protected copy of the text at the moment of quoting from it. Encryption techniques or algorithms allowing to detect any form of tampering with a given text are in various stages of development and will provide other kinds of solutions to this question. All this to say that the question of the authenticity and the integrity of texts is not a trivial problem, but that, at the same time, it is being solved successfully. The point, in the end, is to provide the electronic document with a degree of reliability comparable to that offered by the material existence of printed documents — a reliability enhanced in the latter case by the multiplication of copies.[25]

The points just covered barely begin to scratch the surface of the whole subject, but they already show that the main problems of scholarly electronic publishing are not primarily the concerns of engineers or computer scientists. The difficulties encountered are generally not technical, but correspond rather to social factors that must be fully understood and assessed to ensure a successful innovation. Technology keeps offering a range of possibilities that must then be assessed in terms of social and institutional factors. What is true of scholarly electronic publishing is just as true of the whole communication highway.

3. The transformations of the research system

On several occasions in this paper, I have hinted that digitizing scholarly materials would bring about significant shifts in the research system. My belief in this stems from historical examples, particularly the import of print into the community of scholars at the Renaissance and particularly in the

[25] While I am willing to grant that printed texts are more protected than electronic texts in their present state of storage and diffusion, I would not want to overstate the case. Book piracy has always posed problems to the print industry to the point that, in the nineteenth century, it was not rare to have every copy of an edition signed by hand by the author. Printing, in and of itself, cannot completely ensure the integrity of a text.

17th century. The invention of periodicals corresponded to the somewhat startling idea of applying printing — up to then a tool designed mainly to enhance text conservation — to novelties that, because of their very status, could only enjoy a limited life cycle. This idea became possible because the Republic of Letters, in the 17th century, started to collapse under its own communicational weight.[26] The most striking consequence of this innovation was that it led to a deep transformation in the very structuring of knowledge and our apprehension of its totality.

Until the 17th century, the model of knowledge that clearly dominated everybody's thinking was that of a global, ultimately unifiable, natural philosophy where each piece was supposed to fit both in terms of its subject area, and in terms of its relationship to the whole. With the eighteenth century began a profound change that ultimately led to the rise of a disciplinary approach to knowledge. The great difference with the immediate past was that disciplines could work in relative isolation from each other and find the principles of their coherence, method and theories within themselves. Disciplines, despite their appearance, were not divisions of knowledge, but rather institutions. Turning away from the image of knowledge as a great single whole, disciplines fostered the advent of a new vision that Diderot expressed particularly clearly: they appeared as disconnected spots of light[27] which, from the standpoint of experimental physics (as contrasted by Diderot from that of philosophy) had no reason of ever merging into a unified entity.

Diderot's pronouncement is all the more interesting that it coincides with a series of publications that all present knowledge in new and original ways. Specialized journals multiply in the early 1750's,[28] at the very same time that the production of dictionaries was enjoying a steep increase and Diderot's *Encyclopédie* was beginning its amazing saga. Printed journals, in

---

26 See "Electronic publishing of academic journals and the structure of research results", *op. cit.* (note 9), as well as my other piece, "Why are Electronic Publications Difficult to Classify?:...", *op. cit.* (note 22), p. 18. Jean Sgard, in providing an excellent survey of the French scene, underscores the deep relationship between the periodical and the book forms. See his "La multiplication des périodiques" in R. Chartier and H.-J. Martin, eds., *Histoire de l'édition française. Le livre triomphant (1660-1830)*, 2nd volume (Paris: Fayard/Promodis, 1990) 2nd edition, pp. 246-55.

27 The image is found in D. Diderot's "De l'interprétation de la nature" in *Œuvres philosophiques*, P. Vernières ed. (Paris: Garnier, 1964), p. 189. This book originally appeared in 1753.

28 For example, the *Journal économique* in 1751, *Observations sur la physique* in 1752, *Journal de médecine* in 1754.

particular, added a crucial element to the underpinnings of what would evolve later under the name of disciplines.[29]

Merely suggesting the possibility of a relationship between printed scholarly journals, and the emergence of disciplines is enough to demonstrate the magnitude of the claims that can be reasonably made on behalf of print. By analogy, the shift in communication tools that corresponds to electronic publishing may well foster transformations that are just as important, but still difficult to perceive.

The essential developments to come will not simply take the form of multimedia or hypertextual extensions of print. More fundamentally, electronic publishing favors the advent of an important trend — namely what I would be tempted to call the *fluidization* of documents.[30] This process may take a number of forms, but they all end up with one common consequence: they will affect the ways individuals relate to documents, and, more profoundly, the ways they relate to one another. All that can be done here is a tentative exercise at guessing what the contours of the future may be in this regard.

Let us take one first example: data in the laboratories. In the present situation, the author of a scientific article takes up all her data and extracts from them what is usable to state something significantly new in his domain. Out of all the measurements carried out in the laboratory, the reader will see only a few graphs or tables and he will no know what has been rejected and on what basis. The rule, up to now, is that the author is best placed to know how to edit and present her data in a convincing fashion. The essential is shown, presumably without distorting the complete set of experimental results.

A severe degree of filtering of the empirical data is required by the print form: the publication costs impose the need to be as terse as possible and, as a result, an extremely concise style of writing up research results has developed, particularly in this century. It is unthinkable at present to imagine publishing the whole set of experimental data acquired from the daily efforts in the laboratory. With electronic publishing, however, this whole constraint is essentially removed. Why not publish the crucial moments of an experiment? How is the apparatus to be set up and tested? How is the experiment to be launched? How are the data to be acquired? Publishing these details would simplify the task of verifying experimental procedures

29 I refer again the reader to my article "Electronic publishing of academic journals and the structure of research results", *op. cit.* (note 4) where I develop this point to greater length.

30 This idea of fluidization has been strongly inspired by Stevan Harnad's article, "Scholarly Skywriting and the Prepublication Continuum of Scientific Inquiry", *Psychological Science*, vol. 1 (1990), 342-3, reprinted in *Current Contents*, vol. 45 (November 11, 1991), 9-13.

and data acquisition, and, as a result, the whole scientific process would probably be significantly improved.

In the same spirit, citations to articles could go well beyond bibliographic references; they could in fact quote the whole article or at least the relevant parts and these could appear through hypertextual links.[31] Both the video appendix and the full citation would go a long way to help identify the truly important, original and significant, on the one hand, and it would also make scientific fraud much more difficult to perpetrate. In fact, because of the growing concern with frauds, it might not be too far fetched to imagine these possibilities eventually becoming requirements in scholarly publishing.

Another meaning linked with the "fluidization" metaphor used earlier has to do with the new time dimension introduced in the research process by electronic publishing. By considerably accelerating the pace of publication, electronic publishing gives responses and criticisms a chance to act as relevant feedback for on-going research. In other words, a published critique would no longer act as a belated corrective, but would rather become a *visible* extension of the informal discussions normally taking place among scientists. It is as if the discussion group had enlarged to the size of a whole, formerly invisible, college and placed it into full public view. Discussion, dialogue, controversy, as well as collaboration and *complementarities* can all be stimulated by this new situation. As a result, electronic publishing should almost necessarily lead to a much more intense (and fruitful) discussion of the data produced in the laboratory and to a better exploitation of their potential for the development of theory.[32]

At this point, it is easy to see that the "fluidizing" effect potentially induced into the research system by electronic publishing can also be viewed as the institution of a kind of virtual *seminar*. However, unlike present seminars that are limited in time and space, the new publishing structure would create a global seminar that never stops. In fact, along with the increasingly "fluidized" nature of publications, we should witness the multiplication of "seminars" working across the whole planet.

Like a scholarly journal, the seminar form favors originality and performance, but unlike the journal, its role is not to promote any particular author, but rather to stimulate debates and ease the emergence of new ideas. At the same time, a seminar, like a research team, is built on a collective

---

31 The American organization, OCLC, is beginning to play with a first approximation of this vision in its program designed to publish learned journals with the "Guidon" interface.

32 This also has implication for scientists who do not have access to the needed equipment, for example in Third World countries. This possibility to pore over published data, shortly after their production, in a productive fashion, and not simply after the fact, would allow them to play a significant role at the cutting edge of research and in the designing of its future orientations.

effort, but unlike the research team, the seminar is not explicitly organized on a hierarchical model. It does not exclude it either, by the way; but it can also accommodate other forms of relationships among participants. Finally, a seminar functions through the periodic and structured presentation of results and interpretations in front of its members, and together, they act like a kind of intellectual crucible that has the ability to reshape the theses, ideas and theories that are put to the test. This peculiar process creates a collective consciousness, a form of mental synergy that, as the word "synergy" indicates, goes well beyond the simple addition of individual talents.

In the present situation, governed as it is by the rules of the printed word, all research activities eventually lead to the production of a paper submitted for publication. In the seminar form, it is possible to imagine ways to mimic the publishable paper. For example, virtual seminars might, as issues warrant, decide to create synopses, summaries, syntheses of recent discussions at regular intervals so as to clarify issues, sort out the essential from the inessential, organize the verifications needed, etc. Research, then, would incorporate these new reference points and a new round of evaluation and critiques would eventually lead to another effort to pull together the newer results that resist criticisms.

The fluidized form of the seminar debate is already present within the present research process. However, it is still discontinuous and syncopated because of the pace of the research process contrasted with that of the publication process. Electronic publishing can hope to reduce delays, but it will never succeed in getting rid of them completely. This is because some of the factors involved (peer evaluation, for example) remain beyond its reach. It must be remembered that the publishing of results in some acceptable form will remain crucial for recognition, visibility, and the allocation of research grants. All these operations are intricately linked with the notion of the "individual" and the seminar form will have to take it into account.

We may surmise that between the pure (and idealistic) vision of a "flow" publication system based exclusively upon a generalized seminar form, and the present publishing set up based upon the "batch" printing of papers, will appear a new synthesis that will be marked by new relationships between scholars and by new contours of authorship. This does not mean that authors will disappear, or that present forms of collaboration will vanish. It simply means that the relative importance of the various possibilities relative to being an author or relative to collaboration will shift, and, more precisely, will probably shift in the direction of the seminar form.

Two recent events support the fluidization thesis proposed here. The first one has to do with the cold fusion debate that emerged a few years ago.[33] The results published by two chemists, Pons and Fleischman, instantly stimulated an intense competition among many scientists. As a result, an important fraction of the debate took place via electronic mail and fax machines, as time was very much of the essence in this case. In the end, the matter was, if not settled, at least reduced to a scale that brought it back to the level of normal research questions, and this process was done through the habitual, legitimacy-granting processes of printed papers and refereed presentations to important congresses. However, what is interesting is that the excitement and the controversy surrounding cold fusion immediately generated a good deal of continuous communication that did begin to look like a global, constant seminar. Of course, the seminar, in this case, was quite unruly and people who had no business intervening in this discussion, nevertheless did, thus contributing a fair amount of noise. But, with a bit more policing and a more conscious attempt to co-opt the major players along rules similar to those of peer review, a world-wide electronic forum made up of the best specialists in electro-chemistry and in fusion physics could have debated the question at hand. Parts of this debate did take place inside the noise. In some cases, disciplinary boundaries were transcended and various specialists began to share and appreciate the others' tools and arguments. For a few weeks, it was possible to witness the contours of a possible future for the present research system.

The second event comes from the observation of some of the existing electronic scholarly journals. A number of them are moving in the direction of creating discussion lists that accompany the electronic publication *per se*. For example, *Post-Modern Culture* has created a system, called in Internet parlance a MUD,[34] allowing for both synchronous and asynchronous communication. In other words, participants may leave messages for some or all to see, and readers that are on-line together may communicate in real time with each other. In my own journal, *Surfaces*, we are presently testing a list server that will not only facilitate contacts with our users and readers, but also allow our readers to discuss issues related to the published articles among themselves. In this fashion, an electronic journal adds to its role as a repository of texts and documents, a new dimension as a meeting point for a number of individuals interested in a shared domain.

---

33 A considerable literature has developed around this question, including four book-length studies: John R. Huizenga, *Cold Fusion : the Scientific Fiasco of the Century* (Rochester, N.Y. : University of Rochester Press, 1992); Eugene F. Mallove, *Fire from Ice : Searching for the Truth behind the Cold Fusion Furor* (New York, N.Y. : J. Wiley, 1991); David F. Peat, *Cold Fusion : The Making of a Scientific Controversy* (Chicago : Contemporary Books, 1989); Gary Taubes, *Bad Science : the Short Life and Weird Times of Cold Fusion* (New York : Random House, 1993).

34 MUD or Multi-User Dungeon draws its name from a reference to the famous "Dungeons and Dragons" game, but it actually means the creation of a virtual space where participants can communicate with each other.

Surprisingly enough, these two examples show us also that, spontaneously, and with much greater efficiency, we are now recreating some of the dimensions surrounding the workings of the manuscript text, for example during the Middle Ages. To be sure, the acceleration of communication processes through the use of electronic networks would appear to locate us at the antipodes of the Medieval text. But practices such as glosses, comments and codicils appear anew as files are copied and modified to suit someone's objectives (with all the problems this poses once again to text integrity, as noted earlier). But, beyond the questions of copyright and plagiarism, this spontaneous activity marks the profound tendency for texts to be instruments (and instigators) of communication rather than passive tools of information. In fact, a thesis could well be defended along the following lines: pure information just does not exist; information can play its role only if it is located within a wider context dominated by debates, discussions, *disputationes*, themselves noticed through the presence of comments, criticisms, analyses, interpretative tools and so on.

In trying to build room for debates around the published texts, electronic publishing rediscovers a necessity tied to the very process of intellectual assimilation and creation. This is so true that we find it present even in silent reading with a pencil in hand: what we write then in the margins, what we underscore in the text, what we even hear within our own heads are nothing more than bits of an ongoing debate. In other words, the need for a seminar-like process imposes itself very quickly in any case, and this is why the seminar form, i.e. room for discussion, comments, modifications and interpretations, is a potent force in electronic documents, that will increase in the years to come.

4. Conclusion

The whole academic landscape is presently shifting. Horizons move quickly beyond the eyes' reach and saying that we do not know what is going to happen at least means that we know one thing: academic publishing will *not* go on as it used to. Yet, we are talking here about a sector that tends to be conservative in its ways, that is relatively immune from the sound and fury of day-to-day life and that has already demonstrated an uncanny ability to survive cataclysmic social changes. Sectors less shielded from economic and commercial considerations may feel the winds of change faster and more violently, although no general rule can be given. In the end, it is a fair bet that many forms of human relationships will change deeply. They will probably be transformed at least as deeply as when print started to take hold. Already, new words and expressions appear, new icons punctuate texts exchanged through the networks in a manner that would have been unthinkable only a decade ago.[35] Human interactions based on computer-mediated communications, will find themselves organized according to original forms of space-time, new "geographies", new kinds of inter-cultural exchanges. In an age when, to use Amy Bruckman's felicitous phrase, "identity workshops" multiply, when people literally experiment with themselves by trying on various synthetic reconstructions of personality traits, such possibilities cannot and must not be ignored.[36]

---

35 On this topic, see Brenda Danet and Lucia Ruedenberg, "'Smoking Dope' at a Virtual party: Writing, Play and Performance on Internet Relay Chat", to be published in Sheizaf Rafaeli, Fay Sudweeks and Margaret McLaughlin eds., *Networks and Netplay: Virtual Groups on the Internet* (Cambridge, Mass.: M.I.T. Press, in press). I would like to thank Brenda Danet for having sent me a preprint of this interesting paper.

36 Amy Bruckman, "Gender Swapping on the Internet", *Proceedings INET '93*. *Id.* "Identity Workshop: Emergent Social and Psychological Phenomena in Text-Based Virtual Reality". Both of these texts are available on the Internet and the easiest way to obtain them is to ask Amy Bruckman directly at asb@media-lab.media.mit.edu. I take this opportunity to thank her for having allowed me to study these texts.

Part III

What Law for Electronic Highways?

Dematerialized Transactions on Electronic Pathways : A Panorama of Legal Issues

Copyright, Digital Data, and Fair Use in Digital Networked Environments

Free Speech, Pornography, Sexual Harassment, and Electronic Networks : An Update and Extension

The Protection of Rights and Values in Open-Network Management

Dematerialized Transactions on Electronic Pathways: A Panorama of Legal Issues[1]

Karim Benyekhlef

Many habits will be changed, it is said, as multimedia take over communications pathways. The creation of communications networks carrying numerous types of information should allow users in their homes or workplaces to make purchases, perform banking operations, consult data banks and, possibly, download data files, order films, records or books (electronic editions), etc. Many of these operations are not new to such an electronic framework. European telematics experiments, especially in France using the Minitel, already permit reference to this type of electronic operation. However, these new means of communication (electronic highways) embody the ambition to push the experiment further. The transmission of voice, image, sound and data (Integrated Services Digital Network-ISDN) should lead to much more complex and diversified electronic operations than those occurring on the "traditional" telematics networks.

These new communications pathways have aroused the journalistic interest of the traditional media. Much ink has flowed concerning their technical capabilities and the supposed benefits and dangers of these capabilities. Analysis has often been limited to enthusiastic talk about the wonders of technology. No serious attention has been paid to the many legal issues related to these developments.[2] This is not to diminish the importance of the technical aspects of the phenomenon. Yet, one cannot claim to fully comprehend and understand this phenomenon if one reduces it to only its technical component. Obviously the latter might seem much more spectacular than its legal counterpart. However regardless of how impressive electronic highways may become, it remains undeniable that their integration and acceptance in the social and economic fabric will be dependent notably on the legal guarantees they can provide. In other words, the consumer will only be inclined to use these new services if they can offer a degree of legal security comparable to that provided in the framework of traditional operations. It goes without saying that this security can only be

---

1 This research was conducted with the support of the *Fonds FCAR* and the SSHRC.

2 Here we are obviously not referring to the, especially European, legal community which, with public and private support, has applied itself to these problems. This lack of attention is rather that of the media and the initiators of these new technologies.

E. Mackaay et al. (eds.), The Electronic Superhighway, 93–116.

offered after thorough analysis and consideration of the legal aspects of the new communications pathways.

We thus propose to give a brief presentation of the various legal issues raised by the new communications pathways in the domain of dematerialized transactions. Of course, this domain is only one aspect, among others, of the legal issue of new electronic communications pathways. The term "transaction" suggests that a relation of a commercial nature arises between a user and a service supplier. Most often, this relation is the purchase of material goods by a user through electronic means. This is called "teleshopping". However the term "transaction" can cover other types of operations. Thus, a user can subscribe to certain services which provide, for a fee, certain information (stock market and exchange rates, the timetables of transportation services, transportation purchase and reservation systems, downloading or consultation of books, films or records, etc.). We consider these too to be computer transactions.

The expression "transaction" also covers electronic data interchange (EDI). However, EDI represents a method of transaction proper to companies,[3] and we intend to limit our discussion to physical persons, to consumer-users of electronic services. Thus, computer transactions raise questions regarding evidence, consumer protection, civil liability and protection of the right to privacy. Similarly, it will be appropriate to say a few words about the resolution of conflicts likely to arise in the electronic context. Our discussion will concentrate more on giving a view of the panorama than on presenting definitive solutions and conclusions. This panorama will allow us to visualize the size of the task to be accomplished and the legal difficulties linked to the development of electronic communications networks. Before tackling these themes, we shall briefly describe the emergence and forms of communications networks.

1. Emergence and Forms

Here we will describe the Internet network which is often presented as paving the way for what is to be the electronic highway. Likewise, in light of European experiments, we will describe the various actual forms of telematic operations. This short discussion should allow us to better grasp the relations uniting the actors in this dematerialized universe.

---

3 On this subject, see especially: K. Benyekhlef, *Échange de documents informatisés. Contrat type commenté* (Québec, Publications du Québec, 1991); P. Trudel, G. Lefebvre and S. Parisien, *La preuve et la signature dans l'EDI au Québec* (Québec, Publications du Québec, 1993); S. Baum and H. H. Perritt Jr., *Electronic Contracting, Publishing and EDI Law* (New York, Willey & Sons, 1991); T. Piette-Coudol and A. Bensoussan, *L'échange de données informatisées et le droit* (Paris, Hermès, 1991).

About twenty years ago, the Internet saw the light of day. In fact, it was a network set up by the American Defence Department: the Arpanet network. The main goal of this experimental network was to allow uninterrupted transmission of information regardless of any imaginable catastrophe, including nuclear war.[4] Yet the network seemed fragile. At the same time, given the computer boom, researchers decided to create a single standard in order to allow different computers to communicate with each other. This resulted in the development of an Internet Protocol (IP).[5] In the early 1980's, the National Science Foundation, an American federal government organization, decided to create five super-computer centres and make them available to the whole university community. Thus these five centres were to be shared. It quickly became evident that a problem of communications traffic would arise. Rather than connecting each research unit to one of these five centres, it was decided that regional networks would be created to which the research units would be connected. Obviously, each of these regional networks would in turn be connected to one of the five super-computers. Over the years communications capacities were improved in order to prevent any system overload. This National Science Foundation program was to be the true source of the network of networks which is the Internet.

It is thus clear that the Internet's foundations are set in the will to give the scientific community the possibility to access super-computers for doing research. Researchers, noting that the various networks established could thus communicate with each other (IP), very naturally decided to use them in order to exchange information themselves. Moreover, the great number of networks coupled with the development of "packet switching"[6] permits data or a message to arrive at its destination using one of many available routes. In other words, a message sent from point A to point B does not necessarily take the route A-B. If this route cannot be used for whatever reason, the message can always, in principle, take the route A-C-B or A-C-D-B. This

4 Ed Krol, *The Whole Internet. User's Guide and Catalog* (Sebastopol (CA), O'Reilly & Associates Inc., 1993) at 11. See also: J. J. Quarterman and S. Carl-Mitchell, *The Internet Connection. System Connectivity and Configuration* (Reading, Mass., 1994) at 20.

5 Internet developers, responding to market pressures, began to put their IP software on every conceivable type of computer. It became the only practical method for computers from different manufacturers to communicate", Krol, *supra*, note 3 at 11.

6 "In packet switching, data to be sent over a network is divided into many discrete chunks of data, each usually not more than a few thousand bytes long and each called a packet. Each packet is self-contained and holds all the information required to send it to its final destination. Each packet is routed from one computer to the next across the network until it reaches its final destination. Dedicated computers are normally used to route packets from place to place, much like a smart relay; each of these computers is called a router", Quarterman and Carl-Mitchell, *Supra*, note 3 at 21.

extreme mobility and simplicity of circulation makes this mode of information transmission very attractive.

The Internet network belongs to no one. Krol compares it to a kind of church in which free expression belongs to everyone but in which there is no pope or president.[7] As Krol explains,

> "[t]he ultimate authority for where the Internet is going rests with the Internet Society, or ISOC. ISOC is a voluntary membership organisation whose purpose is to promote global information exchange through Internet technology. It appoints a council of elders, which has responsibility for the technical management and direction of the Internet. The council of elders is a group of invited volunteers called the Internet Architecture Board, or the IAB [...] Internet users express their opinions through meetings of the Internet Engineering Task Force (IETF). The IETF is another volunteer organisation; it meets regularly to discuss operational and near-term technical problems of the Internet."[8]

Of course there are other networks, with far fewer subscribers,[9] in the private sector: CompuServe, Prodigy, etc. Naturally, telephone, cable and television giants attempt to exploit these new technologies for commercial ends, completely foreign to the goals inspiring the Internet.[10] The success of the latter has not failed to attract the interest of these giants regarding the immense potential of the new electronic means of communication.

Telematics, or the coupling of computer and telecommunications technology, is in fact the first general-public use of the new communications pathways. It is a system which certainly appears embryonic given the numerous predicted possibilities of what are known as electronic highways. Yet we should not overlook the reflections this technology has spawned. In effect, while legal thought on telematics is not yet mature,[11] a good number of rules developed in this context are perfectly pertinent in that of electronic highways. How could it be otherwise? Both are cases of assessing the legal system which could be established in the framework of a remote relation between a user and a service supplier. Certainly, the services offered, or

---

7 Krol, *supra*, note 3 at 13.

8 *Ibid.* at 14.

9 It is estimated that there are between 8.9 and 17.8 million Internet users (Quarterman and Carl-Mitchell, *supra*, note 3 at 5); this obviously makes it the largest electronic network in the world.

10 See, among others, Astrad Torres, "*Sur les 'autoroutes de la communication': la ruée des géants de la Finance*", and Herbert I. Schiller, "*Reléguer le bien public sur les bas-côtés*" (Paris, Le Monde diplomatique, March 1994) at 18-19.

11 Regarding Canada's situation in this domain, see P. Trudel and F. Abran, *Un état des questions juridiques posées par l'avènement de la télématique grand public*, Report written for the Ministère des Communications du Québec, Centre de recherche en droit public, Université de Montréal, July 1989.

rather which the communications giants propose to offer, demand the development of new legal solutions fitted to technological change. However, given the present situation, telematics is undoubtedly the most adequate model to be used as an analogy since it carries the seed of the aspirations of the new communications pathways. In fact, it is extremely possible that the term "telematics" will continue to designate, in the years to come, the most technically advanced forms of electronic communications. In this respect, the vocabulary should not obscure the legal stakes underlying dematerialised transactions. Moreover, the term "telecommunications" is defined as follows in the 1982 International Telecommunications Convention: "Any transmission, emission or reception of signs, signals, writing, images and sounds or intelligence of any nature by wire, radio, optical or other electromagnetic systems". This leads Poullet and Monville to say that telecommunications, which with computers composes telematics, "includes classical, new and also future services."[12]

The ends of telematics operations can be professional or concern the general public. A professional goal "relates to the transmission of data within a company or to the outside."[13] EDI, for example, falls under this definition. We will examine instead general-public telematics, in other words, the myriad of services offered to the consumer. Telematics brings together four main actors:

- the user benefits from the service.[14] He or she is thus a physical person who, in general, initiates the telematics.[15]
- the carrier is the public or private enterprise which provides the telecommunications network. It acts as a conduit.
- the supplier or producer is the organisation which collects information,[16] creates files which can be accessed. The supplier thus offers a bank of information or services. In the latter case, these services can take various forms (teleshopping, telebanking, various information services, etc.).
- the server is the computer company which makes a set of equipment and software available to the supplier or producer.[17] The server "thus wholly or partially assumes the duties of putting in electronic form, production, management and advertising of services offered by telematic networks."[18]

---

12 Yves Poullet and Claire Monville, *La demande finale en télématique. Aspects juridiques* (Paris, La Documentation Française, 1988) at 19. [Trans. note: my translation.]

13 *Ibid.* at 24. [Trans. note: my translation.]

14 *Ibid.* at 25.

15 Trudel and Abran, *supra*, note 10 at 29.

16 Poullet and Monville, *supra*, note 11 at 25.

17 *Ibid.* at 72.

18 Trudel and Abran, *supra*, note 10 at 28. [Trans. note: my translation.]

These categories are not closed. In effect, a supplier can also play the role of server. It is then known as an integrated server.[19] Likewise, a carrier can offer telematic services, thus playing the role of a supplier, or it can be a server. In short the distribution of roles is far from exclusive. Yet attributing a role to an enterprise or public organisation has major legal implications since it very often determines its range of liability. In other words, in case of a wrong, it is important to clearly identify the actors in order to determine their degree of responsibility. Naturally, the degree of liability varies depending on the facts of the case, but also on the role played by each actor in the telematic operation. Furthermore, as communications giants rush into the telematic field, their concentrating tendencies could be a cause for changing these categories. It is possible that a single entity will be server, carrier and supplier.

Moreover, telematic services can themselves be classified. To do so is not merely capricious. In effect, "the legal system dealing with these operations depends on the nature of the service".[20] Poullet and Monville identify four main types of computer telecommunications services:

- information services including, for example, information on timetables, prices and calendars; the news; electronic directories;[21]
- teletransaction services including, in particular, banking and financial transactions, orders for consumer goods, hotel and show reservations[22];
- teleprocessing services, which "are operations through which the user attempts to achieve a result through a dialogue with the computer system, in other words a set of data, programs and processes,"[23] (video games, courses, management, accounting, etc.);
- transmission services, which "transfer data, messages, documents, files from one place to another."[24] Communications exchanges are the very purpose of this type of service.

Clearly other classifications remain possible.[25] However we will concentrate on teletransaction and information services. In the latter case, it seems to us that offering information can be, in certain cases, a transaction. The word "transaction" must thus be understood to apply to information.

---

19 Poullet and Monville, *supra*, note 11 at 25.
20 *Ibid.* at 32. [Trans. note: my translation.]
21 *Ibid.* at 48.
22 *Ibid.* at 34.
23 *Ibid.* at 34. [Trans. note: my translation.]
24 *Ibid.* at 35. [Trans. note: my translation.]
25 *Ibid.* at 36-46.

2. Evidence

A dematerialised transaction, for example the purchase of a consumer good, can raise difficulties in evidentiary law. The absence of a written document recognizing the transaction, and the absence of the traditional signature sealing the transaction, are undoubtedly the main problems concerning electronic transactions.[26] The telematic network, through its interactive nature, is used notably for producing juridical acts.[27] However it can also simply constitute the record of certain facts.[28] Quebec evidentiary law, in spite of its French civil origins, has been influenced by common law. Thus computer evidence runs up against principles forbidding hearsay and the best evidence rule, common law concepts, and the civil law principle of the document certifying the juridical act. We must first distinguish between evidence of acts and that of facts. We will also say a few words about signatures.

The new Quebec *Civil Code* deals with evidence of juridical acts in a section titled "Computerized Records".

> Art. 2837. "Where the data respecting a juridical act are entered on a computer system, the document reproducing them makes proof of the content of the act if it is intelligible and if its reliability is sufficiently guaranteed.
>
> To assess the quality of the document, the court shall take into account the circumstances under which the data were entered and the document was reproduced."
>
> Art. 2838. "The reliability of the entry of the data of a juridical act on a computer system is presumed to be sufficiently guaranteed where it is carried out systematically and without gaps and the computerized data are protected against alterations. The same presumption is made in favour of third persons where the data were entered by an enterprise."
>
> Art. 2839. "A document which reproduces the data of a computerized juridical act may be contested in any manner."

---

26 A. P. Meijboom and A. Oskamp, "Evidence", in: Y. Poullet and G. P. V. Vandenberghe (eds.), *Telebanking, Teleshopping and the Law* (Deventer, Kluwer Law and Taxation Publishers, 1988) at 33.

27 Trans. note: "Juridical act" will be used as the translation of "acte juridique". This usage follows the English version of the Québec *Civil Code* even though it seems unlikely that jurists outside Québec will find this term familiar. "Acte Juridique" appears to include legal instruments in the broad sense as well as any action having legal import.

28 Claude Fabien, "*La communicatique et le droit civil de la preuve*", in *Le droit de la communicatique - Actes du colloque conjoint des Facultés de droit de l'Université de Poitiers et de l'Université de Montréal* (Montréal, Éditions Thémis, 1992) at 161.

As Professor Trudel explains, this legislation gives "full recognition as evidence to documents reproducing the data contained in a juridical act entered on a computer system."[29] In conformity with the wording of Article 2837, it must be ensured that the document is intelligible and presents sufficient guarantee that it is reliable. Furthermore, this provision has the effect of excluding the best evidence rule stated in Article 2860. Professor Fabien writes:

Certainly, the best evidence of the act is the "invoice" signed by the client. However, the new *Code* does not seem to impose a hierarchy of means of proof which would render inadmissible a computerized record of the same operation, subject to the quality of its proof of authenticity. Regarding admissibility, Article 2837 appears to be an autonomous provision which can bring into competition, before the courts, a record of operations and the original invoices which were entered in the system.[30]

Transactions concluded through telematic operations, such as teleshopping, thus appear to be covered by this provision. The "document" in Article 2837 must be intelligible, in other words, human beings must be able to understand it. This does not necessarily mean that the document must be on paper. A diskette, for example, can be a document which, when inserted in a computer, presents an intelligible text and not binary computer language.

As well as being intelligible, the document must give guarantees of reliability. This can be achieved in two ways. The first can be found in the second paragraph of Article 2837. This paragraph states that the tribunal, in order to assess the quality of a document, must take into account the circumstances under which the data was entered and the document reproduced. Professor Trudel asserts:

In virtue of this article, the testimony of the person who entered the data is not required. It is a sort of exception to the rule against hearsay. The reliability of the data entry and its reproduction could, for example, be attested by the person responsible for the computer department of the company in question or by an expert. This person will have to demonstrate that the data was entered correctly and that its reproduction on a document was done in the same manner.[31]

The second method for establishing the reliability of a document is stated in Article 2838 in the form of a presumption of reliability when the data entry "is carried out systematically and without gaps and the computerized data are protected against alterations". Thus, it is incumbent

---

29 Pierre Trudel, "*La preuve et la signature dans les transactions dématérialisées selon le nouveau Code civil du Québec*", unpublished paper presented at the Journées de formation de l'Institut des vérificateurs internes, Montréal, February, 1994 at 4. [Trans. note: my translation.]

30 Fabien, *supra*, note 26 at 186. [Trans. note: my translation.]

31 Trudel, *supra*, note 27 at 7-8. [Trans. note: my translation.]

on a system operator intending to use a computerized document against a third party to demonstrate that the data entry is performed systematically and that the data is protected against any alterations. In contrast, if the third party uses a computerized document from the operator and the operator argues that this document is not authentic, it is again the latter who carries the burden of proof since this document has the advantage of a presumption of authenticity.[32]

The legislation regarding the admissibility of dematerialized judicial acts has the advantage of giving the courts discretion respecting computer evidence. Contrary to the agreements financial institutions impose on their clients regarding automatic teller cards,[33] legislation does not elevate computerized company documents to the status of indisputable gospel truth. This re-balancing protects the user of telematic services from being charged with burden of proof which would be, in many cases, impossibly heavy.[34] It remains to be seen whether the rules of evidence are public or not.[35] The possibility of contradicting these rules by agreement could certainly contain the potential for an attack on the equality of the parties. As unrealistic as the legal principle of equality might be, it remains that telematics companies could thus set up an iniquitous system of proof in which the burden would rest only on the user's shoulders. Meijboom and Oskamp show that most European countries give the judge the power to overrule rules of evidence in agreements imposing excessively heavy burdens which are often impossible for users to carry in a computer context.[36]

Articles 2837 to 2839 apply only to juridical acts. We cannot therefore have recourse to them to prove legal facts entered on computer media. However, as Professor Trudel rightly points out, the rules of the new *Civil Code* "are flexible enough to permit evidence to be submitted in the form of documents reproducing data entered on a computerized medium."[37]

The rule prohibiting hearsay, maintained under the new code,[38] is in principle opposed to a material fact entered on computer media, for example

32 Fabien, *supra*, note 26 at 187.

33 See, for example, N. L'Heureux and L Langevin, *Les cartes de paiement. Aspects juridiques* (Québec, P. U. L., 1991).

34 On the burden of proof in the comparative law of dematerialized transactions, see especially Meijboom and Oskamp, *supra*, note 25 at 46.

35 Fabien, *supra*, note 26 at 182-183.

36 The authors cite the cases of Denmark, Italy, Germany and Holland. Regarding the last country, they write: "In the Netherlands, for instance, this is put explicitly in draft article 180 of the Code of Civil Procedure, which states that 'Agreements which set aside law on evidence are not admissible when they concern the proof of facts, which have legal consequences, and are not free to parties. The same is applicable if it would be unfair to call in the agreement'. If this is the case, so the Explanatory Memorandum on the Bill of Civil Proceedings states, the judge may decide to alter the burden of proof", Meijboom and Oskamp, *supra*, note 25 at 50.

37 Trudel, *supra*, note 27 at 9. [Trans. note: my translation.]

38 See Articles 2832 and 2843.

a writing which is a bill, being presented as evidence by any person other than the author of that writing (in other words the person who entered the data.) Yet Article 2870 of the *Civil Code* greatly tempers the effects of this prohibition. Let us examine it:

A statement made by a person who does not appear as a witness, concerning facts to which he could legally testify, is admissible as testimony on application and after notice is given to the adverse party, provided the court authorizes it.

The court shall, however, ascertain that it is impossible for the declarant to appear as a witness, or that it is unreasonable of him to do so, and that the reliability of the statement is sufficiently guaranteed by the circumstances in which it is made.

The reliability of documents drawn up in the ordinary course of business of an enterprise, of documents entered in a register kept as required by law and of spontaneous and contemporaneous statements concerning the occurrence of facts is, in particular, presumed to be sufficiently guaranteed.

The common law exceptions regarding business records and statements made in the normal course of business are recognizable in this provision.[39] This attenuation of the rule of hearsay should facilitate the use as evidence of computerized data noting, in law, a material fact, especially respecting the difficulty in identifying the author of the data entered.[40] Obviously, to be admissible, the reliability of this evidence must be "sufficiently guaranteed". Regarding this provision, Professor Fabien asserts:

This broad exception to the proscription of hearsay should permit the liberalization of the evidentiary use of computer documents for proving facts, especially when such documents are those produced in the course of the activities of an enterprise: records of the times of departure and arrival of trains to prove their punctuality, records of pharmaceutical prescriptions entered in the computerized file of an individual to prove abuse, computerized records of gas or electricity deliveries to prove a certain level of consumption. Indeed, any record which reports facts entered in a computer by a human actor can be admitted as evidence if the reliability of the document is demonstrated and the other conditions for the application of Article 2870 C.C.Q. are fulfilled.[41]

Another rule of evidence stands in the way, in principle, of the admissibility of a computerized document when proving a material fact. This is the best evidence rule. It means that a party must present the original of a document, for example, rather than a copy it may have received by fax. The problem in telematics, as Professor Trudel emphasizes, "comes from the fact that it is possible to maintain that the original in question is represented

39 Fabien, *supra*, note 26 at 177.
40 Trudel, *supra*, note 27 at 10.
41 Fabien, *supra*, note 26 at 177. [Trans. note: my translation.]

by the data contained in the computer in magnetic or electronic form, in other words in a language incomprehensible to common mortals".[42] The version printed on paper of data entered in the memory of a computer would then be only a copy. Here again the new *Civil Code* softens the rigor of the principle of best evidence. Article 2860 states:

A juridical act set forth in a writing or the content of the writing shall be proved by the production of the original or a copy which legally replaces it.

However, where a party acting in good faith and with dispatch is unable to produce the original of a writing or a copy which legally replaces it, proof may be made by any other means.

In consequence, it will generally be possible to submit computerized documents as evidence regarding material facts since the original is not available or has never existed.[43] A party intending to use this provision must demonstrate his or her good faith and diligence. He or she cannot however invoke "simple reasons of convenience to be excused from producing these originals".[44] Nonetheless, according to Professor Fabien, it does not seem that Article 2860 allows the submission as evidence of computerized documents which transcribe data on paper (invoices, account or credit card statements, etc.). Thus a company issuing a credit card could not invoke this article "to avoid producing the instrumental writings signed by the client when he or she uses the card".[45]

Article 2827 of the *Civil Code* defines a signature as follows:

> "A signature is the affixing by a person, on a writing, of his name or the distinctive mark which he regularly uses to signify his intention."

As Professor Trudel emphasizes, the wording of this provision in no way prohibits the use of so-called electronic signatures.[46] A signature plays two roles: it identifies the signatory and expresses his or her intention to adhere to the contents of the instrument.[47] Professor Trudel considers, rightly we think, that in the end an electronic signature plays these two roles. It is of course important to ensure that an electronic signature meets certain criteria of security. The question then becomes technical rather than strictly legal.

---

42 Trudel, *supra*, note 27 at 11. [Trans. note: my translation.]
43 *Ibid.* at 11.
44 Fabien, *supra*, note 26 at 179. [Trans. note: my translation.]
45 *Ibid.* at 179. [Trans. note: my translation.]
46 Trudel, *supra*, note 27 at 12.
47 *Ibid.* at 14.

3. Liability

The issue of contractual or civil liability also arises in telematics. In this respect, it is undoubtedly important to determine whether access to the service is based on a contract. In other words, did the server and the user first agree on the nature, limits, exceptions, restrictions, etc. of the service offered? The existence of a contract governing these issues can help to determine the nature and extent of a wrong, if one occurs. What happens when a user has *free* access to a service without any prior agreement sanctioning such access? The authors of *Lamy informatique* consider that there is a tacit contract since "the telematic merchant is in a permanent state of offer, whether this is manifested indirectly through its advertising or directly in the title page which appears and proposes a menu when a 'connectee' calls. The connected user responds to this offer by 'playing the game' proposed."[48] In any case, the authors believe that in the end this difference is not very important since there is a great deal of similarity between the contractual terms and the standards (by the rule) a judge would be led to consider when there is no contractual relation.[49] While signing a contract for each telematic service used might seem difficult, it is possible to establish a model contract which could be appropriate for the entire range of telematic relations. A user could be required to sign this contract when his or her system is connected. This would increase the legal security of servers and users. However, it is also true that, in any case, the general rules of common law apply, which can thus compensate for the absence of a contractual relation.

Liability in teleshopping can result from three situations: the non-performance by the server of an order made by the user, an order fraudulently made in the name of the user by an unauthorized third party, an infringement on the right to privacy of the user.[50] The last case will be studied separately.[51] Regarding the other two situations, in the absence of any special contractual provisions, the law on obligations prevails. Thus each case must be examined in light of the facts and applicable provisions. In Quebec and Canada there are no special rules on telematic relations. In consequence, in the absence of any specific rule, common law is complementary.

Liability can also be incurred concerning information services. Thus, a user who bases his or her behaviour on erroneous information obtained

---

48 Michel Vivant (ed.), *Lamy droit de l'informatique* (Paris, Lamy S. A., 1993) at 1091, No 1642. [Trans. note: my translation.]

49 *Idem.*

50 M. Schauss, "Issues of Civil Liability", in: Y. Poullet and G. P. V. Vandenberghe (eds.), *Telebanking, Teleshopping and the Law* (Deventer, Kluwer Law and Taxation Publishers, 1988) at 98.

51 See *Infra*, point E.

through telematics (computer transactions) could have grounds to sue. An example which springs to mind is that of a work on edible fruits and plants which led a consumer to mistake hemlock for wild carrots.[52] The French court ruled "that the publisher should have ensured that users could depend on the work and judged its behaviour to be wrongful."[53] Likewise, supplying erroneous information regarding stock markets can make telematics actors liable. Beyond the falseness or inaccuracy of the information supplied, liability may occur when defamatory messages or information circulate in the network. The same argument can be made when information contrary to the provisions of the *Criminal Code* circulate in the network. Think of hate propaganda, obscenity or false news.

When this occurs, the major problem is to identify the telematics actor liable for the wrongdoing. We saw in Part B that many actors play roles in the telematics network and that their operations can sometimes be combined. The confusion or integration of roles (server *and* supplier being the same entity, for example) like the clauses disclaiming responsibility which are found almost systematically in all the national carrier domains[54] make the attribution of and redress for the wrongdoing problematic. In effect, this point is central to the problems since common law (civil and criminal) is relatively well-armed and adapted to treating this type of situation. There is not yet, in Quebec or Canada, any legislative rule likely to permit the disentangling of this functional knot created in the telematics universe.[55]

4. Consumer Protection

Teleshopping raises a number of issues regarding consumer protection. These issues become even more pressing when consumers deal with merchants established in other countries. Remote sales are a domain in which fraud is frequent[56] and thus the consumer must be protected. Besides fraud, other problems such as non-delivery of goods ordered, long delivery delays, slow reimbursement of deposits or amounts paid, the inadequate nature of the good delivered, etc., are common.

It must be admitted that the Quebec *Consumer Protection Act*[57] treats these issues very briefly. Thus, Section 20 of the Act defines the expression "remote-parties contract":

> "A remote-parties contract is a contract entered into between a merchant and a consumer who are in the presence of one

52 Lamy, *supra*, note 46 at 1095, No. 1653.

53 *Idem*. [Trans. note: my translation.]

54 Schauss, *supra*, note 48 at 106.

55 Trudel and Abran, *supra*, note 10.

56 Nicole L'heureux, *Droit de la consommation*, 4th Edition (Cowansville, Yvon Blais, 1993) at 339.

57 R.S.Q., c. P-40.1.

> another neither at the time of the offer, which is addressed to one or more consumers, nor at the time of acceptance, provided that the offer has not been solicited by a particular consumer."

Doctrine recognizes that this provision covers teleshopping. However, it is not clear what is the exact meaning of the last part of the section: "provided that the offer has not been solicited by a particular consumer". In effect, does not a consumer consulting the pages on the screen of a terminal solicit the offer? Perhaps we should consider that when a server advertises products it is always systematically making an offer. It is likely that the latter hypothesis will be the one retained by the courts since it ensures a level of consumer protection which is in conformity with perhaps not the letter but the spirit of the law. Yet in certain cases the consumer may be in a situation in which he or she solicits the offer through communicating, using telematics, with a merchant whose products are not advertised but whose name appears in the electronic directory listing "televendors". This would no doubt require that the provision be clarified regarding technological developments.

Whatever the case may be, if a contract falls under the definition in Section 20, Section 21 then provides that such a contract be considered as concluded at the consumer's address. In consequence, on the view of international private law, the applicable act is the *Consumer Protection Act* and the competent court is that of the consumer's residence. Section 22 deals with inconveniences related to the payment of partial or complete deposits. This provision forbids retailers to request complete or partial payment from the consumer before executing their principal obligation, in other words, before delivering the good. However, the President of the *Office de la protection du consommateur* can exempt a retailer from the requirements of Section 22 on the condition that the latter forwards to the Office a guarantee ensuring "payment of the capital, interest and charges awarded in any final judgment"[58] against it.

It must be admitted that in international private law, Section 21 appears deficient. In effect, the statement of material rules of international private law appears slightly derisory given technological developments. What is the worth of such a mechanism when the server-vendor is established in another country with no business address in Quebec or Canada? Telematics allows transborder purchasing. A consumer with a contract with a Texan server-vendor, for example, will be quite defenceless in case of difficulty.

The Commission of the European Communities has noted the increasingly strong growth of long-distance sales. The *Council Directive of 20 December 1985 to protect the consumer in respect of contracts*

---

58 L'Heureux, *supra*, note 54 at 341. [Trans. note: my translation.]

negotiated away from business premises[59] does not apply to teleshopping.[60] In 1992, the Commission proposed a draft Council directive concerning consumer protection in remote-parties contracts.[61] This draft directive has three goals: to ensure the legal security of the consumer, to ensure the consumer's right to choose (the quality of the information transmitted and the right not to be disturbed by certain kinds of solicitation) and, finally, to ensure reimbursement in case of non-fulfilment of the contract.[62] Furthermore, Article 11 of the draft directive provides that the consumer shall have a period of at least 7 days from the date of reception of the product or service to annul the contract with no penalty. This right of retraction is clearly to the consumer's advantage since it allows the evaluation of the quality of the merchandise and its conformity to advertised claims. The legislation of many European countries, including France, Denmark and Belgium, already contains this right of retraction. Regarding the rules of international private law, the draft directive is limited to stating that members shall provide adequate and efficient means to ensure the provisions of the directive are respected. The very nature of a directive renders it difficult to be more precise.[63] In this respect, Article 5 of the June 19, 1980 *Convention on the law applicable to contractual obligations*[64] states that the law applicable in the case of a contract concluded with a consumer is that of the usual place of residence of the consumer. This provision is echoed in Section 21 of the Quebec act.

Given the growing development of transborder teleshopping operations, it undoubtedly appears necessary to provide for mechanisms to resolve conflicts which can arise between a consumer residing in country A and a

---

59 O.J. (1985) L372/31.

60 "It does not appear that this Directive applies to home-shopping. In particular, Article I provides that the Directive only applies to contracts concluded during an excursion organized by the merchant away from his business premises (which is certainly not the case with teleshopping) or during a visit by a merchant to the consumer's home or place of work where the visit does not take place at the express request of the consumer. Even if one were to equate the process of ordering over a telematics network to a visit by a merchant, it may not be asserted, at least in the case of teleshopping, that this order is placed without the express request of the consumer as the very nature of the medium requires the consumer to voluntarily call up pages on his screen to place an order for goods or services," M. Schauss, "Issues of Contract Law", in Y. Poullet and G. P. V. Vandenberghe (eds.), *Telebanking, Teleshopping and the Law* (Deventer, Kluwer Law and Taxation Publishers, 1988) at 81-82.

61 COM (92) 11 Final-SYN 411 (May 20, 1992).

62 *Ibid., Explanatory Memorandum* at 11-12.

63 Louis Cartou, *Communautés européennes*, 8th Edition (Paris, Dalloz, 1986) in which the authors write on the nature of directives at page 180: "A directive binds all member states to which it is addressed regarding the result, but it leaves national authorities to choose the form and means to achieve it. (Art. 159) A directive can be a general or specific law: but it addresses the member states and is applied through the intermediary of these member states". [Trans. note: my translation.]

64 J.O.J. (1980) L266/1.

server residing in country B. A material rule declaring the law of the consumer's residence to be the law of the contract is not sufficient. There must also be a provision for a mechanism to deal with the inconveniences associated with the fact that telematic operations are no longer located in a set place regarding the territorial jurisdiction of the courts.

5. Protection of Privacy

The establishment of a vast electronic communications network offering users a large number of services is not without danger to the protection of privacy. This theme is not new. Beginning in the 1970s, many European countries developed legislation protecting the individual from the misuse of computer technology. Transactions pose a few specific problems: the possibility of compiling a profile of consumption habits, knowing the financial status of the user (telebanking) and monitoring the consumer's movements (withdrawal cards, sales outlets).[65] Other infringements will undoubtedly occur as the technical potential of electronic communications pathways develops. There are two main issues. On one hand, are the present personal data protection mechanisms adequate given the new technologies? On the other hand, how is the protection of personal data ensured internationally?

In Canada, Quebec stands out. Following the federal government and certain other provinces, in 1982 Quebec passed an act protecting personal information in the public sector.[66] In 1993, one of the events differentiating Quebec occurred: it adopted the *Act Respecting the Protection of Personal Information in the Private Sector*, which came into force on January 1, 1994.[67] The domain of private and public relations is thus, in principle, covered by the two sets of legislation. Obviously, this protection appears partial from the point of view of the whole country since neither the federal government nor the other provinces offer private personal data the same sort of protection as Quebec. Given the interprovincial flow of data, in particular when we consider the new communications routes in which Canada is a *single* market, this absence of protection in the other areas can only decrease the range and efficiency of the Quebec legislation. We will come back to this point when we discuss international protection of nominative information. For now, we shall turn to the question of new technologies and the adequacy of the Quebec legislation.

---

65 Yves Poullet, "Privacy", in Y. Poullet and G. P. V. Vandenberghe (eds.), *Telebanking, Teleshopping and the Law* (Deventer, Kluwer Law and Taxation Publishers, 1988) at 159.

66 *An Act Respecting Access to Documents Held by Public Bodies and the Protection of Personal Information*, R.S.Q., c. A-2.1.

67 S.Q., 1993, ch. 17. This act complements the provisions of Articles 35 to 40 of the Québec *Civil Code*. See Section 1 of the act.

Here we will not study the Quebec act section by section. It is sufficient to say that it affirms the fundamental principles of personal information management which are found in European legislation and international regulations.[68] Do these basic and general principles[69] provide an adequate response to technological change? We must recognize, with Professor Poullet, that these regulations "have fought the risk related to the processing of information received *a priori* by the processing centres"[70] while the dangers posed by the new communications routes "concern data generated *a posteriori* by the use of the service itself".[71] In effect, the services offered on electronic highways are generally interactive. The user must *act* in accordance with the options posted. This *action* is what generates new information about the user and which allows, for example, the compilation of a profile of his or her habits of consumption. Likewise, the definition of "file" found in much European legislation and in the European Convention can pose problems.[72] The development of the integration of computers and telecommunications leads to, among other things, decentralization of operations, making automated processing commonplace, and leading to a diversification of the types of data collected.[73] A Council of Europe committee of experts, working on the new information technologies, is now examining the value of the definition of "automated file" found in the Convention:

---

68 *Guidelines on the Protection of Privacy and Transborder Flows of Personal Data*, adopted by the OECD (1980); the *Convention for the Protection of Individuals with regard to Automatic Processing of Personal Data*, adopted by the Council of Europe (1981); the *Guidelines for the Regulation of Computerized Personal data Files*, adopted by the United Nations Human Rights Commission (1988) and the draft directive of the 1982 Commission of the European Communities: *Proposal for a Council Directive on the Protection of Individuals in Relation to the Processing of Personal Data and on the Free Movement of Such Data*, COM (92) 422 final-SYN 287. See also the *Proposal for a Council Directive concerning the protection of personal data and privacy in the context of public digital telecommunications networks, in particular the integrated services digital network (ISDN) and public digital mobile networks*, COM (90) 314 final-SYN 288. On these two proposals, see Karim Benyekhlef, "Réflexions sur le droit de la protection des données personnelles à la lumière des propositions de la Commission des Communautés européennes", [1992] 2 *Media & Communications L.R.* 149.

69 On the generality, terms and structure of these principles, see Karim Benyekhlef, *La protection de la vie privée dans les échanges internationaux d'nformations* (Montréal, Éditions Thémis, 1993) at 97-146.

70 Yves Poullet, "Le marché de l'information. Aspects contractuels: les clauses de confidentialité", unpublished text, Namur, p. 42. [Trans. note: my translation.]

71 *Ibid.* [Trans. note: my translation.]

72 It should be noted that in the Québec act there is no definition of the expression "automated file". The Québec act has the advantage of targeting personal data in whatever medium. The act is thus not constructed on a computer model of protection of nominative information.

73 H. Burkert and M. Rankin, "The Future of the OECD Privacy Protection Guidelines: Building Trust in Electronic Data Networks" (Paris, OECD, June 1989) ICCP (89) 14 at 5.

It may be, however, that the notion of file as used in the Convention suggests centralised storage and processing and is not in keeping with the new reality of distributed processing and networks which allow data to be dispersed and yet linked up at will through the possibility of computer to computer, or terminal to computer, dialogue.[74]

The idea that personal data are stored and organized in a file, located in a precise place, has been exploded. The notion of file is not appropriate. Today data is scattered (in various locations) and thus it is no longer found in a single organized set (a file). Yet the traditional notion of a file fulfilled the requirements of transparency and easy access of data by the person who was the subject of the file.[75] The Committee of Experts of the Council of Europe proposes the concept of "logical file". That data is not located in a single place and is scattered presents no obstacles to the creation of a virtual file. In other words, it is possible, especially through coupling, to reunite dispersed data to make a single ordered set. This then becomes a potential file.[76] Who would perform these operations? This is where the notion of "file controller" comes into play. The provisions on file controllers found in the OECD guidelines[77] and the European Convention[78] are essentially similar. It is a physical or moral person empowered to decide on the goals, recording and use of data. File decentralization makes the identification of a file controller complex.

The notion of file controller[79] is primordial in the general mechanism for protecting personal data because it is the pivotal point defining the effective extent of the rights of the person who is the subject of the file (the principle of individual participation). The Committee of Experts considers that the concept of file controller remains globally valid. It believes that the last known user can be considered to be responsible:

Accordingly, a distributed, decentralised processing system may still give rise to a person or body ultimately responsible for particular "files" if regard is to be had to the ultimate authorised user of the data - is it a PTT, or a cable company operator, or a service provider, or an electricity company? Even if the ultimate authorized user so identified - and for this reason it is

---

74 Council of Europe, *New Technologies: A Challenge for Privacy Protection?* (Study prepared by the Committee of Experts on Data Protection, (CJ-PD) (Strasbourg, Council of Europe, 1989) at 35 (hereafter "*New Technologies*").

75 *Ibid.* at 24. See also Jon Bing, "Impact of Developing Information Technology on Data Protection Legislation", OECD, Paris, DSTI/ICCP (86) 5, February 1986 at 14-31.

76 *New Technologies*, *supra*, note 72 at 25.

77 Article 1a).

78 Article 2b).

79 The Québec act does not explicitly define this term. However, it imposes various duties and obligations on those possessing data. Thus it is presumed that there is a physical or moral person who is ultimately responsible for operations concerning personal data.

essential that the roles of the various actors involved in any telematic service should be clearly communicated to the user - operates a distributed data processing system it should still be possible to regard him/her as in control of all processing operations in regard to a particular file and in particular as being the repository of the sum total of personal data located in a network - the so called "logical file".[80]

Moreover, the Committee refers to network managers. These technological changes have a certain effect on the fundamental principles of personal information management.[81] However it is equally appropriate to note that the generality of fundamental principles fortifies them against obsolescence when faced with new technology. Regarding the European Convention, the Committee of Experts asserts:

At the outset the point should be made that the Convention's principles have the value of generality. As with constitutional and international guarantees of human rights, the principles of data protection are set out in a manner which allows adaptation to evolving situations.[82]

Remember that the fundamental principles found in the Quebec act are, in the end, philosophical statements which define the stakes by imposing limits. However it must be recognized that the development of specific rules can prove necessary in order to clarify, in a practical, operational framework, the application of fundamental principles. The development of such rules is related to the sector-based approach used in recent years by the Council of Europe. We know that the goal of the various recommendations adopted in specialized sectors (direct marketing, medical data, social security, for example)[83] is to complete and define the general mechanism of the European Convention. The sector-based approach is not permitted under the Quebec legislation. In other words, the act does not recognize the possibility of developing specific rules proper to a sector through regulations developed by the *Commission d'accès à l'information* or of controlled self-regulation on the Dutch model,[84] for example. The development of norms governing the new technologies falls under this sector-based perspective. The possibility of completing the general provisions of the act with norms appropriate to the new communications pathways can only ensure a right to respect for privacy adapted to technological change. Such sector-based norms can be, furthermore, brought up-to-date regularly. This flexibility is a clear advantage compared with the long, ponderous process of adopting legislation.

---

80 *New Technologies*, *supra*, note 72 at 25-26.

81 For an examination of these effects, see Benyekhlef, *supra*, note 67 at 370-376.

82 *New Technologies*, *supra*, note 72 at 31.

83 On these recommendations, see Benyekhlef, *supra*, note 67 at 322-336.

84 *Ibid.* at 75 and ss.

Let us now briefly examine the issue of international protection of personal data. The new electronic communications pathways ignore national boundaries. The mobility of information makes national means of protection extremely fragile. It is thus very easy to transmit and store data in a foreign country which has no legislation on the protection of personal data or where the legislation is particularly lax. Thus the letter and the spirit of national legislation is avoided through the export of personal data. While there may be those who purely and simply desire to escape national law, it must also be recognized that in order to conduct business, companies must sometimes export data to other countries. Most European legislation contains provisions meant to prevent undue export of personal data. National law thus submits the export of nominative information to certain controls or conditions in order to prevent its provisions from becoming derisory.[85]

The Quebec act contains no such provision. It has no explicit answer to the problems caused by the extremely high international mobility of personal data. Quebec legislation is clearly deficient in this respect since the United States, the main destination of personal data from Canada,[86] gives only fragmentary protection to nominative information in the private sector. The same can be said about the federal government and the other Canadian provinces. Thus, just when new electronic communications routes are being established, when the mobility of information is increasing, the Quebec act ensures only *territorial* protection to personal data concerning its citizens.

Section 17 of the Quebec act is the only provision concerning transborder transmission of personal data:

> "Every person carrying on an enterprise in Quebec who communicates, outside Quebec, information relating to persons residing in Quebec or entrusts a person outside Quebec with the task of holding, using or communicating such information on his behalf, must take all reasonable steps to ensure:
>
> (1) that the information will not be used for purposes not relevant to the object of the file or communicated to third persons without the consent of the persons concerned, except in cases similar to those described in sections 18 and 23;
>
> (2) in the case of nominative lists, that the persons concerned have a valid opportunity to refuse that personal information concerning them be used for purposes of commercial or philanthropic prospection and, if need be, to have such information deleted from the list."

---

85 *Ibid.* at 245-273.

86 R. Laperrière, R. Coté, G. Lebel, P. Roy and K. Benyekhlef, *Crossing the Borders of Privacy. Transborder Flows of Personal Data from Canada* (Ottawa, Department of Justice, 1991) 212 and ss.

Transborder transmission is neither prohibited nor subject to conditions requiring equivalent protection. Section 17 absolutely does not enshrine the principle of equivalence found in European legislation.[87] It simply states that the data communicated must not be used for ends different from the original goals. Likewise, the importer shall not communicate the data except in the cases provided for by the act itself. Legislators have perhaps too much confidence in the good faith of the importer. Moreover, it is assumed that the exporting Quebec company will sign a contract with the non-Quebec company, whether or not it is in the same group, in order to guarantee the prescriptions of the act. This is how, it seems, the words "all reasonable steps" in Section 17 must be interpreted. What happens if the importer disregards the prescriptions of Section 17? Should the Quebec company be punished? Nothing is less likely. If the Quebec company took all *reasonable steps*, in particular by signing a contract, it is difficult to see how it could be held responsible for a failure of the other contracting party. In this respect, the *Commission d'accès à l'information*, responsible for applying the act, seems poorly equipped to prevent such a case from occurring. In effect, it could not prohibit transborder communication or subject it to certain conditions because the act is silent on these points. These are perhaps the only means able to prevent this type of situation.

Furthermore, even if we consider that Section 17 grants a certain form of protection to transmitted data, the wording of the section forces us to note that only data relating to citizens residing in Quebec can benefit from this presumed protection. Data concerning a citizen of Germany, Holland or Canada (not residing in Quebec) is not protected if it is stored in Quebec. This is utterly contrary to the spirit of European legislation and to Article 1 of the European Convention. In this legislation, it is clearly provided that legislative guarantees apply to all physical persons regardless of their nationality or place of residence.

It is obvious that the development of electronic highways intensifies the urgency of the need to create a normative framework protecting personal data. In North America, such a framework appears even more imperative given the virtual non-existence of norms concerning personal data in the private sector. One solution, among others, would be for Canada and the United States, next to adopting legislation in due form, to adhere to the European Convention. In Article 23, this agreement provides for the possibility of countries which are not members of the Council of Europe to adhere to it. Thus following this agreement would have the notable

---

87 The principle of equivalence can be defined as follows: a country shall not oppose the transmission of personal data to another country provided the latter ensures protection of personal data which is equivalent in substance to that in the exporting country. This principle is also enshrined in international legislation: see Article 17 of the OECD guidelines, Article 12 of the European Convention and Article 26 of the draft directive of the Commission of the European Communities.

advantage of ensuring adequate and efficient protection for personal data circulating in the international communications networks.[88]

6. Conflict Resolution

A normative framework proper to telematics is not defined in Canada. We must thus take recourse, as we have just seen, to common law in order to sketch out the solutions to problems raised by dematerialized transactions. It goes without saying that a great many aspects have not been treated in this study, such as issues linked to freedom of expression and access to the network,[89] the control of certain information exchanges in the name of public interest or national security,[90] etc. Here again a normative framework must be established in order to ensure use of the new communications pathways is, legally speaking, optimal and secure. The term "normative framework" is intended to be neutral. In other words, it does not necessarily presuppose legislative intervention. Other modes of regulation can be imagined. As Trudel and Abran emphasize, "in telematics, parliaments and ministers must determine in what form the norms within their competence will be stated."[91] There are a number of forms: codes of conduct, guidelines, free or controlled self-regulation, regulation by an administrative organization, ministerial directives, strict or flexible legislative action, etc. The development of a normative framework is however but a step, though certainly an essential one, in the general supervision of the new communications pathways. It is equally important to determine the mode of conflict resolution. This issue is often, but not always, largely shaped by the choice of normative framework. For example, the legislative route might be favoured and arbitration be provided for as the mode of conflict resolution rather than recourse to judicial tribunals. Many combinations are possible.[92]

In fact, the approach chosen depends on the policy. It is true that this choice is fraught with practical considerations. Furthermore, the choice of a normative framework undoubtedly depends on the aspect one intends to govern. Now, these aspects are very diverse in the new communications pathways. Dematerialized transactions cannot be regulated in the same way

---

88 On the international cooperation provided for by the European Convention in the application of the fundamental principles regarding personal information management, see Benyekhlef, *supra*, note 67 at 352-357.

89 See, among others, E. J. Naughton, "Is Cyberspace A Public Forum? Computer Bulletin Boards, Free Speech, and State Action", [1982] 81 *The Georgetown L.J.* 409 and Henry H. Perritt Jr., "Tort Liability, the First Amendment, and Equal Access to Electronic Networks", [1982] 5 *Harvard Journal of Law & Technology*, 65.

90 Karim Benyekhlef, "La souveraineté nationale et le contrôle des échanges internationaux d'informations", [1991] 25 *Revue Juridique Thémis*, 434.

91 Trudel and Abran, *supra*, note 10 at 15. [Trans. note: my translation.]

92 Henry H. Perritt, Jr., "Dispute Resolution in Electronic Network Communities", [1993] 38 *Villanova L.R.* 349.

as freedom of expression on electronic bulletin boards, or access to the network for such ends. The first aspect requires, it seems, more active intervention since it has to do with protecting the user from co-contractors which are often much more powerful. There is an unbalance to be corrected.

Regarding the nature of the mode of conflict resolution in dematerialized transactions, one is inclined to believe that the law courts are best qualified to ensure user protection. Yet, it seems that in this context a more flexible formula would be more appropriate. In effect, we must avoid the situation in which the user takes legal action to recover small amounts of money or to annul a contract the object of which is minimal: a small sum, everyday consumer merchandise, etc. In this respect, the telematic actors could agree to refer all suits to a sort of network ombudsman. In principle, the ombudsman would have the power to decide electronic conflicts. Obviously, there would be the possibility of providing for appeal, and recourse to law courts could be limited to cases analogous to those involving issues of judicial control over administrative acts.[93]

The exact nature of the formula is of little importance. What is important is to favour flexibility, simplicity and economy in conflict resolution. The electronic environment, through its speed and incessant change, seems to require this type of intervention. Internationally, moreover, the establishment of a flexible method of conflict resolution in the communications networks would have the advantage of reducing the difficulties associated with the many legal systems and competent jurisdictions. This path must be explored.

7. Conclusion

This overview has allowed us to identify several points of tension between the legal and the technical. These points of tension are in fact the technological advances with which the law has not yet caught up. While common law can get around many difficulties, it remains that a normative framework proper to the new communications pathways must be instituted, in particular for reasons of legal security. As was mentioned in the introduction, this legal security is essential to the efficient development of the communications networks. There remains much to be done. In effect, the aim of our discussion was to underline the many issues which doctrine must submit to careful analysis in the coming years. This task is all the more difficult in that the technology is continually changing. The development of a-technological norms, in other words norms independent of the state of the technology at a given point in time, is undoubtedly the goal for which we must strive. This normative quest must not be strictly legal. Other disciplines

93 *Ibid.* at 362-363.

must be associated. This is an investment which should permit the development of solutions fulfilling the expectations of the third millennium.

Copyright, Digital Data, and Fair Use in Digital Networked Environments

Pamela Samuelson

Starkly divergent views exist as to the future of copyright and of fair use in a world of digital networked environments. Among those making end-of-copyright predictions are John Perry Barlow,[1] a Grateful Dead songwriter and co-founder of the Electronic Frontier Foundation, and Nicholas Negroponte, head of the Media Lab at the Massachusetts Institute of Technology.[2] Barlow's recent article in WIRED magazine, was subtitled "Everything You Know About Intellectual Property Is Wrong". This is not a very popular concept among copyright lawyers, publishers, and many authors, and it is not a position that this article espouses. Even so, it is worth noting that copyright law is a relatively recent construct in the history of the law, one that responded to circumstances arising from a particular stage in the evolution of technology for manufacturing written works.[3] As technology for producing and disseminating informational works evolves, it seems reasonable to assume that the law will continue to evolve as well. It is at least possible that the evolution will take us beyond copyright, but that obviously remains to be seen.

The view that digital technologies pose no threat to copyright law received a hearty endorsement at a March 1993 symposium on "The Impact of Digital Technologies on Copyright Law", sponsored by the World Intellectual Property Organization at Harvard Law School.[4] To stir interest in the conference, the organizers mailed to prospective attendees a set of questions that the symposium would address, as well as a set of tentative answers. The mailing asked, for example, whether there was "any need for modification of the philosophy behind, and the basic principles of, the law

---

1 John P. Barlow, The Economy of Ideas: A Framework for Rethinking Patents and Copyrights, 2.03 *WIRED* 84 (March 1994).

2 Nicholas Negroponte, The Bit Police: Will the FCC Regulate Licenses to Radiate Bits?, 1.2 *WIRED* 112 (May/June 1993).

3 The first copyright statute was the English Statute of Anne of 1710. Printing presses that had made it possible to manufacture multiple copies of books in far less time and with far less expense than had previously been possible were the technology that gave rise to the perceived need for a copyright law. See generally L. Ray Patterson, *Copyright in Historical Perspective* , Nashville : Vanderbilt University Press (1968).

4 See World Intellectual Property Organization, Proceedings of the WIPO Worldwide Symposium on The Impact of Digital Technology on Copyright and Neighboring Rights (1993) (cited as "*WIPO Proceedings*").

E. Mackaay et al. (eds.), The Electronic Superhighway, 117–126.

of copyright and neighboring rights because of the advent and impact of digital technology", and went on to say that "[a] negative answer is proposed to this question".[5] Since the organizers of this symposium did not invite anyone to speak who had ever questioned the future of copyright in the digital age, it came as no surprise that virtually all of the speakers gave firm (rather than tentative) "no" answers to the questions posed, as one might expect from a program that featured a well-known set of copyright professionals and representatives of today's strongest copyright industries[6]. Virtually all of the speakers reassured themselves and the audience that copyright would continue to be as important as it is today and would not be changed by these technologies, although it might occasionally need to be strengthened.[7]

One thing I found curious about the WIPO symposium was that a number of speakers offered glowing predictions of radically new kinds of works that would be created by digital technologies; these works would be produced and distributed in radically new ways, opening up radically new market opportunities for producers and publishers of information products; the one thing that would be constant in this sea of radical change was copyright.[8]

When I later read John Barlow's article in WIRED magazine, images of the WIPO symposium speakers came to my mind when I read this passage: "Legal efforts to keep the old boat [of copyright] floating are taking three forms: a frenzy of deck chair rearrangement, stern warnings to the passengers that if she goes down, they will all face harsh criminal penalties, and serene, glassy-eyed denial."[9] Had Barlow attended the WIPO symposium, I suspect he would have considered the talks given there as prototypical instances of glassy-eyed denial.

1. Copyright Has Survived Previous New Technologies

Copyright has, of course, evolved to deal with new technologies in the past. Photography, sound recordings, and broadcasting have all posed some challenge for copyright law and theory, for both technological reasons and

---

5 World Intellectual Property Organization, General Information and Provisional Program, at 5 (Oct. 8, 1992).

6 Among the speakers at the conference were Jason Berman, President of the Recording Industry Association of America, Robert Hadl, Vice-President and General Counsel of MCA, Inc., and Gloria Messinger, Managing Director of ASCAP. Well-known copyright professionals on the program were Jon Baumgarten and Morton David Goldberg.

7 See, e.g., Nicholas Garnett, The Music Industry, Electronic Delivery, and Copyright, *WIPO Proceedings*, *supra* note 4, at 101-117.

8 See, e.g., David Baron, "Digital Technology and the Implications for Intellectual Property", *WIPO Proceedings*, *supra* note 4, at 29.

9 Barlow, *supra* note 1, at 85.

for reasons having to do with evolving notions about what "authorship" was. Yet, copyright law--sometimes supplemented or supplanted by neighboring rights legislation--is generally thought to have survived these new technologies. Even though copyright's adaptation to these technologies sometimes required adoption of some "*sui generis*" (of its own kind) rules, previous new technologies have not threatened the viability of the core concepts of copyright law. Those who believe that copyright law will evolve without serious difficulty in the new digital environment look to this historical experience as a source of reassurance about copyright's potential to evolve to deal with digital networked environments.[10]

I will leave to my readers the task of judging whether this is so, or whether the nature of digital data and of networked environments is of a sufficiently radical character that these phenomena will, in time, transform or render obsolete the copyright concept with which we are today so comfortable.[11] Weighing against the historical argument, however, is the observation that traditional copyright law has regulated the reproduction and distribution of physical copies of works (and this was true of photographs, sound recordings, and motion pictures), whereas networked environments tend to regulate access to and use of digital data.[12] Perhaps this means that there is not as much commonality between the previous technologies that copyright has swallowed and digital networked environments which many copyright lawyers are intent on helping copyright to swallow—lest copyright be swallowed by these networks.

2. In the Digital Medium, Works are more Equivalent

The observation about digital data with which I will begin is that digital is a medium. This matters for a number of reasons, among them because the digital medium may upset the complex classification system that copyright laws have evolved for dealing with particular types of works.[13] Copyright classifications have historically been quite medium-specific, and have had important implications for the extent of protection that the law would provide. Some exclusive rights are, for example, available to certain classes

---

10 See, e.g., Morton David Goldberg, Copyright and Technology: The Analog, the Digital, and the Analogy, *WIPO Proceedings*, *supra* note 4, at 37-54.

11 I have previously suggested that the term "copyright" may continue to be used, even though the content of that law may change so substantially as to be unrecognizable to those who know it in its present incarnation. See Pamela Samuelson, Digital Media and the Changing Face of Intellectual Property Law, 17 *Rutgers Computer & Technology Law Journal* 323 (1990).

12 See, e.g., Pamela Samuelson & Robert J. Glushko, Intellectual Property Rights for Digital Library and Hypertext Publishing Systems, 6 *Harvard Journal of Law & Technology* 237 (1993).

13 See, e.g., Paul Geller, The Universal Electronic Archive: Issues in International Copyright, *WIPO Proceedings*, *supra* note 4, at 213-215.

of copyrighted works but not to others.[14] Certain limitations on the scope of a particular exclusive right are available to some classes of works, but not to others. The library archival copying privilege of U.S. copyright law, for example, applies to literary works, but not to motion pictures.[15] Moreover, how "thin" or "thick" a scope of copyright some works will have is dependent on the kind of work it is. Sound recordings, for example, have such thin copyrights that infringement can only occur by exact reproductions,[16] whereas copyrights in other works can be infringed by less literal copying.[17]

In digital form, all copyrighted works--pictures, sounds, texts, music, or movies--consist of strings of bits. All, therefore, fit the definition of "literary work" under U.S. law.[18] This may lead to a general flattening out of the classification scheme of copyright law and the elimination of special medium-specific rules about how copyright law will be applied to particular categories of works. One potential advantage of this may be a greater simplicity in the law of copyright and a lesser need to go to copyright lawyers for a finely honed opinion on the application of some special exception.

A potentially more destabilizing consequence of digitization may arise from the fact that in digital form, works can be more than one kind of work. Bits are just bits; they don't know and don't care whether they are a literary work, a musical work, or a pictorial work until certain instructions execute that will render them as one kind of work or another. How the bits are processed will determine what kind of work will be perceived to exist. A stream of bits that was seemingly created as an audiovisual work can, for example, be processed to produce a musical work. The Canadian performance artist David Rockeby posts video cameras so that they will record the movements of persons walking into the space where the camera views converge. Rockeby's "very nervous system" produces musical sounds corresponding to the movements.[19] Neither Rockeby nor the persons who compose music by moving in the system perceive that an audiovisual work has been created; what they perceive is music. Scientific visualization programs allow researchers to assign visual symbols to different kinds of numerical data, thereby converting what would generally be viewed as a "literary work" into a "pictorial work".[20]

---

14 17 U.S.C. §106(4), (5).

15 17 U.S.C. §108.

16 17 U.S.C. §114.

17 See, e.g, *Sheldon v. MGM Pictures Corp.*, 81 F.2d 49 (2d Cir. 1989) (novel infringed by taking of plot elements for motion picture).

18 17 U.S.C. §101 (definition of "literary work").

19 Rockeby demonstrated this system at the annual conference on computer-human interaction sponsored by the Association for Computer Machinery (ACM) in 1990.

20 Scientific visualization programs are routinely demonstrated at the ACM's annual conference on computer graphics.

Bits can also be processed so that viewers perceive them to be more than one kind of work at the same time. A few years ago, I saw a demonstration of a tool to aid in the interpretation of digital data. With this tool, graphical information could, for example, be processed to produce sounds.[21] The demonstration began with viewing a chart that depicted the distribution of men (represented by one graphic symbol) and women (represented by a different symbol) in scientific fields by rank and salary. With the aid of this tool, one could assign different sounds to different graphical symbols (e.g., a deep base sound for the male symbol, a high piccolo sound for the female symbol). After programming the tool in this way, one could then run the cursor over different parts of the chart, and could thereby "hear", as well as see, the higher concentrations of men in the senior rank and salary positions. Suddenly, the chart became a kind of musical work.

This example is interesting in itself, but it also raises interesting copyright questions. If the author of the chart has not authorized use of this tool on the chart, could he or she sue the user of the tool for copyright infringement? After all, the user has arguably created a derivative work of the chart? Or could he or she sue the developer of the tool for contributory copyright infringement? I believe that the doctrine of fair use can be extended to deal with this kind of situation.[22] If the purpose of the use is research-oriented (to better understand the chart), the nature of the copyrighted work is factual (as was true of the chart), the amount of transformation is modest and transitory, and there is no significant potential for harm to the market for the copyrighted work, it is reasonable to assume that use of the tool on the chart would be fair and noninfringing. The developer of such tools are unlikely to be held liable for contributory infringement because the tools are capable of so many noninfringing uses that it would be difficult to show any intent to contribute to infringements.[23]

3. The Plasticity of Works in Digital Form

The "singing chart" illustrates a more general characteristic of works in the digital medium: their plasticity. The assumption of the print world--which also holds for other traditional copyright media--is that works are fixed in a tangible medium, and will remain so. Many countries, Canada among them, have adopted moral rights rules aimed at ensuring that works will remain in

21 For a paper discussing this tool, see Stuart Smith, R. Daniel Bergeron & Georges G. Grinstein, Stereophonic and Surface Sound Generation For Exploratory Data Analysis, *Proceedings of ACM Conference on Computer-Human Interaction*, at 125 (1990).

22 This set of issues is discussed at length in Pamela Samuelson, Fair Use for Computer Programs and Other Copyrightable Works in Digital Form: The Implications of Sony, Galoob, and Sega, 1 *Journal of Intellectual Property Law* 49 (1993).

23 Id.

the same pristine state as the day they were born. An aid to the enforcement of moral rights is the physicality of traditional copyright artifacts which impede somewhat their transformation.

Works in digital form are inherently plastic. As the singing chart illustrates, works in digital form are easily transformed from one form to another. They are also easy to alter, even without a change in the character of the work. With the right tools, it is easy to digitally edit photographs, texts, or anything else--and to do so in a manner which cannot easily be detected. (This is one reason why photographs, video tapes, and even documents may be less useful as evidence than they once were. It is simply so easy to alter them and make what appears to be a perfect original.)[24] Because of this, it is clear that the digital medium causes a shift in the balance of power between authors and publishers, on the one hand, and consumers of copies of copyrighted works, on the other. Consumers are no longer passive recipients of a physical text which they can only read or look at. Armed with digital tools, consumers are now users capable of taking an active role in interacting with texts to enhance the usabililty of them.

There will surely be a need to restrict some plastic uses of works in digital form as copyright infringements. However, fair use and fair dealing doctrines may be increasingly useful as flexible instruments with which to balance the interests of authors, in the continued fixity of their works, and the interests of owners of copies of copyrighted works, who may want to take advantage of digital tools to enjoy the plasticity of works in the digital medium. They may also be useful when dealing with other situations arising in digital networked environments, such as making noncommercial copies of some copyrighted texts distributed on the Net.[25] Countries that do not have fair use or fair dealing doctrines may find it more difficult to adapt their copyright laws to dealing with questions posed by digital technologies because they lack a balancing mechanism of this sort. Since it is necessary to make copies of digital works in order to use them, a copyright law that regards all uses of digital versions of copyrighted works as infringements may be too rigid to be enforceable or to command respect.

---

24 See Don E. Tomlinson, *Computer Manipulation and Creation of Images and Sounds: Assessing the Impact* (Annenberg Washington Program/Comm. Policy Studies, Northwestern University, Evanston IL) (1993).

25 See Pamela Samuelson, Copyright's Fair Use and Digital Data, 37 *Communications of the ACM* 21 (Jan. 1994).

4. Automatic Generation of Works in Digital Form

The digital medium also permits new works to be created for which no human author can readily be designated.[26] One example of this is the music created by users of David Rockeby's "very nervous system". Other examples can be found in the computer programs that have been created for the sole purpose of allowing users to generate music, pictures, or simple texts. The products of these programs are not works that the programmer directly created. Rather, they are works that the programmer simply made it possible to create. One application domain likely to be very commercially significant as automatic generating technologies improve is natural language processing tools that can perform automated translations of texts.[27]

Yet another automatic generation technology that is already important is that which permits the automatic creation of databases. It is possible to program a computer system to detect certain phenomena at certain intervals and to record this information in digital form. Databases of this sort, consisting of geological and other data, have become increasingly important for commercial as well as for scientific purposes.

Programs that can automatically generate other works pose difficulties for copyright law principally because this law has always assumed that protectable works will have human "authors" who were directly responsible for every word, line or note of which the works consist. Although the automation responsible for their creation means that no human author can readily be designated for such works, commentators have been reluctant to say that no one should own rights in them because of the commercial value the automatically created work may have.

Some U.S. commentators have argued that copyright can be used to reach products of automatic generator programs.[28] Continental Europeans who take copyright's "originality" standard very seriously can be expected to press for a "*sui generis*" (of its own kind) solution to this problem. Indeed, the Europeans have already proposed a new form of intellectual property law for automated databases.[29] Even England which has no difficulty offering copyright protection to works lacking in creative

---

26 This set of issues has been the subject of much commentary in the law review literature, among which is Pamela Samuelson, Allocating Ownership Rights in Computer-Generated Works, 47 *University of Pittsburgh Law Review* 1185 (1986).

27 See, e.g., Makoto Nagao, The Machine Translation System and Its Possible Intellectual Property Implications, *Proceedings of SOFTIC's Third International Symposium on Legal Protection of Computer Software* 277 (1991) (cited as "*SOFTIC Proceedings*").

28 See, e.g., Arthur R. Miller, Copyright Protection for Computer Programs, Databases, and Computer Generated Works: Is Anything New Since CONTU?, 106 *Harvard Law Review* 977 (1993).

29 See Proposal for a Council Directive on the Legal Protection of Databases (1993) (OJ 93, Pt C, 308/01; COM (93) 464 final - SYN 393).

authorship on account of the "sweat of the brow" that must generally be invested to bring uncreative works into being (such as a data compilation) has a sui generis provision on computer generated works, giving the user responsible for generation of the work 25 years of rights to copy and commercially exploit it.[30]

Whether these works are eventually brought within the body of copyright law or protected by a sui generis regime, there will very likely need to be some sort of fair use or fair dealing limitation on the scope of the intellectual property rights in generated works, so that users who are not rightsholders can make reasonable uses of them. Indeed, the proposed EC database directive would give users of unoriginal databases a right to make fair extractions from the database contents.[31] This provision is notable, in part, because most European countries do not have general fair use provisions in their copyright laws.

5. Technological and Contractual Means for overcoming Digital Replicability

An well-recognized problem digital technologies pose for copyright arises from the ease and low cost with which multiples copies can be made and distributed in digital form, especially in a networked environment.[32] What makes this ease of copying and virtually costless distribution so frightening to copyright owners is that digital copies are perfect replicas of the original. Unlike the products of previous reprography technologies, digital copies are not degraded in quality. This means that any copy of a digital work is capable of serving as a virtual factory for reproduction of many perfect copies. Unless one can force manufacturers of digital reprography technologies to produce less-than-perfect copies, as was done with digital audio tape recording devices, there is a real danger that copyright owners will be unable to enforce their rights in digital works. Inability to control copying and distribution of works in digital networked environments helps to explain why so few commercial publishers have begun distributing copyrighted works "on the Net".

One promising body of research aimed at addressing this problem focuses on the development of technological means for protecting copyrighted works in digital form.[33] Some researchers are studying systems

---

30 See Christopher Millard, Advanced Computer Systems and Their Output, *SOFTIC Proceedings*, *supra* note 27, at 439-444.

31 See Article 8, Proposed Directive, *supra* note 29.

32 See, e.g., Samuelson, Digital Media, *supra* note 11.

33 In April 1993 the Coalition for Networked Information, the Interactive Multimedia Association, the John F. Kennedy School of Government of Harvard, and the Massachusetts Institute of Technology jointly sponsored a workshop on research initiatives of this sort. See Proceedings, Technological Strategies for Protecting

for encryption of the contents of digital works, with decryption available only after payment has been received.[34] Some are investigating the embedding of digital signatures in seemingly unimportant portions of digital pictures or movies, so that regardless of the digital manipulation that might be done to parts of these works, it would still be possible to detect that the subsequent work derived from the first work.[35] Perhaps digital works will eventually be able to report back to their rightsholders if the user is abusing access rights in these works.

Another promising area of research focuses on the potential for increased use of "header contracts" in digital networked environments.[36] Most of the commercial electronic information providers today already rely heavily on contracts and control over access to the digital information they purvey as a way to guard against market-destructive copying of their assets. In digital networked environments, a user may send out a request for access to a certain kind of information. In the future, intelligent agents operating either for information providers or for the user could search various repositories on the Net to determine whether information corresponding to this person's needs is available, and if so, on what terms. The intelligent agent could then forward to the user the various "headers" sent to it by information providers. If the user replied to a particular header as a means of ordering the information, the user would thereby have bound him- or herself to the terms of permitted use designated in the header. Software developers like the idea of such contracting with customers, for it would seem to overcome the enforceability problems that have beset their efforts to limit uses by means of "shrink wrap licenses" that so often come with packaged software sold in mass market outlets.

If copyright comes to an end in the digital networked environment, it will likely be as a consequence of the use of technological means for protecting digital works in networked environments and of header contracts. If works are protected against unauthorized copying by means of technology and contract law, there may be nothing for copyright to do, except perhaps to serve as a kind of *deus ex machina* justifying the use of technological and contractual means for protecting works in digital form. Even if copyright continues to serve at least a ceremonial role in the protection of texts and other works in networked environments, header contracts and technological protections of digital works in networked environments may spell the end of

---

Intellectual Property in the Networked Multimedia Environment (Jan. 1994) (cited as "*IMA Proceedings*").

34 See, e.g., Gary N. Griswold, IMA Proceedings, *supra* note 33, at 169-178 and Marvin A. Sirbu, Internet Billing Service Design and Prototype Implementation, *IMA Proceedings*, *supra* note 33, at 67-80.

35 See, e.g., Kineo Matsui & Kiyoshi Tanaka, Video-Steganography: How to Secretly Embed a Signature in a Picture, *IMA Proceedings*, *supra* note 33, at 187-296.

36 See, e.g., Henry J. Perritt, Jr., Permission Headers and Contract Law, *IMA Proceedings*, *supra* note 33, at 27-48.

fair use. After all, the header will have informed the user about what uses can be made of the work, and the user will have contracted to use no more than this. Encryption of the work may also make it impossible to borrow any part of someone else's work without paying for it.

It would be ironic if the principal role that copyright came to serve in digital networked environments was to protect encrypted works against decryption (that is, ensuring that copyrighted works cannot be read rather than, as has been its traditional function, to promote the dissemination of knowledge). Any effort to decrypt a digital work would necessarily require intermediate copying of the encrypted version. Such copying would arguably be beyond the decryption privilege established in the U.S. in the *Sega v. Accolade* case[37] and would certainly be beyond the decompilation privilege established in the European directive on computer software protection.[38]

6. Conclusion

It is obviously too early to tell what impact digital technologies will have on copyright law or on the fair use doctrine. In some respects, copyright and fair use seem to have a bright future; in other respects, they seem to have a dim future.

Which of these futures will occur depends on public policy decisions that will be made in coming years. The outcome of these decisions will, in turn, depend on the willingness of those who favor broad user rights to formulate proposals that will balance their interests and the interests of rightsholders. They must also engage in political action to gain broad support for their proposals. If the history of copyright legislation teaches any lesson, it is that those whose commercial interests are deeply affected by public policy initiatives about intellectual property rights can be expected to lobby hard for any initiatives that would extend their rights and against any initiatives that would limit their rights.

37 *Sega Enterprises, Ltd. v. Accolade*, Inc., 977 F.2d 1510 (9th Cir. 1992) (making intermediate copies of computer program code was fair use because the user had a legitimate need for gaining access to the information and it was available in no other manner).

38 Article 6, Council Directive 91/250 on the Legal Protection of Computer Programs, 1991 O.J. (L. 122) 42.

Free Speech, Pornography, Sexual Harassment, and Electronic Networks: An Update and Extension[1]

Richard S. Rosenberg

The Internet has indeed become an important worldwide resource and given the estimated 20 million users and more than 25,000 sites it is not surprising that a number of issues have arisen that pose difficult questions for both users and system administrators. In an earlier paper,[2] the concern with so-called pornographic text and images was discussed and an approach was proposed. For the present purposes, the major points in this paper will be reviewed, some of the findings updated, and new issues introduced.

This update will review recent events at a number of Canadian Universities including the Universities of Waterloo, McGill, and Carleton and the Scarborough campus of the University of Toronto. For some reason, the last few months have witnessed a renewed interest in the issue of pornographic postings over the Internet. A possible reason to explain this situation will be proposed later in the paper. In an attempt to briefly characterize an approach to dealing with offensive material on the Internet, six basic principles, divided into two groups, were proposed in Rosenberg.[3] These adhere strongly to the principle of free speech, as the hallmark of an open and democratic society:

Administrative Principles

(1) Do not treat electronic media differently than print media, or traditional bulletin boards, merely because they can be more easily controlled.

---

1 Free Speech, Pornography, Sexual Harassment, and Electronic Networks. *The Information Society*. Oct.-Dec. 1993, 9(4):285-331.
Acknowledgments
Many have helped shape my thinking on these difficult issues. Appreciation is offered to students in my graduate class on the social impact of computers: Tara Ehrcke, Kurt Hoppe, Ed Knorr, Sue Rathie, and Peter Smith; as well as to some of the students in my undergraduate class. Thanks as always go to Sheryl Adam. Of course the views expressed here are my own.

2 Richard S. Rosenberg. 1993, Oct.-Dec. Free Speech, Pornography, Sexual Harassment, and Electronic Networks. (1993) 9/4 *The Information Society* 285-331.

3 Richard S. Rosenberg. 1993, Oct.-Dec. Free Speech, Pornography, Sexual Harassment, and Electronic Networks. *The Information Society* 9(4):285-331, p. 287.

E. Mackaay et al. (eds.), The Electronic Superhighway, 127–158.

(2) Do not censor potentially offensive material on networks: Encourage the use of sexual harassment procedures, if appropriate.
(3) Be aware of your responsibility with respect to the uses and misuses of your facilities. However, do not use cost of services as an excuse to censor and limit access.
(4) Trust, and educate, people to be responsible.

Social Principles

(1) Issues will proliferate beyond the ability of organizations to control them by rigid policies.
(2) Occasional offensive postings do not detract from the benefits of electronic networks.

Arguments in support of these principles were presented and discussed at length. They ranged from in principle arguments about the importance of free speech to the practical impossibilities of limiting or preventing access to newsgroups containing offensive postings, even if such newsgroups could be identified. Also stressed was the importance of an ongoing program of education to remind users that they were members of a community with a shared set of values that included a concern for the feelings of others, especially in public places. And finally, if all else failed, sexual harassment procedures could be invoked to redress gross insensitivity or sheer malicious behaviour. It is believed that free speech is such an important right that it must be defended as vigorously as possible and other measures taken to deal with possible negative side effects. The report of the Task Force on the Appropriate Use of Information Technology at the University of British Columbia (the author's university), delivered in December 1992,[4] certainly makes a significant statement, consistent with this analysis:[5]

> "Among its specific recommendations, the committee said that the university should: ensure that its efforts to create an environment in which all members treat each other with respect extend to facilities and activities associated with information technology; provide access to *all* [italics added] newsgroups and more broadly, the Internet as a whole, for all members of the University community; should make it clear that the user bears the primary responsibility for the material he or she chooses to access, send, or display on the network and other computing systems; educate the University community about

4 UBC Report, 1992, Dec. *Report of the Task Force on the Appropriate Use of Information Technology*, The University of British Columbia, Vancouver, B.C., Canada. (Copies of the report and appendices may be obtained by contacting Shirley Marcus: phone: (604) 822-6122; e-mail: marcus@unixg.ubc.ca).

5 Richard S. Rosenberg. 1993, Oct.-Dec. Free Speech, Pornography, Sexual Harassment, and Electronic Networks. *The Information Society* 9(4):285-331, p. 325, fn. 12.

the benefits of access to the Internet and information technology, as well as the form of and need for responsible use of these resources; and establish Sexual Harassment and Human Rights policies in which victims need not bear the entire responsibility for initiating correction of offenses under those policies. The policies should attempt to deal with causes as well as symptoms."

In the sections to follow, recent events at some Canadian universities will be described, as will the concern with sexual harassment over the net and new developments in the unpleasant area of child pornography. Attempts to limit the abusive postings of certain well known Usenet regulars have been greeted with some concern but with considerable relief as well. Comments about the movement towards censorship in Canada in both the print and electronic media will complete this paper.

1. A Canadian Update

Two years ago the issue of censoring supposed pornography on Usenet seemed to be an every day event in Canada. Newspaper stories described occurrences at the universities of Waterloo, Toronto, Manitoba, Simon Fraser, and British Columbia. In most cases, the apparently sudden discovery of pornographic text or pictures was brought to the attention of university administrators, who behaved in a variety of ways. Some suspended the identified newsgroups and subsequently appointed committees to explore the issue of appropriate use of computing facilities. In one case, at the University of Toronto, vice president (computing and communications) David Sadlier declined to be a censor, arguing that since active steps must be taken to view possibly offensive material, the university would take no action.[6] Simon Fraser University decided to restrict access to certain newsgroups in the alt.sex hierarchy. The University of British Columbia adopted a policy (given in part above) that placed the primary responsibility upon the user. It would seem that existing policy at the University of Waterloo contributed to this decision. A controversy had arisen at Waterloo, in 1988, over offensive jokes appearing in rec.humor.funny and a committee had been appointed to study the issue and make recommendations. Consider the following:[7]

- In May 30, 1991, the report of the Advisory Committee on Network News was released by Dr. Johnny Wong, associate provost (computing and information systems). All banned newsgroups (referred to as newsgroups not currently

---

6 Rosenberg 1993, p. 308.
7 Rosenberg 1993, p. 307

supported) were restored and a designated liaison person was appointed to deal with complaints related to the contents of electronic mail and news articles. Among the recommendations made by the advisory group are the following:[8]

"The University of Waterloo adopt and widely publicize the principle that, in sending E-mail or in posting an article to a newsgroup, it is the user and not the University, who assumes responsibility.

The University adopt and widely publicize the principle that it is the user, not the University, who is responsible for his or her decision to read a mail message or an article posted to an electronic newsgroup.

The University's primary news-server continue to receive all newsgroups generated internally and all newsgroups which arrive over the networks to which the University is connected."

Thus the University of Waterloo adopted a rational set of principles with respect to a non-censorship policy. Further to the above, it also outlined procedures to deal with complaints about specific postings, but these seem to involve directing objections to the source of the postings. No mention is made of the possible invocation of sexual harassment procedures, although reference is made to the role that could be played by the ethics committee, the university computing committee, or the dean of a faculty.

1.1 THE UNIVERSITY OF WATERLOO RETREATS

On the front page of the *Globe and Mail* of Saturday, February 5, 1994, there appeared a brief story with the headline, "College drives sex titles off info highway". The first two paragraphs are as follows:[9]

> "Canada's best-known computer-science [sic] school has banned from its campus five electronic bulletin boards that deal with violent sex and pornography.
>
> The University of Waterloo, which for six years resisted censoring the sometimes lurid discussion groups carried on the Internet system, said it made the move this week because of

---

8 Kadie, 1992a, June 5. Last year U. Waterloo restored as a.s.b. Posted on *alt.sex*. Message-ID: <1992Jun5.020530.12305@eff.org>.

9 Gooderham, Mary. 1994, Feb. 5. College Drives Sex Titles off Info Highway. *The Globe and Mail*. p. A1.

> concerns that the contents contravened laws on pornography and obscenity."

The following people at the university were quoted: spokesman Martin Van Nierop, "The university is trying to protect freedom of expression as much as possible, [b]ut when it goes beyond what's in the Criminal Code then we have to draw the line;" Sally Gunz, a professor of business law and chairwoman of the six-member ethics committee that recommended that the five bulletin boards be dropped; "The issue is not for technological people to solve, it's for legal people to solve, it's for society to solve", and Tammy Speers, a member of the Womyn's Centre Collective, that complained last year "that the newsgroups were blatantly violent and sexist", "We are talking about the worst child pornography you could imagine. These newsgroups were completely infringing on our right to a safe education".

If a personal comment may be permitted, I felt betrayed by the actions taken at the University of Waterloo. Its 1991 policy was reasonable, placed the responsibility on the user, and included a role for the ethics committee. Unfortunately, the ethics committee recommended that the five newsgroups be banned. Given that offensive material has been available for years and that the issue has been debated for years, why did Waterloo take this unexpected step that reversed an existing policy? The answer is related to the Canadian Criminal Code as the following letter from the President of the University of Waterloo, James Downey, to the deans, academic department chairs and directors of schools, and academic support department heads, dated January 31, 1994, reveals:[10]

> "Last fall I became aware that certain newsgroups on the Internet carried material which was *almost certainly obscene* [italics added] and therefore contrary to the Criminal Code. Advice from the University solicitor was unequivocal: under the Criminal Code it is an offence for anyone to publish or distribute obscene material, and the University is running a risk of prosecution if it knowingly receives and distributes obscene material. In these circumstances I felt the University had to act to protect itself."

The specific newsgroups banned were alt.sex.bondage, alt.sex.bestiality, alt.sex.stories, alt.sex.stories.d (discussion), and alt.tasteless.[11] Note that all of these newsgroups consist of text and that none of the newsgroups carrying pornographic pictures were included in the ban. Furthermore, any regular alt.sex aficionado could name many more newsgroups that are

10 Kadie 1994a, Feb. 3. Obscenity - Waterloo focused on medium rather than message. As posted to *alt.comp.acad-freedom.talk* . Message-ID: <2irpui$aga@eff.org>.

11 'Obscene' Newsgroups Dropped. 1994, Feb. 19. *University of Waterloo Gazette* . p. 1.

equally as offensive and tasteless as the ones named above. President Downey announced the setting up of the following process related to newsgroups and concerned specifically with the issue of obscenity in electronic form:[12]

> "Complaints concerning newsgroups which contain material considered to be obscene are to be referred to the Ethics Committee. The Ethics Committee, with advice from legal counsel as appropriate, will make a recommendation to the Vice-President, Academic & Provost for the removal of any newsgroups it judges to be carrying obscene material. Requests to have a restricted newsgroup reinstated would also be handled by reference to the Ethics Committee. Any member of the University community requiring access to a restricted newsgroup for *academic purposes* [italics added] can make application to the Vice-President, Academic & Provost."

To be consistent, surely President Downey should have also invited suggestions about which books, magazines, and tapes "which contain material considered to be obscene are to be referred to the Ethics Committee". In fact, in November 1993, Dr. Jim Kalbfleisch, Vice-President, Academic and Provost, "issued an order to librarian Murray Shepherd to discontinue access to certain articles in foreign newspapers containing information about the Teale/Homolka trial, citing a publication ban imposed by Judge Francis Kovacs".[13] Thus, whereas obscenity is to be rooted out on Usenet newsgroups, at Waterloo, it is not to be sought and controlled in libraries, but material that might violate a judicial ban is to be identified and removed. It will be seen later in this paper that even McGill University did not institute any kind of library censorship based on a legal opinion that it was impractical to do so.

The new process also neglects to mention any criteria for determining which newsgroups should be banned. Rosenberg[14] suggests the difficulties inherent in this unwelcome task:

> "From both a practical and theoretical perspective, censorship is a bad idea and in a very real sense unenforceable, short of restricting all access to nonlocal networks. Deciding to restrict a certain class of newsgroups based on their supposed content may be easy for alt.binaries.picture.erotica or alt.sex.bondage but what about alt.censorship and talk.rape? What about discussions of pornography and the use of explicit references?

12 Kadie 1994a.

13 Jeffrey Shallit. 1994a, Feb. 6. Electronic Frontier of Canada press release. As posted to *alt.comp.acad-freedom.talk*. Message-ID: <CKtrwB.MKL @watserv1.uwaterloo.ca>.

14 Rosenberg 1993, p.311.

> How many newsgroups must be regularly monitored and how many instances of objectionable postings must be accumulated before a given offensive newsgroup is added to the delete list? What are the criteria for labeling a posting offensive? Who is to be responsible for applying them? Will there be a censorship board that reviews newsgroups, responds to complaints, sets standards, and evaluates qualifications? Will such a board hold open hearings, hear appeals, and regularly publish a list of banned newsgroups, or will it operate in secrecy? Under pressure, will the board extend its mandate to control and censor newsgroups that offend any narrow interests? In any case, as long as access to the network is in force, anyone can do a remote login to a site that has a more liberal policy, if an account can be obtained at such a site or a friend at such a site can E-mail choice postings. Networks connect people in a variety of ways."

President Downey concluded his statement with the following somewhat less than ringing defense of free speech:

> "I am mindful of concerns about the principles of free speech and expression in an academic environment. Universities, however, are not above the law and their policies and procedures should not be contrary to the law. It is important to note that, while the Charter of Rights and Freedoms provides for free speech, that freedom is subject to limitations that are deemed to be responsible in a free and democratic society. In February of last year, the Supreme Court of Canada upheld obscenity provisions of the Criminal Code as being of justifiable restriction on freedom of expression in order to protect, in particular, women and children from the harm of violent, degrading, and dehumanizing pornography."

This letter has been extensively quoted because the decision and policy enunciated represent a dramatic change in a previous enlightened approach to the problem. Other events will be described before a more comprehensive overview is presented, but it should be noted that no other universities in Canada, as far as can be determined, have justified any actions they may have taken with respect to the removal of certain newsgroups, on these grounds. Does this mean that they have wilfully ignored legal opinion at Waterloo as if it is not relevant to their own situation? In any case, Waterloo's actions confirmed for American free speech advocates, on Internet, that Canada had once again "wimped out" and could not be counted on to seriously defend free speech. Postings appeared on a variety of newsgroups, offering resources so that deprived Canadians could access their favourite banned newsgroups. Two Canadian professors, Jeffrey Shallit at Waterloo and David Jones at McGill, announced the creation of a Electronic Frontier Canada,[15] an offshoot of the Electronic Frontier Foundation, a United States organization dedicated to the defense of free speech and other social concerns, especially privacy, on electronic networks. Finally, questions were raised about the role played by the Ontario government's Framework Regarding Prevention of Harassment and Discrimination in Ontario Universities. Was this policy being used as a justification for the limitation of free speech?

1.2 Carleton University and the University of Guelph Check Files for Banned Material

The issue of free speech does not always turn on pornography, although it sometimes seems that way given the amount of discussion on the topic. The following items were reported over Internet and no independent confirmation is available; however, neither have any contradictory postings been intercepted. Consider the posting by Yerxa:[16]

> "Hi All:
>
> I need some help. As most probably know much of the material about the Homolka/Teale case is being suppressed in Canada under court order. I have a few questions about how far this can go. The university (Carleton) has been deleting E-mail and files in directories which have (it seems) references to the case. The deletions are arbitrary and not restricted to banned material. For instance, I sent a copy of the court order (Kovacs) to a friend and it was immediately vapourized..."

Yerxa also questioned the legal right of the university to unilaterally search through students' files and then to arbitrarily remove them. A few days later, Kadie[17] reposted the following brief note:[18]

> "The University of Guelph is now scanning all incoming mail for refrences [sic] to Paul Bernardo and Karla Homolka. THIS INCLUDES PRIVATE MAIL! Already, two subscrbers [sic] to my mailing list have asked me to scramble their mail.

15 Shallit 1994a.

16 Shawn W. Yerxa. 1994, Jan. 30. Canadian University Deleting files. Posted on *alt.censorship*. Message-ID: <CKGJtH.Azp@freenet.carleton.ca>.

17 Kadie 1994b, Feb. 8. Guelph is scanning all incoming mail for Possible Ban Breaks. Posted to *alt.comp.acad-freedom.talk* . Message-ID: <CKwtwA.9BE@cs,uiuc.edu>.

18 I have been informed in personal communication from Jeff Shallit that Guelph University has denied that such an action ever took place. This situation points out the obvious care that must accompany the use of Usenet postings and the corresponding difficulty in verifying the accuracy of such postings.

- Abdul

Teale Tales Mailing List (an49117@anon.penet.fi)"

"Abdul" is the anonymous name of a person who is providing information for a mailing list of subscribers who do not wish the name of their provider to be known. This message had been originally posted to the following newsgroups: alt.fan.karla-homolka, alt.pub-ban, alt.pub-ban.homolka, alt.censorship, alt.journalism. The first and third of these are not carried by most Canadian universities because clearly they do carry material that would violate the judicial publication ban, but what about the other newsgroups? Only a vigilant administrator, however, would discover possible illegal postings on the other newsgroups. And only extremely diligent system administrators would scan incoming e-mail messages to determine if they contained information about suspect topics. Is this what we want our system administrators or their employees to be doing? Of course, the very serious issue of right to privacy is central to the actions taken at Guelph and Carleton, but given that the focus of this paper is on free speech, no further mention will be made other than to note that the question of privacy protection on electronic networks is currently a very hot topic in the United States.

Note that the library analogy is instructive. Can anyone imagine that a committee could be appointed at a university to examine the library holdings to determine if they contained books, magazines, newspapers, or reports that might offend some person, group, organization, or even the courts. (Well administrators at the University of Waterloo could and they did require librarians to prevent public access to offensive articles in foreign newspapers and magazines, as noted above.) The library analogy has been championed for some time by Carl Kadie, the ubiquitous Usenet regular and indefatigable defender of free speech principles. Recently, he delivered a speech at the conference, *Computers, Freedom, and Privacy '94* titled "Applying Library Intellectual Freedom Principles to Public and Academic Computers."[19] Kadie quotes from the Library Bill of Rights: "Materials should not be proscribed or removed because of partisan or doctrinal disapproval", and provides this gloss, "In other words, don't remove something because it is offensive to many or even yourself. If you believe that the principles of intellectual freedom developed for libraries apply to public access computer sites, you should not remove the newsgroup". There is much more, but the point is clear, or should be, the recent contrary actions of some universities notwithstanding.

19 Kadie. 1994c, March 27. Applying library principles to computers. As posted to a number of newsgroups including *alt.comp.acad-freedom.talk* and *alt.censorship* . Message-ID: <2n4n15$d0@eff.org>.

1.3 McGILL UNIVERSITY TAKES ACTION AGAINST SOME NEWSGROUPS OR DOES IT ?

In January of this year, Alan Greenberg,[20] Director of Computing and Telecommunications at McGill University, defended McGill against the following report, by a McGill Professor, David Jones, of actions to be taken:

> "In a surprise move, a McGill Computing Centre staffer announced that all McGill Usenet newsgroups will be "audited". Newsgroups of "questionable value" will be deleted. The decision will be made solely by this one individual. Apparently, there are no guidelines, no committee, and no academics or librarians involved at all. (One hopes censorship within libraries is not similarly handled) An edict was simply sent out today. The audit will begin Jan. 24. Apparently it is a done deal."

Mr. Greenberg's response is quite lengthy but enough will be quoted to indicate the nature of the defense:[21]

> "- Our news partitions are filling up. We felt that it was better to focus on groups that were of interest instead of simply reducing retention periods (again). Clearly we will need to support the growing news volume in the long term, but it is not completely obvious that we can let it grow without some control.
>
> - The proposal was to remove hierarchies and groups that were not of interest. The posting identified the hierarchies that we were questioning. Many were geographic groups that we felt might not be actively used at McGill. . .
>
> - We made it clear that we have not decided on the exact method to determine which groups to carry, and we asked for suggestions and comments..."

The argument that the limits on storage require that some (many?) newsgroups therefore must be deleted are not particularly novel nor convincing. Consider the view expressed in Rosenberg[22] with regard to this position:

---

20 Alan Greenberg. 1994, Jan. 20. Re: Decision made to arbitrarily censor Usenet at McGill. As posted to *alt.censorship*, *alt.comp.acad-freedom.talk* , and *can.general..* Message-ID: <16F44F572S85. ALAN@VM1.McGill.CA>.

21 Greenberg 1994

22 Richard S. Rosenberg. 1993, Oct.-Dec. Free Speech, Pornography, Sexual Harassment, and Electronic Networks. *The Information Society* 9(4):285-331, p. 289.

> "In regard to the third principle [see above], a number of institutions, when confronted with the issue of offensive material on the network, have taken the position that given the expense of receiving, storing, and distributing network news, it is not possible to accommodate all the newsgroups. Thus they have reserved the right to withhold those groups that have generated the most controversy, namely the apparently sexually oriented ones. By adopting this position they hope to avoid any debate over the real issues. Managers of extensive and costly computer and communications facilities certainly have the right and indeed the responsibility to define conditions of use as well as standards of behaviour. They are rightly concerned about the possible use of university computers for profit by students and faculty. They are also justified in their concern about the copying of software or that students may be uncomfortable about the display of sexually-oriented images on public workstations. Many universities require users to sign a statement before receiving a computer account, affirming their awareness of and agreement with university computer use regulations. These regulations are usually posted in all public areas. All these measures seem to be an appropriate way to deal with the possible negative outcomes of the public display of sexually-oriented material."

The current situation at McGill is not known but the views of legal advisor Raynald Mercille are not encouraging. Mr. Mercille was asked two questions about legal opinions, that he gave late in 1993, with respect to the availability of information, about the Karla Homolka trial, which might fall under the judicial ban and the banning of certain Usenet newsgroups. The questioner's name is not given, but Kadie[23] carried both the questions and Mr. Mercille's response. It is noted in the question and confirmed by Mr. Mercille that,

> "According to your December 3 memo to Ms. Groen, you note that the following actions are specifically *not* prohibited:
>
> * receipt of information
> * possession of information
> * providing access to information
> * reading information on a computer screen
>
> In addition, you pointed out that it is simply not practically possible to monitor all sources of information on campus to watch out for so-called "banned material". Because of all these

23 Carl M. Kadie. 1994b, Feb. 8. Guelph is scanning all incoming mail for Possible Ban Breaks. Posted to *alt.comp.acad-freedom.talk.* Message-ID: <CKwtwA.9BE@cs, uiuc.edu>.

> reasons, you concluded that, for example, there is no legal concern associated with the McGill Libraries receiving and making available foreign news articles in the library. Thus, information that it might be wrong to "publish" is nonetheless readily accessible to any member of the McGill community and is in fact allowed, as a matter of policy.
>
> In a related decision, except instead of print media it was electronic media, you recommended that a campus-wide "ban" on an electronic newsgroup be maintained. The key distinction, from my reading of your arguments, rests on this notion of "publication". By default, electronic news articles are propagated to neighbouring institutions using Usenet News software. It is this propagation that may be similar enough to publication that was the primary concern."

Mr. Mercille's concern was that the steps the university must take to prepare newsgroups for accessibility by other institutions would constitute an act of publishing and therefore would be in violation of the judicial ban on publication. But what about access by local users, the McGill community? Why are they also banned from receiving and viewing the suspect newsgroups? Simply put, the process for the McGill community is exactly the same as for connecting institutions and hence the ban must be applied to McGill as well. In support of his opinion, he first argued that to allow open access by McGill but not by other Quebec institutions would smack of elitism, special status, and "inter-institutional censorship". The second supporting argument is worth considering:

> "Second, a decision to favour local users to the exclusion of non McGill users should have taken into consideration the factor of the public's perception. Some USENET users may take great pride in the fact that they can do what they want: this is a case where the lack of self restraint combined with the pride of their mission could prove to be their downfall. This is an area of fascinating freedom yet unregulated by government. Those who push that freedom to its limit may be inviting state regulatory intervention...
>
> By pulling the plug on the newsgroup globally, although he was forced to, Vice-Principal Tavernas ironically preserved the very freedom you now enjoy. By contrast, an unbridled approach or a cunning evasion could possibly hasten the elimination of that freedom."

Let me apologize in advance for my lack of legal training, but are we to believe that freedom is best preserved by not exercising it or by exercising it so carefully as not to offend, or arouse the attention of, government? Raising prior restraint to a virtue is not only embarrassing it is also a losing strategy. A vigorous exercise and defense of all rights, including free speech, is vital in preserving an open and democratic society. To do anything less is to cower before the power of the state and to yield without challenge what is most important and to be valued in life. The McGill decision has elevated the print media above the new electronic ones with respect to free speech protection and given the comments about the practical difficulties of monitoring libraries, strongly suggests that because it is seemingly easy to censor newsgroups and not libraries, newsgroups are indeed censored.

It is both interesting and curious that officials at the University of Toronto have directed sharp criticism at the McGill search policy. This policy extends the putative right of university officials to search computer files to mail, closed briefcases, etc., under certain circumstances:[24]

> "U of T officials say McGill University's controversial right to access policy is extreme.
>
> A recent McGill memo states that university officials have the right to access all materials on its property including "mail, closed briefcases, or similar containers". It also stated that in certain cases, a professor's home could also be searched.
>
> David Cook, U of T vice-provost, says the McGill policy is totally contrary to U of T's.
>
> "Our policy protects the freedoms of the individual. Faculty members have some protection relating to personnel files just as students have"."

It seems that in order to justify its right to search computer files for banned material, McGill sought to embed this right into a broad range of rights it took upon itself to enunciate. In spite of the outrage expressed by the University of Toronto, its Scarborough Campus proclaimed a computer policy not unlike McGill's.

1.4 Scarborough Campus, The University of Toronto, Institutes Strict Controls

The Guidelines for Use of Computing Facilities at the Scarborough College Computing Centre were updated on November 25, 1993. The implications

24 Annetta Somar. 1994, March 31. Profs slam McGill search policy. *The University of Toronto Varsity*. (Also posted by David Jones to *alt.comp.acad-freedom.talk* on April 3, 1994. Message-ID: <2nnb9p$ 2cr@ghost.McRCIM.McGill.EDU>.

of this updated policy, as stated by Computer Centre, were reported by Jones:[25]

> "WHAT DOES THIS MEAN?
>
> 1) You are allowed to use the computer systems to aid in the completion of all your courses.
>
> 2) You are allowed to use mail to correspond with associates around the university and around the world.
>
> 3) You are allowed to use the resources of the computer system to further your academic pursuits.
>
> 4) You are not allowed to talk, telnet, or ftp to computers not on Scarborough Campus. You are not allowed to possess *pornography* in any form, files which are *unacademic*, files which are to be used for subverting the system, files which may be *deemed offensive by any one person, or one group*. Needless to say, you are not allowed to use anyone else's account (anywhere in the world)!
>
> 5) If you have any files which are "*unacademic*" you must *IMMEDIATELY remove them from the University's computer systems*. (italics added)."

Points 4) and 5) are of particular interest in the present context. Assuming that no definitions have been provided for such terms as "pornography", "unacademic", and "offensive", the burden is presumably on students to censor themselves. It is also not clear how system administrators will check for violations of the Guidelines. These guidelines deprive students of free speech and privacy protection and place upon them the burden of making very difficult judgments. Note that the university does not place similar restrictions on library materials, perhaps because there are no pornographic or offensive books or magazines in the libraries at the Scarborough Campus. Treating students as second class citizens adds precious little to their education. Monitoring their computer files diminishes the role of the University in fostering a collegial atmosphere of open and free inquiry. Scarborough's actions embarrass all Canadian universities.

1.5 SOME FINAL COMMENTS

Why the need to monitor, control, expunge, or deny access to, material on electronic networks, that may be offensive and controversial. It could be obscene, it could involve harassment, sexual, racial, or otherwise, it could

[25] David Jones. 1994a, Jan. 18. U of Toronto (Scarborough) introduces drastic computer policy. As posted on *alt.comp.acad-freedom.talk* . Message-ID: <2hhrs5$3ne@ghost.McRCIM.McGill.EDU>.

threaten, it could reawaken terrible memories, it could deny the reality of the Holocaust, or it could aggressively challenge accepted beliefs. Certainly in the case of censorship directed toward material related to the Karla Homolka trial, the existence of a judicial ban places a legal responsibility upon newspaper publishers, radio and television station owners, as well as a variety of university administrators, not to make available in part or in whole any of the banned material. In spite of relentless, off-the-wall criticism from U.S. free speech enthusiasts, Canada's laws must be obeyed, or changed by traditional methods. All of this, however, requires that each medium, whether paper or electronic, be treated exactly the same. The fact that electronic networks, more specifically Usenet newsgroups, can be more effectively controlled than books or magazines, itself a debatable proposition, does not mean that they should be. Perceived adherence to the law should not be driven by efficiency considerations. There may, of course, be other considerations that motivate the actions taken by university administrators.

Consider another censorship story that seems to belie yet again previous remarks about libraries being somewhat immune to restrictive actions:[26] "... In Ontario anyway, (where the court-ordered blackout occurred), subscribers to Infomart online searching services were warned at login that if they attempted to access stories about the trial, the lines would be dropped". Again, however, the censorship is applicable to electronic systems, not books. The comparable situation would be to require librarians to either censor library materials beforehand, either by whiting out or clipping offensive material, or refusing to provide help for requests for the material, and then breaking off any further interaction with the patron. Although there are reports of librarians actually whiting out stories in foreign newspapers, such actions are offensive to most librarians and presumably would be carried out only under extreme circumstances. It is easier just to terminate subscriptions to newspapers and magazines that have ever carried suspect material, even if such actions are generally disapproved.

One of the other factors in the assault on free speech is the creation of an atmosphere that instead of fostering open debate inhibits the expression of controversial opinions. In this regard, consider the following memorandum (SUBJECT: Computer Pornography) sent to the presidents of Ontario colleges and universities in September 1992, by Deputy Minister [presumably of Higher Education] Bernard Shapiro:[27]

---

26 Chris Syed. 1994, March 31. Re: Microfilm censored at McMaster University Library. As posted to *alt.comp.acad-freedom.talk* . Message-ID: <CnJJ82.B8H @gpu.utcc.utoronto.ca>.

27 Kadie. 1992b, Oct. 20. Ontario does/doesn't ban material at universities. As posted on *alt.comp.acad-freedom.talk*, *soc.culture.canada*, and other newsgroups. Message-ID: <1992Oct20.181236.15507@eff.org>.

> "It has recently come to my attention that computer systems at Ontario's colleges and universities, normally used for the exchange of information between academics and scientific researchers, may be providing access to pornographic and/or racist material through international computer networks.
>
> It is the ministry's position that publicly-funded post secondary institutions in Ontario should have appropriate policies or procedures in place to discourage the use of their computing systems for purposes of accessing or sending racist or pornographic materials. Furthermore, offensive material should be removed when it is identified, and appropriate sanctions should be in place to deal with offenses.
>
> I realize that private computer companies offer their subscribers access to international computer networks and that virtually anyone in Canada with a computer and a telephone link can gain access to this material. Nevertheless, I do not believe that publicly-funded institutions should be seen to support either access to, or distribution of offensive material.
>
> It is my expectation that each institution will have policies and procedures in place to discourage the use of its computer systems for access to, or sending of, racist and/or pornographic material. Please write me at your earliest convenience indicating your institution's policies and plans in this regard.
>
> Thank you for your early attention to this very serious issue."

Apparently, this document should be viewed as advisory because the ministry has no power to impose policy on autonomous colleges and universities, but the tone certainly suggests that they would be well advised to have procedures in place in the near future. What are the options for institutions to "discourage … accessing or sending racist or pornographic materials", for the removal of such material "when it is identified", and what "sanctions should be in place to deal with offences?" The obvious response by cautious administrations is simply to remove newsgroups that they believe carry occasional, a few, or frequent postings, that are or could be interpreted by one or more individuals or groups as being racist or pornographic. In addition there are to be sanctions in place to be used against individuals that access or send the offensive material. Are these two acts to be treated equally? Why should accessing pornography on Internet be punished? Why should reading racist postings be an act deserving sanctions? What if I repost a racist message to publicize the kinds of views currently in circulation? Should I be punished? What has happened to the free and open debate of controversial, even offensive ideas? What has happened to free and open inquiry if certain ideas cannot be accessed, saved, or transmitted to others?

Censorship is a bad policy; consider Rosenberg's[28] defense of the second principle:

> "The second principle is clear: No censorship. Free speech protection is not absolute and there are occasions when compromises must be made, but censorship of selected newsgroups by system managers does not warrant such a compromise. No one is required to read or view material on the network. A definite decision must be made to receive and a definite action must be taken to retrieve this material. No prior restraint should be initiated. However, the consequences of viewing certain material in public places may well be detrimental to the well-being of some people. Women who find it offensive and whose feelings are ignored in attempts to improve unpleasant situations can initiate sexual harassment procedures. Such actions may not be easy, however, and may further subject women to abuse. Furthermore, what constitutes sexual harassment in the workplace is still being defined and the burden placed on women to voice their displeasure may indeed be heavy. Use of public computing facilities does not license anyone to display material that others, not necessarily women, may find offensive. Ignoring the expressed discomfort of others may open one up to charges of harassment, sexual or otherwise. By the same token, private reading or viewing of material that some might find offensive is not sufficient cause to deny ready access to all."

Approximately a year later, the Ontario government announced "policy guidelines to prevent harassment and discrimination at colleges and universities ... on all grounds covered by the Ontario Human Rights Code".[29] To quote from Calamai:[30]

> "What the original report didn't make clear is that the Ontario government has actually laid down detailed rules for what may be said in a university classroom, for what may be cited by professors, for what reading materials libraries may have on their shelves, for what art can be shown and taught.

28 Rosenberg 1993, p. 288.

29 Peter Calamai. 1994, Jan. 23. Universities Kowtow to Big Brother. *Ottawa Citizen* , Editorial page. (Also posted on *alt.comp.acad-freedom.talk* , January 26, 1994. Freedom in Ontario. Message-ID: <CK9295. 82J@freenet.carleton.ca>.).

30 *Id.*

> Nothing may now be spoken, read or displayed on a university campus in Ontario, for example, if it "creates a negative environment for individuals or groups" and is of a "significant nature".
>
> Equally verboten are "gestures, remarks, jokes, taunting innuendo, display of offensive materials, offensive graffiti, threats, verbal or physical assault, imposition of academic penalties, hazing, stalking, shunning or exclusion"."

It should be clear that the purpose of the principles given at the outset of this paper is to foster an open and equitable environment in which to pursue academic interests. Ostensibly, the purpose of this Ontario policy is the same, but the attempt to articulate a complete and comprehensive set of guidelines seems to have the appearance of stifling open inquiry and academic pursuits. It offers a ready target for those who wish to maintain dominance by males, by whites, in short by the traditional power structure. The attempt to eliminate inequity by instituting a policy of "zero tolerance" of a "negative environment" on campus,[31] which employs the dangerous tool of censorship (self and otherwise), can easily have the opposite effect. The cumulative effect of Ontario policies in this area may lead to, and some would say has already led to, a reliance on suppression and censorship and the creation of a fearful environment, the antithesis of open and free inquiry.

2. Harassment on the Net

It may be instructive to turn away, at least temporarily, from a preoccupation with pornography as the main focus of censorship, towards another free speech issue, namely problems associated with harassment on the net, including sexual, racial, and other forms.

2.1 Sexual Harassment

Some would claim that the Internet is anti-female, in a variety of ways. First and foremost are newsgroups carrying pornographic pictures mostly of women, albeit in coded form, such as alt.binaries.pictures.erotica and newsgroups carrying pornographic stories in which women are often presented in very unpleasant circumstances. But beyond these rather obvious examples, women may be directly harassed in a variety of ways: offensive e-mail, "flamed" or just put down in newsgroups, and insulted in IRC (Internet Relay Chats) interactions. It is however very difficult to determine how pervasive such incidents are. In one attempt to estimate the frequency of such events, the British science and technology writer, Mike Holderness,

---

31 Bill Graham. 1994, February 14. Don't sell academic freedom short. The *Globe and Mail*, p. A19.

posted a survey request on October 10, 1993 to various newsgroups asking for information and opinions about sexual harassment. Results were reported in an article published in the *Times Literary Supplement* of December 24, 1993. In addition Holderness[32] presented the raw data from 32 responses: of these 18 were identified as women and they reported 6 incidents of targeted, personal e-mail harassment, 8 of other kinds of harassment , including IRC insults, and 2 flames following newsgroup postings. The 12 men reported a total of 8 incidents: 2 direct e-mail, 1 other, and 5 flames. It is of interest that the two men reporting e-mail harassment had gender ambiguous names. It is difficult to evaluate such data given that some 20 million people around the world use the Internet.

There are some legal issues involved in excessive flaming, that is, in outrageous criticism that may be seen as a public insult as compared with excessive e-mail that may be seen as private harassment. As Victor Cosentino, a Washington lawyer puts it:[33] " ... flaming in private E-mail may be the equivalent of illegal telephone harassment, and flaming in a public news group or discussion board may be defamatory". He further notes that, "The relative anonymity and socially detached nature of on-line communications allow people to say things on-line that they would never think to say in person. ... We can hurt and defame people and possibly become legally liable. We can have our privacy breached or our words taken out of context, twisted, or falsified. The solution is to treat the virtual world like the real world - because it is".

Personal experience may not be reliable but there is some indication that another form of harassment exists, that is, men taking over the discussion in newsgroups ostensibly created by and for women. For example, soc.feminism and alt.feminism have more than their fair share of men not only contributing to the discussion of women's issues but frequently dominating the discussion. Soc.feminism is a moderated newsgroup, which means that all postings must be filtered by a moderator, currently a women, who is criticized and berated on occasion for not acceding to the wishes of male participants. It is as if women cannot be permitted to deal with feminist issues without a continual confrontation with men with attitudes. The net culture is definitely dominated by men - they set the agenda and the style - and women who wish to participate must play by their rules. A subtle and sometimes not so subtle pressure exists to play the game by male rules. Does this situation constitute sexual harassment and if so should steps be taken to even the playing field? Maybe and probably not. The electronic frontier will be tamed and women will become more equal or else most will abandon this domain or be satisfied with a marginal role.

---

32 Mike C. Holderness. 1994, Jan. 10. SUMMARY: Harassment on the Net survey. As posted on *comp.org.eff.talk* . Message-ID: <2gscfj$p46 @swan.doc.ic.ac.uk>.

33 Victor J. Cosentino. 1994, March. Virtual Legality. *Byte* . p. 278.

2.2 RACIAL AND POLITICAL HARASSMENT

To defend free speech may mean to defend the rights of others to make pronouncements that are personally painful. In this regard, there exist a number of Internet regulars, who single-mindedly post a stream of messages to many newsgroups, which others find offensive, tiresome, and finally, irrelevant. A brief introduction to the worlds of Dan Gannon and Serdar Argic is unavoidable.

Dan Gannon has a mission: to post as many anti-holocaust messages as possible and to as many newsgroups as possible. For years, Gannon has been providing a forum for revisionists to spout their line that the holocaust did not happen. And for years, two or three hardy souls have responded with postings that dispute every claim made by Gannon. Gannon reprints papers from a "journal" specializing in revisionist history with pretensions of objective scholarship. He regularly reposts his own pieces and on occasion has posted more than five pieces a day. On March 10, Gannon[34] posted a special diatribe on the occasion of a perceived restriction in his otherwise open access to the Internet. Part of this plea follows:

> "Administrators at Netcom have told me I cannot post any more messages about Holocaust Revisionism to any newsgroups except certain newsgroups they have specified. I have no choice but to comply.
>
> There is a lobby which opposes any critical examination or questioning of the "Holocaust story" or of Israeli policy...
>
> Following are the ONLY newsgroups Netcom says I am still allowed to post to:
>
> alt.revisionism, talk.politics.misc, soc.culture.german, soc.culture.jewish, soc.rights.human, alt.discrimination, alt.cons-piricy, alt.illuminati, alt.individualism, alt.mindcontrol, alt.poli-tics.correct, alt.politics.reform, and alt.censorship."

Does this step taken by Netcom smack of censorship, a less serious restriction but still severe, a slap on the wrist, or a minor inconvenience? Gannon acts as if he has been mortally wounded and believes that he has been punished by those offended by his postings and furthermore, that the restriction to ten newsgroups will seriously impair his effectiveness. He subsequently argued that the Internet's legendary forbearance has broken down resulting in a limitation of his free speech. There was some disagreement in responses to the Netcom action, but the majority felt that Gannon deserved what he got and that he had not really been overly damaged by the ten newsgroup limitation. Note that one of the select

34 Dan Gannon. 1994, March 10. Locked Out of Usenet Newsgroups! Posted to alt.censorship. Message-ID:<9403102243.A2439wk@banished.com>.

newsgroups is soc.culture.jewish and that Gannon messages posted there will continue to cause considerable emotional pain and arouse a feverish response, exactly the purpose of his efforts. In this instance the Internet community seems to have acted with some resolve after a long period of inaction not to exclude a user but instead to *mildly* admonish him in response to complaints that his activities were too pervasive. In another case, however, the community seems to be paralyzed.

Serdar Argic purports to be a person of Turkish heritage, whose mission in life is to set the record straight with respect to Turkish historical events. He is primarily concerned with convincing the world that the Turkish massacre of Armenians, early in this century is historical fiction and that on the contrary, Armenians have been systematically murdering Turks. That they have managed to convince the world that they are the deeply injured party is to be seen as a triumph of their ingenuity and deviousness. Argic's method is to post vast quantities of material scanned in from the books of supposedly reputable historians accompanied by jargon-laden political polemics. He rarely responds to criticism or advice no matter how well intentioned and he regularly takes advantage of news events to establish the most tenuous connections with his primary concern. Argic has been asked politely to voluntarily restrict his postings to appropriate newsgroups, but to little effect. Argic greeted the recent massacre in Hebron not with sadness or concern but with yet another opportunity to abuse Armenians and their supposed hatred towards Islam. Many have believed that Serdar Argic is really a collective of individuals who have been able to develop tactics to defeat the Internet posting rules and thus render it almost impossible to discover the source of the messages. More recently, however, he has been identified as Mr. Ahmet Cosar, a graduate student at the University of Minnesota and a concerted effort has begun to direct complaints to the local system administrator, but difficulties are anticipated.[35]

However unpleasant postings by Gannon and Argic may be, they pale in comparison with more recent, single shot examples, which raise the stakes in the free speech debate. Someone called Lane Wright, upset by a recent television show "60 Minutes", which offered a forum for revisionists, including the Canadian and German representative Peter Zundel, posted at least two quite virulent anti-Semitic messages, because he felt Jews had not been accurately portrayed and revisionists had not been allotted sufficient time to make their case. In the first posting, Wright[36] asked the following questions:

---

35 Douglas W. Jones. 1994, April 7. Re: 'Serdar Argic': Racist remarks? Defamation? Supply info ... As posted on *alt.comp.acad-freedom.talk*. Message-ID: <2o145r$br8 @nexus.uiowa.edu>.

36 Lane Wright. 1994, March 21. Who Controls "60 Minutes"? As posted to *alt.censorship* . Message-ID: <9403212018.A6252wk@banished.com>.

> "Why no story about how Jews eventually have been despised by every society they entered since the beginning of time? Why no speculation as to a relationship between this and the Talmud and Torah teaching young Jews to lie to, steal from, cheat and even kill filthy gentiles?"

His second posting followed up these questions with a number of supposed revelations, found in the Talmud, about how Jews view their gentile neighbours and how they are taught and even commanded to commit the actions mentioned above. In Canada, Wright would probably have been charged with a violation of the "Hate Laws;" in the U.S., Wright was more or less ignored on the Internet except for a few vigorous responses.

The last of these examples is the worst, in terms of the degree of extreme hatred and sheer ugliness expressed. It purports to represent the views of something called OEM, Organization for the Execution of Minorites [sic] and lists about a page of unbelievably crude, offensive, and racist so-called "nigger" jokes, followed by very violent, threatening doggerel, none of which will be reproduced here. A name is attached to the posting, Vincent Allen Krause at the University of Michigan,[37] but there is some question about whether or not any sane individual would actually attach his real name to such a posting. In fact Mr. Krause has denied his involvement and awaits an investigation at the University of Michigan to clear him. It appears that the violence expressed here goes beyond speech, as it talks about using a shotgun to inflict untold damage, burning, crushing, performing castration, and blasting with a 44 magnum. This posting was sent to several newsgroups including alt.censorship, the haven of choice for some of the worst products of the human imagination. However, upsetting this posting is, it must be considered speech and therefore protected, unless its call to commit violence can be proven to go beyond protected speech. U.S. law in this area currently rests on the Supreme Court 1969 decision in the *Brandenberg* case:[38]

> "In the 1969 case of *Brandenberg v. Ohio*, the Supreme Court struck down the conviction of a Ku Klux Klan member under a criminal syndicalism law and established a new standard: Speech may not be suppressed or punished unless it is intended to produce "imminent lawless action" and it is "likely to produce such action". Otherwise, the First Amendment protects even speech that advocates violence."

---

37 Vincent Allen Krause. 1994, April 6. Nigger Jokes. As crossposted from *alt. activism* to *alt.censorship*. Message-ID: <2nt77d$pf2@lastactionhero.rs.itd. umich.edu>.

38 Carl M. Kadie. 1994e, April 6. Re: What to do about this guy. As posted to *alt.comp.acad-freedom.talk*.. Message-ID: <Cnv360.3wF@cs.uiuc. edu>.

The system administrators at the University of Michigan in responding to complaints, of which there will be many, may choose to remove or suspend the computer privileges of the named individual, given that he actually made the posting. It is interesting that many respondents have simply said that anyone can post anything they wish, whenever they wish, wherever they wish. Free speech, in their opinion, is unrestricted, an unrealistic position given that such a situation does not obtain in the real world, beyond the Internet. If devotees of electronic networks wish to have rights equal to other media, they cannot realistically demand more rights.

3. Other Issues

The Internet is indeed a global network and therefore one shouldn't be too surprised by this recent reposting:[39]

> "The new newsgroup "alt.recovery.catholicism" is illegal in many countries. Italy, Brazil, Spain, Ireland (Republic), Portugal, and several predominantly Catholic countries have demand [sic] its removal."

With respect to the benefits of the emerging "Global Village", Rosenberg[40] makes the following point:

> "One of the main virtues of networks like Internet is that they are international; transmissions are sent around the world as easily and quickly as next door. They have altered the way research is carried out, not fundamentally but sociologically. They appear to have reduced time and space and to have forced a confrontation of an aggressive culture with many previously isolated and inward-looking ones. What is open for discussion and debate in the United States is not necessarily fair game elsewhere. In the United States, one important consideration of decisions with respect to the judgment of pornography or obscenity, has been the determination of community standards. For international networks, community standards multiply rapidly to the point that no one can assume to know that what "plays in Peoria" will "play in Dublin". The concept of international standards of good taste begs description.

In this section a number of disparate issue will be discussed including the distribution of child pornography over networks and bulletin boards and a recent, interesting Canadian event.

---

39 Timothy C. May. 1994, March 31. This newsgroup is illegal! As posted on *comp.org.eff.talk*. Message-ID: <tcmayCnJx0A.58A@netcom.com>.

40 Rosenberg 1993, p. 292.

3.1 CHILD PORNOGRAPHY AND BULLETIN BOARDS

One area in the concern with obscenity that appears to have near universal agreement is the condemnation of child pornography - books, magazines, videos, and material on bulletin boards (BBs) - including its creation and dissemination. BB system operators (sysops) as well as system administrators at universities and elsewhere are obviously concerned with their responsibility if suspect material is being transmitted over their systems. A number of sysops have been arrested in the U.S. and Canada and charged with disseminating child pornography. It is claimed by some free speech advocates that such charges are used to intimidate sysops whose other holdings, while objectionable to certain groups, are within the law. What is the responsibility of sysops and system administrators? Mike Godwin, online legal counsel for the Electronic Frontier Foundation in the U.S., attempted to discuss this question in a recent article, Godwin:[41]

> "[Re: Online obscenity] In short, you can't constitutionally be convicted merely for possessing obscene material or for distributing obscene material you didn't know about.
>
> [Re: child pornography] For all practical purposes, the law of child pornography is wholly separate from the law of obscenity … child porn laws are not aimed at *expression* at all. Instead, they are designed to promote the protection of children by trying to destroy a market for materials, the production of which requires the sexual use of children … In sum, then, the child porn statutes create additional problems for the system administrator who wants to avoid criminal liability and minimize the risk of a disruptive search and seizure."

The Canadian law in this area is more stringent than in the U.S. In fact, the U.S. Supreme Court has "agreed today to decide whether the Federal law against child pornography requires the Government to prove that those who distribute or receive sexually explicit films or photographs of minors are aware that the performers are not adults."[42] In 1992, a Federal appeals court ruled "that because the Federal law does not require proof of such knowledge, the law violates the First Amendment's guarantee of free speech". Greenhouse further notes that "Under Supreme Court precedents the First Amendment bars obscenity convictions without proof that the defendant is aware of the character of the obscene material". Thus system administrators may be better off not trying to track down and expunge all

---

41 Mike Godwin. 1994, March/April. The Law of the Net. Sex and the Single Sysadmin: The Risks of Carrying Graphic Sexual Materials. *Internet World.* pp. 56-62.

42 Linda Greenhouse. 1994, March 1. Supreme Court to Consider '77 Child Pornography Law. *The New York Times.* p. A8.

"obscene" material. For this purpose, being considered a bookstore is better than being a newspaper or broadcasting company.

If the above issues are not troublesome enough, another one has created a deep concern in the public at large. On a regular basis, reports appear of the use of BBs by child molesters, who establish initial contact with unsuspecting children, typically boys, and then over time gain their confidence to the point that personal meetings follow. For example, the following story is illustrative:[43]

> "A Santa Clara prosecutor says a Cupertino man pleaded no contest to charges he used a computer bulletin board to contact a 14-year-old boy with whom he later engaged in sadomasochistic sex ... Santa Clara County Sheriff's Department investigators say Deatherage, a computer engineer, met the 14-year-old boy through a computer bulletin board and arranged to meet him."

How common such occurrences are is unknown, but they are frequent enough to create a sense of danger associated with BBs. Parents are sure to monitor their children's activities, because in addition to stories of lurking child molesters, stories of the ready availability of pornography are also prevalent. Given that parents are already concerned with books, magazines, television, and video, the extension to computer BBs is neither surprising nor a major burden. Note that another area of concern is video games for which both sex and violence have become highly publicized issues. Having children, usually boys, inflict various degrees of violent actions on scantily clad women, is disturbing to say the least. Finally, the emergence of pornography on interactive CD-ROMs is yet another indication of how intimate the relationship between sex and technology is.[44]

3.2 ANOTHER CANADIAN EVENT: *WIRED* RECALLED

On March 24 1994, the following posting appeared in the newsgroup alt.wired:[45] "Bookstores throughout Ontario, Canada are pulling WiReD 2.04 (April '94) from their shelves because it violates the Homolka/Teale ban". Using the gopher retrieval mechanism, I was able to access the gopher files for *Wired* magazine and read the article which caused the removal of *Wired* from the newsstands in Ontario (and from British Columbia newsstands as well) and the *Wired* news release of March 23. In the news

---

43 No Contest Plea in Computer Bulletin Board Molestation. 1994, April 6. As posted on *clari.tw.computers*. Message-ID: <VdeatherageU4A6505 pp@clarinet.com>.

44 John Tierney. 1994, Jan. 9. Porn, the Low-Slung Engine of Progress. *The New York Times*. Section 2, p. 1.

45 M. Dulcey. 1994, March 24. Re: WiReD Magazine - Banned in Canada. As posted on *alt.wired*. Message-ID: <mdulcey.764536138@BIX.com>.

release, *Wired* described the contents of the 400 word article, justified its publication, decried the ineffectiveness of the ban, criticized Canada's recent seizure of gay and lesbian periodicals, and proclaimed its support of free speech. The release then went on to provide explicit details of how the article in question could be obtained via e-mail, gopher, or World Wide Web. Gopher was employed once again to retrieve the short article "Paul and Karla Hit the Net".

As expected, a tidal wave of postings flooded such newsgroups as alt.wired, alt.censorship, comp.org.eff.talk, and alt.comp.acad-freedom.talk. The majority condemned Canada for its apparent violations of free speech, compared its behaviour to the common acts of repressive countries, quoted unfavourable American newspaper articles about the ban, offered access to archives in the U.S. devoted to Teale/Homolka lore, and generally portrayed Canada as having betrayed the basic principles of a free and open democracy, to say nothing of its stupidity in attempting to enforce such a ban, given the pervasiveness and power of world wide electronic networks, especially the Internet. Although students at the University of British Columbia had reported purchasing copies of the April issue of *Wired* attempts by the author to do the same were futile. Reports appeared that copies were available in eastern Canada with the offending page torn out. Finally a copy was purchased on April 8, with a 2" diameter green sticker on the cover bearing the words: "Material in this Issue is BANNED in Canada". The article on page 28 appeared in its entirety except for a black sticker, with white text, that concealed about 5 lines. The text of the sticker is given as follows:

> "Information in this article has been removed to conform with a Canadian court ban. For a discussion of censor-ship issues, check out WIRED Online.
>
> See page 115 for addresses."

22 words were censored. These will not be included here. *Wired* presumably incurred costs of about $50,000 in pulling the magazine and covering up the offending words. At the cost of spending too much space on this event, a few additional remarks will be offered. At almost the same as this story was being reported the following appeared in a local newspaper:[46] "Meanwhile, Niagara Region police say Karla Teale, expected to be a witness in her husband's case, will be kept in a special cell at police headquarters in St. Catherines during Paul Teale's preliminary hearing". As far back as December 2, 1993, the following information was available:[47] "Ms.

46 Tom Blackwell. 1994, March 24. Defense, prosecution lawyers clash as Teale hearing slated. *The Vancouver Sun* , p. A4.

47 Rudy Platiel. 1993, Dec. 2. Lawyers argue over Homolka ban. *The Globe and Mail* . p. A2.

Homolka was convicted in July [1993] of two counts of manslaughter and sentenced to 12 years in prison". A number of facts could be inferred from this information that would be related to the censored material, but no more will be said in print.

Two fundamental principles, namely free speech and the right to a fair trial, have once again collided. The judiciary, with the Kovaçs publication ban, has once again favoured the right to a fair trial, and has argued that the ban will be lifted shortly after the trial. Thus, free speech is not being banned, merely postponed, although there is a perception that certain details will never be made public. Most Canadians are still in the dark about the details of Karla Homolka's trial because of the ban, but many thousands, with access to the Internet, know the complete story, in spite of the best efforts at many universities to prevent access. Is there a lesson in all this? Perhaps, that it is and will continue to be impossible to control information. It is contradictory, in the same breath, to attempt to control information and to advertise the wonders to be brought by the "Information Superhighway". The issue is being forced, and rearguard actions notwithstanding, the global dissemination of information will render practical efforts to control information mute.

One last point: Wired is not unique; "The British edition of Elle Magazine is being pulled from Toronto store shelves because of fears it ignored the ban on reporting details of Karla Homolka's manslaughter trial. R. M. Distribution which supplies Elle to stores in the Toronto area, is pulling the magazines on the advice of its wholesaler, said spokeswomen Melissa Boscariol."[48]

4. Conclusions

The problem of reconciling rights is difficult and often results in apparent unfairness, whether it is free speech versus the right to a fair trial or free speech versus the violation of the civil rights of women by the ready availability of pornography, as is argued by many women and men. In the former case, the publication ban on reporting events associated with the judicial decision in the Karla Homolka trial has been hotly debated in Canada and has resulted in steps taken by a number of university administrators to limit access to certain newsgroups on the Internet and to restrict access to certain foreign publications. In addition, in some cases universities have asserted their right, and indeed obligation, to search user computer files to ensure that the university is not legally liable for information held in those files, which could be in violation of the Criminal Code with respect to obscenity. Thus, another right, privacy, not usually

48 David Jones. 1994b, March 27. There's more! British edition of "Elle" banned in Canada. As posted on *alt.censorship*. Message-ID: <2n5go1$3nk@ghost.McRCIM.McGILL.EDU>.

formally enunciated in the law, is sacrificed for purposes of satisfying other more urgent requirements. International magazines have been pulled of newsstands because of a fear that they contain banned material, an act resulting in a flurry of criticism of Canada, especially over the Internet, as having little regard for free speech.

System administrators and BB sysops (pardon the cyberspeak) regularly face the need to make compromises between their responsibility to provide adequate services to their users and clients and their concern that their systems are carrying possibly offensive and even illegal information. In this regard, they share the ongoing concerns of broadcasting and print editors and publishers. However, there are differences in that while personal property, consisting of books and magazines, is normally not open for inspection, computer files can be examined at the discretion of system administrators. Another important factor, a social but not a legal one, is the frontier mentality of the Internet. This global culture, barely ten years old, originating in the U.S. and still infused with U.S. values, is adamant in its support of an absolute interpretation of U.S. civil rights - free speech, privacy, the right to purchase and own guns without government interference, and of course the unrestricted right to participate in the Internet and to make full use of the available resources.

Thus whenever a collision occurs between these and other rights and events anywhere in the world, the Internet culture springs into action, denouncing the violators and mobilizing opposition. Local, fairly narrow actions may be highlighted and their visibility so raised that minor, relatively harmless events assume temporary importance. Initiators may be embarrassed and victims castigated for their passivity and implicit compliance. Of course, there are situations for which this spotlight plays a beneficial and transforming role - witness the 1989 events in Tiananmen Square in Beijing, during which communications instantaneously appeared over the Internet. Short of cutting off world wide communication links, no event will go unreported. Local containment may be an option but even this choice will not go unnoticed. The conclusion is clear: information is almost impossible to control.

The implications for government, the legal system, educational institutions, and others is less clear. But for very practical reasons, any attempts to limit access to information will likely be doomed to failure and may have the side effect of bringing the "offending" institution into disrepute. An open information policy that in general eschews prior restraint and relies on the after the fact impact of the controversial information upon which to take action, may be the preferred policy. It is not without risk and should not be seen as a panacea. Thus, at universities, instead of restricting access to certain newsgroups or searching student files (and rarely those of professors) because of concern with pornographic material, a better approach, as advocated here and elsewhere, is to establish an atmosphere of collegiality and awareness, not through injunction, but through education and a demonstration of the benefits of an open and equitable environment. If unfortunate incidents do occur, and they will, sexual harassment procedures may be employed as well as other appropriate institutional and legal sanctions.

The concluding paragraph to Rosenberg[49] seems an appropriate way to conclude this paper as well:

> "We find ourselves at the beginning of an age of world-wide networks. Up to now, the operating rules have been largely self-imposed and behavior has been self-regulated. However, as financial opportunities are recognized by the major communications companies and information providers, the control of networks, or many of them, will be assumed by these private corporations. They will establish the rules and the costs, as have such companies as Prodigy and CompuServe. Whatever the future holds, it is necessary to defend free speech, open access, and a fair and equitable environment. This article has discussed a variety of issues associated with pornography, censorship, and free speech and a way has been proposed to deal with material that may be sexually offensive, namely sexual harassment procedures coupled with an ongoing educational program. How well this putative solution works remains to be seen but all of us in the network community must demonstrate an active interest in maintaining a real community of trusting and trusted users."

Postscript

> "A group based in Buffalo, N.Y., says it will sell any Canadian 30 pages of banned material from the Karla Homolka trial for $20 (U.S.).
>
> Calling itself the Citizens Coalition for Responsible Government, the group made the offer late last week through an international computer-network bulletin board."[50]
>
> The Homolka - Bernardo Murders; The Government of Ontario in Canada does not want you to read this media release.
>
> The Ontario socialist government of Premier Bob Rae has ordered a court publication ban on the trial proceedings of Karla

49 Rosenberg (1993, p. 322

50 Homolka information for sale. 1994, April 11, *The Globe and Mail* , p. A4.

> Homolka and her husband Paul Bernardo who are accused of the most heinous murders in Canadian history …
>
> It is the government of Ontario's intention to hold Bernardo's trial after this falls [sic] elections and avoid any public electoral responsibility. The Citizens Coalition for Responsible Government accuses the government of Ontario of a cover-up, the details have been attached.[51]

Bibliography

Anon87679. 1994, April 10. The Homolka/Bernardo Murders. As posted anonymously on *alt.censorship*. Message-ID: <135303Z10041994 @anon.penet.fi>.

Blackwell, Tom. 1994, March 24. Defense, prosecution lawyers clash as Teale hearing slated. *The Vancouver Sun* , p. A4.

Calamai, Peter. 1994, Jan. 23. Universities Kowtow to Big Brother. *Ottawa Citizen* , Editorial page. (Also posted on *alt.comp.acad-freedom.talk* , January 26, 1994. Freedom in Ontario. Message-ID: <CK9295. 82J@freenet.carleton.ca>.)

Cosentino, Victor J. 1994, March. Virtual Legality. *Byte* . p. 278.

Dulcey, M. 1994, March 24. Re: WiReD Magazine - Banned in Canada. As posted on *alt.wired*. Message-ID: <mdulcey.764536138@BIX.com>.

Gannon, Dan. 1994, March 10. Locked Out of Usenet Newsgroups! Posted to alt.censorship. Message-ID:<9403102243.A2439wk@banished.com>.

Godwin, Mike. 1994, March/April. The Law of the Net. Sex and the Single Sysadmin: The Risks of Carrying Graphic Sexual Materials. *Internet World.* pp. 56-62.

Gooderham, Mary. 1994, Feb. 5. College Drives Sex Titles off Info Highway. *The Globe and Mail* . p. A1.

Graham, Bill. 1994, February 14. Don't sell academic freedom short. The *Globe and Mail*, p. A19.

Greenberg, Alan. 1994, Jan. 20. Re: Decision made to arbitrarily censor Usenet at McGill. As posted to *alt.censorship*, *alt.comp.acad-freedom.talk* , and *can.general*. Message-ID: <16F44F572S85.ALAN@VM1.McGill.CA>.

Greenhouse, Linda. 1994, March 1. Supreme Court to Consider '77 Child Pornography Law. *The New York Times.* p. A8.

Holderness, Mike C. 1994, Jan. 10. SUMMARY: Harassment on the Net survey. As posted on *comp.org.eff.talk*. Message-ID: <2gscfj$p46@swan. doc.ic.ac.uk>.

Homolka information for sale. 1994, April 11, *The Globe and Mail* , p. A4.

---

51 Anon87679. 1994, April 10. The Homolka/Bernardo Murders. As posted anonymously on *alt.censorship*. Message-ID: <135303Z10041994 @anon.penet.fi>.

Jones, David. 1994a, Jan. 18. U of Toronto (Scarborough) introduces drastic computer policy. As posted on *alt.comp.acad-freedom.talk* . Message-ID: <2hhrs5$3ne@ghost.McRCIM.McGill.EDU>.

__________. 1994b, March 27. There's more! British edition of "Elle" banned in Canada. As posted on *alt.censorship*. Message-ID: <2n5go1$3nk @ghost.McRCIM.McGILL.EDU>.

Jones, Douglas W. 1994, April 7. Re: 'Serdar Argic': Racist remarks? Defamation? Supply info ... As posted on *alt.comp.acad-freedom.talk* . Message-ID: <2o145r$br8@nexus.uiowa.edu>.

Kadie, Carl M. 1992a, June 5. Last year U. Waterloo restored as a.s.b. Posted on *alt.sex*. Message-ID: <1992Jun5.020530.12305@eff.org>.

________. 1992b, Oct. 20. Ontario does/doesn't ban material at universities. As posted on *alt.comp.acad-freedom.talk* , *soc.culture.canada* , and other newsgroups. Message-ID: <1992Oct20.181236.15507@eff.org>.

________ .1994a, Feb. 3. Obscenity - Waterloo focused on medium rather than message. As posted to *alt.comp.acad-freedom.talk* . Message-ID: <2irpui$aga@eff.org>.

________. 1994b, Feb. 8. Guelph is scanning all incoming mail for Possible Ban Breaks. Posted to *alt.comp.acad-freedom.talk*. Message-ID: <CKwtwA.9BE@cs,uiuc.edu>.

________. 1994c, March 27. Applying library principles to computers. As posted to a number of newsgroups including *alt.comp.acad-freedom.talk* and *alt.censorship* . Message-ID: <2n4n15$d0@eff.org>.

________. 1994d, Feb. 12. McGill U. treating computer media differently than paper media. Posted to *alt.comp.acad-freedom.talk* . Message-ID: <2jj9rbjsfeff.org>.

________. 1994e, April 6. Re: What to do about this guy. As posted to *alt.comp.acad-freedom.talk*.. Message-ID: <Cnv360.3wF@cs.uiuc. edu>.

Krause, Vincent Allen. 1994, April 6. Nigger Jokes. As crossposted from *alt. activism* to *alt.censorship.* Message-ID: <2nt77d$pf2@lastactionhero. rs.itd.umich.edu>.

May, Timothy C. 1994, March 31. This newsgroup is illegal! As posted on *comp.org.eff.talk.* Message-ID: <tcmayCnJx0A.58A@netcom.com>.

No Contest Plea in Computer Bulletin Board Molestation. 1994, April 6. As posted on *clari.tw.computers*. Message-ID: <VdeatherageU4A6505 pp@clarinet.com>.

'Obscene' Newsgroups Dropped. 1994, Feb. 19. *University of Waterloo Gazette* . p. 1.

Platiel, Rudy. 1993, Dec. 2. Lawyers argue over Homolka ban. *The Globe and Mail* . p. A2.

Rosenberg, Richard S. 1993, Oct.-Dec. Free Speech, Pornography, Sexual Harassment, and Electronic Networks. *The Information Society* 9(4):285-331.

Shallit, Jeffrey. 1994a, Feb. 6. Electronic Frontier of Canada press release. As posted to *alt.comp.acad-freedom.talk.* Message-ID: <CKtrwB.MKL @watserv1.uwaterloo.ca>.

___________, 1994b, April 4. Text of a letter on the library and Canadian publication bans. Posted on the ALAOIF List server (American Library Association Office for Intellectual Freedom).

Somar, Annetta. 1994, March 31. Profs slam McGill search policy. *The University of Toronto Varsity.* (Also posted by David Jones to *alt.comp.acad-freedom.talk* on April 3, 1994. Message-ID: <2nnb9p$ 2cr@ghost.McRCIM.McGill.EDU>.

Syed, Chris. 1994, March 31. Re: Microfilm censored at McMaster University Library. As posted to *alt.comp.acad-freedom.talk* . Message-ID: <CnJJ82.B8H@gpu.utcc.utoronto.ca>.

Tierney, John. 1994, Jan. 9. Porn, the Low-Slung Engine of Progress. *The New York Times*. Section 2, p. 1.

UBC Report, 1992, Dec. *Report of the Task Force on the Appropriate Use of Information Technology*, The University of British Columbia, Vancouver, B.C., Canada. (Copies of the report and appendices may be obtained by contacting Shirley Marcus: phone: (604) 822-6122; e-mail: marcus@unixg.ubc.ca).

Wright, Lane. 1994, March 21. Who Controls "60 Minutes"? As posted to *alt.censorship* . Message-ID: <9403212018.A6252wk@banished.com>.

Yerxa, Shawn W. 1994, Jan. 30. Canadian University Deleting files. Posted on *alt.censorship*. Message-ID: <CKGJtH.Azp@freenet.carleton.ca>.

The Protection of Rights and Values in Open-Network Management

Pierre Trudel
in collaboration with Robert Gérin-Lajoie

Like any evocation, the idea of an electronic highway has great metaphorical power. Thousands of units of information rushing down high-capacity routes! The metaphor's mobilizing effect is undoubtedly largely responsible for its success. What could be a better source of enthusiasm, in this time of economic stagnation, than this project symbolizing a new industrial wave with the flood of hopes and promises it carries! Yet this is the time to systematically identify the nature of the challenge, in Canada, of ensuring respect for human rights and the fundamental values affected by the circulation of information in open networks.

The fact that cyberspace transcends national boundaries and permits the existence of planet-wide virtual spaces[1] does not imply the disappearance of concerns about the circulation of pornographic material, hate propaganda, pirating of protected works or the dissemination of private information. In one way or another, we must identify the means of resolving contradictions which breathe life into conflicts about behaviour and information circulation in open networks.

When supervising new phenomena, the law starts with the ways in which they are analogous to known situations. The law already contains a set of principles meant to regulate information distribution and exchange. The goal of legal research is precisely to identify how these principles apply to new situations.

Yet traditional techniques and approaches for regulating information circulation in public spaces must be re-examined to determine the degree to which they are capable of producing the necessary balances between the need to circulate information, the protection of human rights and the preservation of fundamental values of democratic societies. The goal of this paper is to describe how open electronic communications networks affect the protection of human rights and values dear to our pluralist, democratic societies.

---

1 Di Lello explains that: “"virtual" is a term of art in computer technology, signifying the phenomenon of something purely electronic substituting for a physical object or event”. See: Edward V. DI LELLO, “Functional Equivalency and its Application to Freedom of Speech on Computer Bulletin Boards”, (1993) 26 *Columbia Journal of Law and Social Problems* 199 at 216.

E. Mackaay et al. (eds.), The Electronic Superhighway, 159–193.

Information circulation creates interactions between agents. Thus it can create conflicts. Most often, norms aim to solve those conflicts likely to come up. The networks are at once places of transmission, communication and transaction. They suppose the establishment, through authority or spontaneity, of propriety, of norms and of mutually accepted rules. It follows that the issue is not so much whether there will be norms to supervise the operation of electronic highways, but rather what sort of norms are likely to develop to ensure a balance between the various conflicting rights and values.

Perritt identifies three zones of conflict which almost always come up at some point in the environments of open networks. He writes that:

> "As networks grow, the following kinds of disputes are almost certain to arise: (1) someone not yet on the network wants to get on and on more of the people already on the network want to keep him out; (2) someone wants to stop certain kinds of traffic moving on network (or to recover damages because the traffic in moving) and the person moving the traffic wants to continue moving it; (3) someone on the network believes that someone else on the network has not lived up to his or her commitments."[2]

In order to situate the norms with diverse origins which could play a role in the prevention and resolution of such conflicts, the rules concerning access to the networks and the conditions of such access must be examined. The rules governing the content carried and those covering transactions between users must also be studied. In the present paper, we will be concerned mainly with rules dealing with information transmitted or circulating in the networks.

The new cybernetic space, "cyberspace",[3] calls for a revision of the way we view legal supervision of information production, transmission and

---

2 Henry H. Perritt Jr., "Dispute Resolution in Electronic Networks Communities" (1993) 38 *Villanova L.R.* 349-401 at 353.

3 This expression is often used in American writings on the subject. Our usage follows that of Laurence Tribe in "The Constitution in Cyberspace: Law and Liberty Beyond the Electronic Frontier", where he writes that "I am using the term "cyberspace" much more broadly, as many have lately. I'm using it to encompass the full array of computer-mediated audio and/or video interactions that are already widely dispersed in modern societies - from things as ubiquitous as the ordinary telephone, to things that are still coming on-line like computer bulletin boards and networks like Prodigy, or like the WELL (Whole Earth 'Lectronic Link")..." See: Laurence Tribe, "The Constitution in Cyberspace: Law and Liberty Beyond the Electronic Frontier", Keynote Address at the *First Conference on Computers, Freedom & Privacy*, March 26, 1991, Jim Warren & Computer Professionals for Social Responsibility, posted on the Gopher Cyberspace; see also, Edward J. Naughton, "Is Cyberspace A Public Forum? Computer Bulletin Boards, Free Speech and State Action" (1992) 81

circulation. Such a redefinition would not necessarily break with all traditional ways of viewing norms of conduct: it could find its roots largely in the norms emerging and observed in the present environments of electronic communication. This approach allows flexible supervision compatible with the conditions of pluralist societies to be fostered.

The integration of computer components in traditional media has favoured the establishment of new possibilities and new services such as direct access to data bases and electronic commercial transactions. These electronic information services bring together media, technologies and contents, the effect of which is the generation of a multitude of new virtual environments, services and applications. Various technological advances have allowed people to interact more rapidly and more frequently. Synergy can be created between the media possibilities which were independent of each other until now: video documents can be integrated in data banks, texts can be exchanged through electronic mail, they can be modified, written collectively. Sounds and pictures can be added, as can videos taken from servers situated on the other side of the earth.

In terms of its normative framework, the novelty of electronic communication lies in the fact that it tends to federate the various known contexts of information transmission and exchange. There is no longer a conversation or a mass transmission: there can be both at once. They can mix together to modify the nature of both, and the way in which the issue of their legal supervision must be approached.

The types of communication which permit the emergence of open networks are not really new in themselves. Their novelty lies in their power to transform existing services or create different possibilities. Formerly captive spectator-listeners become increasingly active: they can access a wealth of written and audio-visual information, somewhat as if they were in a library.[4]

Georgetown L. J. 409; Dan L. Burk, "Patents in Cyberspace: Territoriality and Infringement on Global Computer Networks", (1993) 68 *Tulane L.R.* 1.

4 Department of Communications, *New Mediums...New Choices*, Department of Supply and Services Canada 1992, 47 p.; Organizaton for Economic Cooperation and Development, *Convergence entre technologies de communications: Études de cas de l'Amérique du Nord et de l'Europe de l'Ouest*, Paris, *Politiques d'information, d'informatique et des communications*, No. 28, 1992, 149 p.; NEUSTADT, Richard M., Skall, Gregg P. and Hammer Michael, "The Regulation of Electronic Publishing" (1981) 33 *Federal Communications Law Journal* 331; Salgrado, "Regulating a Video Revolution" (1989) 7 Yale L. & Pol'y Rev. 516; Scott, Michael D. and Talbott, James N., "Interactive Media: What is it, Why is it Important and What do I Need to Know About it?", (1992) 11 *Computer/Law Journal* 585; Stern, Jill Abeshouse, Krasnow, Erwin G. and Senkowski, R. Michael, "The New Video Marketplace and the Search for a Coherent Philosophy" (1983) 32 *Catholic University Law Review* 529; Wachtel, Mindy Elisa, "Videotex: A Welcome New Technology or an Orwellian Threat to Privacy?" (1983) 2 *Cardozo Arts and Entertainment L.R.* 287.

of these environments operate simultaneously as modes of transmission, distribution and exchange. Thus they can offer the of communicating with one or more correspondents, the chance to make information available to many users. These possibilities are so powerful that the relation between the user and the information available resembles both an electronic library and a transmission network programmed by the transmitter. To this is added the possibility to combine, relate, reorganize and copy many types of information. Furthermore, the networks themselves are interconnected, which provides all users with a very wide reach. Finally, it is possible to communicate with people without requiring them to be at a set place at a set time.

Control of the legal aspects of a phenomenon like open-computer-network communication does not follow from passing a plethora of laws and regulations, or from instituting an organization with a vocation of legal evangelicalism! Such control comes through establishing the ability to adapt, as rapidly as possible, the whole legal system in order to contribute to the development of legal knowledge in the domain of computer-network communication. The chance the development of these new tools will be oriented towards respect for the rights and interests of the greatest number is thus increased. This is a completely separate component of the true development of information technologies. Just as research and development are the cornerstones of innovation and efficiency in terms of technology and content, research on legal supervision techniques is paramount to ensuring the emergence of an appropriate, realistic and effective framework for this global communications environment.

1. Reasons for rules of conduct

Rules of conduct limiting access to networks or controlling the circulation of messages affect freedom of expression. They must thus be sufficiently justified. Most often, decisions to limit freedom of expression are made because of requirements implied by respect for other rights and values. To invoke such reasons to justify its limiting freedom of expression is to argue in support of rules imposing controls or sanctions following the transmission of information.

The legal framework has its source in those, often contradictory, values it attempts to reflect. It cannot thus be analyzed if these values are disregarded. These values are captured by the law, which sometimes turns them into notions charged with legal meaning and consequences. These values assign rights and obligations to those considered responsible for information put into circulation.

Understanding the rules supervising a phenomenon like open-network communication supposes knowledge of the underlying reasons for the envisaged or foreseeable rules. In a way this is knowledge of the reasons leading to the adoption of the rules, the reasons which make them "rational".

The representations of reality held by agents and decision-makers, the imperatives dictated by the concerns "public opinion" expresses at various times, certainly play a major role in the emergence and crystallisation of arguments perceived as legitimate reasons for intervening in an issue. For example, our contemporary societies place a great deal of importance on protection of human dignity, equality, proper operation of the judicial system, protection of privacy.

Reasons may be based on the missions assigned to a network, for example, a computer network devoted primarily to teaching and research will be regulated so as to favour such use. The values perceived to require protection can be reflected in these reasons. Thus these reasons are not identical in the various sites existing on the planet: there are differences in values, sensitivity and culture.

Now we must ask about the legitimacy of intervention at the level of local networks. Should this legitimacy be based on arguments for restricting expression traditionally accepted as reasonable, or should it find support in a new set of arguments special to the borderless, planet-wide environment of open networks.

2. Regulatory techniques

We call "regulatory techniques" the various means used by those who wish to impose behaviour norms on those taking part in an activity. By adopting one or a combination of regulatory techniques, the authorities charged with perfecting policies manage to define and predict the relationships between the rights, obligations and interests of the various parties implicated in information circulation.

In general, there is no single approach to stating the rights and obligations of individuals or to stating the precepts which will guide the behaviour of participants in an activity. The analysis of regulatory techniques aims to identify the various possibilities for policy establishment rather than to fall back on the reflexes of habit and resort to regulations or other familiar tools where they are inappropriate.

Knowledge of regulatory, para-regulatory and professional practices is necessary to understand the law and the operation of an environment like that of electronic highways. The norms under examination here concern activities taking place in a situation which dictates certain rules of play. Regulation and especially self-regulation are thus striking aspects of a legal framework which is rarely outlined in legal texts. Most often, inferences must be made from the general principles of common law.

Thus, in order to study the possible regulatory techniques applicable to a phenomenon, one must possess sufficient information on the fundamental aspects and operation of available regulatory techniques. This information is required to attempt to make behaviour conform to the goals of the reasons underlying the legal rules. Two main lines mark the norms supervising information exchanges and the various activities occurring on open networks. The first is that they are stated through general principles and vague notions. The second has to do with where these norms are stated: they are very often found in the policies of network managers.

2.1 Recourse to General Principles and Standards

Stating the rights and obligations of agents with respect to immaterial realities remains a challenge for the law. It is ill at ease prescribing norms from models developed to deal with material phenomena. Furthermore, the reason for regulating the universe of open information networks is much more a global result than a mechanical application of legal rules. The regulation and supervision mechanisms must thus target obtaining the adjustments and conformity required by respect for essential values.[5]

This undoubtedly explains, in part, the recourse to broad formulations, to general precepts and to after-the-fact judgments which seem to constitute the preferred regulatory technique in these cybernetic universes. When there are laws which apply to such environments, they are generally stated in broad terms and reserve a great deal of space for the concrete evaluations of agents in the field.[6]

In an open environment where national frontiers are transcended and the notions of time and place are redefined, it is difficult to determine *a priori* how the various principles, values and goals stated in general policies or laws could be attained concretely. Regarding this, Daniel Gifford writes "These value-referents reflect (...) the inability of the legislature to speak more precisely."[7] It is as if the realities the law intends to confront were so numerous, complex and volatile that it is impossible to supervise them more precisely. The kind of formulation which employs vague notions responds to a need for adaptability: one of the most difficult for law to fill.

No guarantee of a balance between the contradictory requirements existing in open-network environments can be founded on approaches based

---

5 Bernard Guillou and Jean-Gustav Padioleau, *La régulation de la télévision* (Paris, CNCL, *La documentation Française*, 1988) at 44.

6 Regarding laws relative to the protection of privacy, see: Karim Benyekhlef, *La protection de la vie privée dans les échanges internationaux d'information* (Montréal, Éditions Thémis) at 65 and ss; Ruel Torres Hernandez, "ECPA and Online Computer Privacy" 41 Federal Communications Law Journal 17.

7 Daniel J. Gifford, "Communication of Legal Standards, Policy Development, and Effective Conduct Regulation" (1971) 56 *Cornell L.R.* 409 at 419.

on the quest for precise "rules" of law. This kind of approach is moreover difficult because we are dealing with a universe undergoing constant change. Thus how could one state clearly, precisely and definitively, what is permitted and what is forbidden when the environment of the networks is undergoing continual transformation.

Often what is required is an approach which is less reassuring, more complex, but infinitely more likely to truly attain this balance between the contradictory values which must be reconciled. Vague notions, and ideas with variable contents are essential to allow the law to remain in contact with practices and changes. Since rights and freedoms cannot be defined in a vacuum, it is essential to write the rules related to fundamental rights while remaining open to all circles which reflect on and engage in activities concerning these rights.

This is why norms are often stated using vague notions, standards. What is meant by "standard" is a flexible norm founded on an intentionally undetermined criterion. This technique is appropriate for situations in which it is difficult to formulate *a priori* rules on the behaviour which subjects of law should have.[8] The transmission of information, characterized by its rapid evolution and the importance it gives to creative activity, adapts poorly to detailed rules. In Rials's terms, standards are presented as "*des instruments de mesure en termes de normalité.*"[9] This is what makes them special; it is also what makes them ambiguous. Normality, in pluralist societies, is ambiguous.[10]

In sum, in volatile environments like cybernetic spaces, it is not very realistic to expect that the wording of laws or regulations can define once and for all what one may and may not do. Rather, regulation states broad principles and leaves their concretization to a continuous process of dialogue, discovery and experimentation. Such a regulatory process is moreover typical of open networks. Dialogue and controversy contribute to

---

8 Al Sanhoury writes that "*A la fixité et la rigidité de la règle, s'oppose avantageusement la souplesse et l'adaptabilité du standard.*" ["To the fixity and rigidity of the rule, the flexibility and adaptability of the standard can be opposed advantageously."] A.-A. Al-Sanhoury, "Le standard juridique" in *Recueil d'études sur les sources du droit en l'honneur de François Gény*, Volume II (Paris, Librairie du Recueil Sirey, 1935) at 144; Pierre Trudel, "Le standard de programmation de haute qualité dans la législation sur la radio et la télévision" (1989) 34 *R.D. McGill* 203-233.

9 Rials, Stéphane, "Les standards, notions critiques du droit" in Chaim Perelman and Raymond Vander Elst (Dir.), *Les notions à contenus variables en droit* (Brussels, Travaux du Centre national de recherches en logique, 1984) at 43. Translator's note: "instruments of measure in terms of normality".

10 Pierre Trudel, "Le rôle de la loi, de la déontologie, et des décisions judiciaires dans l'articulation du droit à la vie privée et de la liberté de presse" in Pierre Trudel and France Abran (eds.), *Droit du public à l'information et vie privée: deux droits irréconciliables?* (Montréal, Éditions Thémis) 181-202 at 195.

the regulation of the discourse which flows in a continuous, multidirectional stream.

The meaning of fundamental rights and other notions used to decide the rights and obligations of the participants in an environment as volatile as that of open networks is defined in diffuse systems[11] such as morals, ideologies, common beliefs, or generally accepted beliefs. No source of law, and this includes legislation, could act in a definitive way on the emergence of the conceptions and ways of seeing which combine and recombine spontaneously. This is why arguments and concepts are refined through the maintenance of a lively environment in which the various conceptions and value systems can confront each other.

Conflicts and distinctions between fundamental rights occur in diffuse systems just as they do in dense systems such as the political system, clearly legal institutions and, above all, the practices which develop in the environments made up of these networks. They reveal themselves in deontology and sometimes crystallize in government legislation through the intervention of judicial decisions or other authorities called upon to resolve conflicts. All these systems contribute, in their own way, to determining the meaning of the rights and freedoms in a given context and to refining the rules which are followed there.

Open networks bring a large number of users together. These users are grouped into different communities. It is at the level of these communities that regulation is experimented with, stated, applied and discussed. Given this situation, we can hardly expect that regulation be expressed through government legislation. Rather, the legal systems of the various states will limit themselves to stating fundamental values and should take into account that these values will be defended and promoted in user communities which are virtual.

In open networks, there is no obligatory link between national laws and users. In effect, it is impossible to say that each user is under the jurisdiction of the provisions of the legislation of the country in which he or she is located. The user might in fact be in Quebec and take part in a discussion group which is directed from Amsterdam.

In contrast, a community of users can *de facto* or by choice find itself under the jurisdiction of foreign legislation. The laws which appear most appropriate to communities of users will be those they choose and follow

---

11 See Philippe Jestaz, *Le droit*, 2nd ed. (Paris, Dalloz, 1992) at 26 and ss.: "*Le droit, avec son réseau serré de règles et d'institutions, est un système compact, de surcoît imbriqué avec d'autres systèmes sociaux. Certains sont aussi denses que lui (...) le système politique et les moeurs, (...) d'autres paraissent plus diffus (...) la morale et l'idéologie (...)*" ["The law, with its tight network of rules and institutions, is a compact system, interwoven moreover with other social systems. Some are just as dense as it (...) the political system and customs, (...) others appear more diffuse. (...) morals and ideology (...)"]

more spontaneously. This accounts for the more or less marked tendency towards standardization the law.

Faced with the challenges resulting from the need to protect human and fundamental rights in network environments, it is possible to envision two main legal approaches. The first approach is the perfecting of specific regulations determining the obligations of network users, especially respecting personal data.

At the macro-judicial level, this means examining the state intervention strategies for taking action on a given set of reasons. In the first place, the growing importance of national and international standardization organizations cannot be overlooked. These organizations, sometimes basing their views on technical norms, state sets of precepts which end up being imposed in spite of their constraining character. This process of "over-normalization" plays a major role in the emergence of norms in technical environments.

When defining a national policy on a given phenomenon for which one has taken care to identify the underlying reasons for state intervention, it must be decided whether it is appropriate to:

- hold to the principles of common law;
- intervene by means of criminal law;
- create a regulatory and supervisory organization;
- state broad principles while leaving authorities to apply them, or make precise statements regarding the rights and obligations of agents;
- resort to self-regulation;
- set up "awareness" campaigns.

Taxation and financial mechanisms are another way to apply public policies. In this sense, they are unhesitatingly considered a regulatory technique.

In sum, the macro-judicial analysis of regulatory techniques must weigh strategies of norm statement and evaluate approaches to ensure the decoding and application of such statements.

At the micro-judicial level, in other words at the level of the application by each actor with a certain decision-making power, analysis of regulatory techniques is also necessary. Such actors must identify the means compatible with the context, susceptible to contribute to applying the reasons. They must also identify the micro-reasons which come up at the level of the application of the broad policies which can be outlined in general writings.

Here again it is undoubtedly appropriate to take the time to state the principles which must be followed by those participating in network activities. Furthermore, recourse can be taken to preventive techniques, educational programs, statements of principle, and ethical norms.

Supervision is another means by which respect for norms can be ensured. Supervision can be continual or by "spot-check", it can be done following explicitly identified complaints, following a report during routine procedures or according to a sophisticated general or targeted monitoring program. Supervision poses major problems concerning balancing values linked to protecting confidentiality and other values which can be affected by certain activities of agents in a network. For this reason, it is often necessary to frame it in a process offering guarantees against arbitrariness.

Warnings given to those who do not respect the norms are no doubt, in themselves, part of the regulatory activity. Of course, actual sanctions, such as account closures, etc., are the ultimate disciplinary measures.

By adopting a policy encouraging dynamic deontological reflection in communications circles in open networks, one increases the chances of fostering the development, within the user community, of critical behaviour, or even reflexes, and of consideration of the values and interests present. Such an approach presupposes increasing the training of all those who make decisions relating to information transmission and regulation in these environments.

2.2 POLICIES OF NETWORK MANAGERS ("*SITE POLICIES*")

Those who control a site in the network can adopt policies on access to the site, acceptable behaviour and prohibited acts. Most university institutions have policies or regulations defining the rights and prerogatives of those who use their computer facilities. These policies are based on reasons often following from a desire to promote rational use of institution resources, respect for fundamental rights and human dignity. For example, McGill University has adopted a regulation concerning the users of its computer services. This text sets out that:

> "McGill Computing Facilities (MCF) are defined as any computer, computer-based network, computer peripheral, operating system, software or any combination thereof, owned by McGill of under the custody or control of McGill University. Equipment and Software purchased from research funds administered by McGill are owned by McGill University unless otherwise specified in the research grant or contract.
>
> All McGill staff, students and other users of the MCF shall:
>
> 1- Recognize that MCF are strictly intended to support the academic mission and the administrative functions of the University and assume full responsibility for using these facilities in an effective, efficient, ethical, lawful and polite manner.

2- Use only those facilities which are in the public domain or for which they have obtained explicit authorization, at McGill or at any other location accessible through a network.

3- Take all necessary steps to protect the integrity of MCF. In particular, the users shall not share with others the access codes, account numbers, passwords or other authorizations which have been assigned them.

4- Respect the copyrights of owners of all software and data they use.

5- Respect the policies established by the administrators of external networks such as RISQ, CA*net, NSFNET when using such networks. They shall also respect the policies established by the administrators of local computing facilities at McGill.

6- Respect the privacy of E-mail and other user files carried and stored in MCF or at any other location accessible through a network.

7- Not use the MCF for conducting private business or for personal financial gain, unless specifically authorized.

8- Not use the MCF for any unauthorized or illegal purpose, such as destruction or alteration of data owned by others, interference with legitimate access to computing facilities or harassment of users of such facilities at McGill or elsewhere, unauthorized disruption of MCF, attempts to discover or alter passwords or to subvert security systems in MCF or in any other computing facility.

9- Properly sign or make traceable any remote access to MCF, any E-mail, message or file transfer initiated on MCF.

10- Take all reasonable steps to protect the integrity and privacy of the software and data made available to them.

Users should recognize that authorized McGill personnel may have access to data and software stored in MCF while performing routine operations or pursuing systems problems. Users should further recognize that, as specified in the relevant administrative policies at McGill, authorized personnel have the obligation to take appropriate steps to ensure the integrity of MCF and to ensure that the present regulations are observed.

Any violation of these regulations will be prosecuted in conformity with the relevant University policy (Code of Student

Conduct, Personnel policies, etc.) and the principle of due process."[12]

The policies of certain institutions provide for the special case of harassment resulting from use of computer networks. Recently, the Government of Ontario issued a directive concerning universities. In it we find:

> "In developing their local policy and procedures, institutions are encouraged to review best practices already present in the post secondary system and material in the Council of Regents Harassment Task Force Report. This information will be provided to any interested stake holder group by the Ministry. In writing their policies and procedures, institutions will have to balance legal soundness and accessibility for users. The product should be easy to read, easy to understand, and easy to use. Those developing policies and procedures should write simply, clearly, and use plain language.
>
> The government will provide $1.5M to the post secondary sector to support the development and production of training packages, data collection models, ongoing evaluation models, an external audit model and process, the development and production of educational materials for all constituent groups and regional training and information sharing workshops."[13]

Rosenberg advocates flexible policies. He bases his view on the need to preserve free expression and to attempt to educate people rather than repress them. He recommends six principles for network managers:

"A. Administrative principles

1. Do not treat electronic media differently than print media, or traditional bulletin board, merely because they can be more easily controlled.
2. Do not censor potentially offensive material on networks: Encourage the use of sexual harassment procedures, if appropriate.
3. Be aware of your responsibility with respect to the uses and misuses of your facilities. However, do not use cost of services as an excuse to censor and limit access.
4. Trust and educate people to be responsible.

B. Social principles

---

12 "Regulations for Users of McGill Computing Facilities", taken from *Computer and Academic Freedom*, gopher EFF.

13 Ontario, Framework Regarding Prevention of Harassment and Discrimination in Ontario Universities, in Gopher, Computer and Academic Freedom Archives and Info.

1. Issues will proliferate beyond the ability of organizations to control them by rigid policies.
2. Occasional offensive postings do not detract from the benefit of electronic networks."[14]

He adds that the censorship reflex may be the first to appear. In effect, it is often easier to resort to authoritarian solutions when responding to complaints of those who feel offended by certain behaviour or transmissions. He explains that:

> "Experience indicates that under pressure, administrators at public institutions may be willing to sacrifice free speech over networks to appease loudly expressed concerns about pornography corrupting the morals of otherwise innocent students. On the opposite side it might be argued, unsuccessfully I would maintain, that networks are a special case with respect to free speech because they are so pervasive and so difficult to monitor for material that might be ruled illegal because of a violation of community standards."[15]

The magnitude of the work necessary to ensure supervision by site managers can prove considerable. As Rosenberg explains:

> "Posting to given newsgroups can be cross-posted to other, less threatening, ones. So for example an item in alt.sex might also appear in alt.censorship. The job of making sure that no offensive postings appear anywhere on the network would be formidable, far beyond the capability of any site. But suppose that the number of these cross-postings is limited and not a real concern. Is everything safe for the university and its students and staff? Probably not. The more enterprising people will do a remote login (i.e. connect from the home site to another site), even in a different country, that carries the desired newsgroup, having first acquired a computer ID (identification codeword) and password at that site. Once downloaded, postings from this newsgroup are then available for distribution at the home site."[16]

A site can decide to eliminate access to a group or list etc., but this access can be obtained through another available site, which offers links to the forbidden site. In sum, there are considerable practical limits on the ability to suppress messages in an environment of open, interconnected networks. A

---

14 Richard S. Rosenberg, "Free Speech, Pornography, Sexual Harassment, and Electronic Networks", *The Information Society* Oct.-Dec., 1993 9(4) 285-331.

15 *Ibid.*

16 *Ibid.*

report by the University of Western Ontario brings out the extent of the problems faced when one hopes to limit access to information available in certain Internet bulletin boards:

> "A partial filtering of postings to the system based on presumed content (eg. based on the title of the newsgroup to which a posting is made) would not significantly impair access, and might generate additional network traffic. Moreover, there is the matter of the legitimacy of censorship (however ineffective) based on presumed or possible content rather than actual content. The CUC judges that, in general, the campus community would be against such arbitrary censorship. This course of action is, therefore, not acceptable either.
>
> [...]
>
> Given the volume of daily postings to the entire News system, it is not feasible for anyone to read all postings before they are placed on the system. However, should a specific posting be received by a user of the system and its content judged to be possibly illegal, the CUC agrees that it is reasonable to expect that there be a procedure for that individual to follow that could lead to the posting in question being removed from the University's local feed (even though that would not prevent users from gaining access through remote feeds). Even if this is granted, however, questions remain, including: How do we determine whether a posting is or might be judged to be illegal? and How can timely decisions regarding this matter be made, given that all postings are automatically removed from the local feed after a few days in any event?"[17]

Given the mammoth resources which would be necessary to suppress information in this context, very serious reasons would have to support the rules to be applied in this way. However, it must be noted that Canada has a tradition of frequent recourse to censorship as a reflex to resolve these difficulties. The environments of open networks suppose the development of less rudimentary methods to confront conflicts resulting from the circulation of information.

A number of conflicts are preventable by stating the policies followed by site managers in case of conflict. While there has not yet appeared a review of the tenor of these policies, that of the University of Western Ontario provides for the following:

---

17 University of Western Ontario, Department of Computing and Communications Services, Computer Users' Committee, *Report on Usenet Policy*, May 12, 1993, alt.comp.acadfreedom.talk, message-ID: <2drlpc$qk0@eff.org> also posted on Gopher EFF.

1. The Computer Users' Committee (CUC) is responsible for reviewing and approving all Usenet-related policy proposals from Computing and Communications Services (CCS), including those relating to the newsgroups to be carried in the University's local feed.
2. In its publications regarding Usenet, CCS should make it clear that the individual user bears the primary responsibility for the material that he or she chooses to send or display on the network or on the University's computer systems.
3. Anyone who wishes to lodge a complaint regarding the content of a particular newsgroup posting should file a complaint with CUC in accord with the following procedure:

   (i) A complainant should register his or her complaint with the News Manager in CCS. The complaint should be in writing, preferably via e-mail, and should define the newsgroup and the posting of concern and specify how the material was obtained by the complainant.

   (ii) The News Manager will immediately forward this material to the CUC, through the Director of CCS, and the Chair of the CUC will call a meeting within two days of its receipt. The CUC will solicit a legal opinion if necessary. The Committee might take the following actions: reducing the time that the posting of concern remains on the local feed; reducing the time that the newsgroup in question remains on the local feed; asking CCS to assist the complainant to contact the individual who posted the material in order to register a complaint. Copies of the decision, including reasons, will be sent to the Director of CCS and to the complainant, and relevant action will be taken by CCS through the Director.

   (iii) Appeals of CUC decisions may be made to the Director of CCS in writing, who will forward it to the University Computer Council (UCC), along with copies of the original complaint, as well as the CUC decision. UCC will review this material and make its decision on the appeal through a simple majority vote. This decision will be forwarded to the Director of CCS and the appellant, and the original complainant if this is not the same individual.
4. All administrators of CCS and other campus computing systems should continue to be responsible for following up on reported abuses of the information technology resources under their control by the faculty, staff and students of the University who are users of their system(s), including abuses

of the Usenet system such as the posting of possibly offensive or illegal material.

5. Anyone wishing to lodge a complaint regarding suspected abuse of the information technology resources of the University by a member of the University community, should contact the administrator responsible for the system on which the abuse took place or, if it is unclear or unknown who that person is, or if the abuse is of a more general nature, the Director of CCS.[18]

There is not yet any systematic typology of the policies followed in the various circles providing access to open networks, though it is possible to see certain tendencies. In order to prepare the establishment of such a typology and appreciate the real extent of such policies, it is imperative to identify how the issue of defending rights and values in open networks presents itself. For this, the variety of contexts and the diversity of the roles played by the various agents in such a universe must be considered.

3. Contexts

Electronic communication takes place in different contexts. Some of these contexts make obvious the roles and responsibilities of network suppliers and communications carriers, while others place more direct emphasis on the relations created between participants in this virtual space.

In order to better understand the emergent norms in these virtual electronic environments, the principal types of contexts they present today and the possibilities they promise must be identified. Four main types can be identified from the situations often evoked as foreshadowing communication by electronic highways.

Four contexts seem to cover the range of situations in which the rights of individuals are brought into question and for which there is felt to be a need to resort to norms to prevent or control conflicts. First, there are centrally-controlled networks destined for the public such as cable networks and the various improvements likely to make them interactive. Second, there are completely open networks like the Internet. Third, there are the relations between network managers and, fourth, the relations between users creating contexts and situations in which the intervention of rules of conduct is necessary.

[18] *Ibid.*

3.1 CENTRALLY-CONTROLLED NETWORKS

The first context is that of networks with relatively identifiable control, such as cable networks or telematic services offered to the public or to groups of professionals. These networks are controlled by a single, well-identified body.[19] The places of transmission and those of reception are fairly clear and the division of roles is quite well defined. Transmission is completely controlled by the enterprise offering the content. This content is delivered to subscribers following choices made by them from those offered automatically. For example, in the UBI project or its present forerunner, Vidéoway, the focal point, by which communications pass is the server at the head of line of the cable network.[20] This is a centralized system: subscribers gain access to the network through cable television companies, which provide the network and give access to various contents and services.

These environments permit access to information, communications, transaction, pay, control and supervision services. Included in information services are publicly available services such as information and video servers: such services are very similar to familiar information transmission services. For example, radio and television are presently considered entities transmitting information to the public, and legislation concerning them reflects this role.[21]

Communications services include message services, mail, and electronic mail boxes. In transaction services, one finds T.V. shopping and electronic funds transfers. Pay services include games and so-called "intelligent" transaction-type services such as T.V. medicine and T.V. education services.

---

19 Pierre Trudel and France Abran, *Droit de la radio et de la télévision* (Montréal, Éditions Thémis, 1991) 1180 p. at 325 and 764-771.

20 It is, given the present state of Canadian law, difficult to imagine that the services offered through cable companies completely escape control by these firms. Cable distribution must, unless the CRTC rules otherwise, be done in an effective way by the license-holder or, in fact, by its employees. Furthermore, it itself must own and operate its equipment and facilities. Section 4 of the *1986 Regulation on Television Broadcasting* requires that the license-holder possess and operate its local head of line, its amplifiers and its subscriber outlets. When the company is authorized to offer specialized or pay-television services, it must also own the decoders or other coding equipment and, in the case of an addressable security system, the computer controlling this system. These obligations, targeting the actual operation of the enterprise and the possession of a minimum of certain facilities, reflect the Council's attitude regarding the need for license-holders to exercise determining control over their firms in order to fulfil their official obligations. The Council wants to ensure that license-holders are accountable, to the public and the Council, for providing the services and the fees imposed. See: Pierre Trudel and France Abran, in *Droit de la radio et de la télévision* (Montréal, Éditions Thémis, 1991) at 713; CRTC, Public notice 1983-82, April 22, 1983, *Proprété du matériel de prestation de services de télévision payante par les entreprises autorisées de télévision par câble*.

21 Trudel and Abran, *op. cit.* at 292 and ss.

Finally, there are the so-called control and monitoring services such as remote reading of electricity consumption and remote home monitoring.[22]

The electronic highway model presently proposed by cable television companies has relatively well-defined transmission and reception functions. However, many factors contribute to pushing this model towards greater openness as interconnection possibilities multiply. This makes transmission and reception functions more difficult to define. In effect, it is less and less possible to identify the place and the typical features of transmission and reception functions. As this tendency becomes more accentuated, we move closer to the context of completely open networks, of which the Internet seems, for now, to be the most complete prototype.

3.2 DECENTRALIZED OPEN NETWORKS

The completely open network model is the second case under consideration. Such a model is marked by the absence of a centralized area able to control the content carried on the network, or more precisely on the interconnected networks. The technological environment allows one to be simultaneously, concomitantly or successively, producer, consumer, transmitter, receptor, place of transmission and place of reception.

The conjunction of the set of functions of the interconnected networks such as the Internet has lead many authors to consider it a world-scale cybernetic space. "Cyberspace" appears much more decentralized than the services the cable television companies have in view. In itself, the Internet is an open network: one enters, leaves, transmits and receives information without any centralized control. Often access is gained from a local network. It contains a multitude of places of information transmission, of servers, while the models derived from cable television currently rest on the assumption of control and a clearly identifiable place at the head of the line of each cable network.

The Internet is a network of networks: all linked users can, with the appropriate computer equipment, offer services and content.[23] There can be no centralized control over those travelling in the network. Each Internet component is at once a place of reception and, potentially, of transmission. However, to enter the Internet, one must, in one way or another, link up with

---

22 André Martin, *Portrait d'ensemble de l'industrie de la télématique*, Québec, Ministère des communications, Direction de l'information électronique et de la télématique, February 1989 at 2; Yves Poullet and Claire Monville, *La demande finale en télématique - aspects juridiques* (Paris, La documentation française, 1988) at 27; Baum, Michael S. and Perritt Jr, Henry H., *Electronic Contracting, Publishing and EDI Law* (New York, John Wiley Sons Inc, 1991) 871 p.

23 Krol, Ed, *The Whole INTERNET-User's Guide and Catalog* (Sebastopol CA, O'Reilly & Associates Inc., 1992) 376 p.; Kehoe, Brendan P., *Zen and the Art of the INTERNET - A Beginner's Guide to the INTERNET* (Chester PA, 1992) 96 p. and appendices.

one of the many networks which are part of it. The network is in a way the doorway to this global environment.

In the Internet, control is performed at the component level, in other words, at the level of local networks, the link suppliers, those who have a certain possibility to monitor what passes to and from the network they control or over which they have some authority. At this level there can be various forms of supervision and verification of conformity of use and messages to the norms in effect in the *milieu* where the network is located.

In open networks, the effective control possibilities are in the hands of those who administrate the various sites between which interconnections exist or can exist. Network managers can determine if they must allow connections with sites which do not seem to respect certain rules.

3.3 RELATIONS BETWEEN USERS AND NETWORK MANAGERS

The third case concerns the relations between the users of local networks and the managers of these networks. Since network managers are the gatekeepers to open electronic environments, the relations they maintain with their users are the source of the emergence of certain norms and regulatory processes which could provide a balance between freedom of expression and the protection of human and other fundamental rights.

Given this situation, network managers seem like gatekeepers who are sometimes asked to become police officers in order to protect intellectual property rights and moral values. Their intervention can be based on explicitly formulated policies or on complaints judged legitimate. This brings into question the framework of their intervention and the limits which should be placed on their powers and prerogatives.

The regulations followed in this kind of context are often linked to the missions of the networks. They are designed for the ends of a company, or a research or teaching institution; or to further the goals of an enterprise. Network managers justify their intervention in the name of protecting the network's mission and also guaranteeing its integrity.

3.4 RELATIONS BETWEEN USERS

Finally, the fourth case has to do with relations between users. Familiarization with the Internet reveals that it is made up of communities of users which have their usages, rules of etiquette, understanding of what it permitted and what is unacceptable.[24] It might be supposed that rules of etiquette and proper usage emerge in order to facilitate harmonious relations between users. Informal communities can develop generally accepted rules

24 Henry H. Perritt Jr., "Dispute Resolution in Electronic Networks Communities" (1993) 38 *Villanova L.R.* at 349-401.

of conduct without any real legal intervention or government regulations, but this spontaneous emergence of norms occurs only under certain conditions. Among the most important is the existence of the prospect of continuing relationships.[25] Now, relations may be continued in certain situations, such as in networks of university researchers; they are much less stable in networks built around more evanescent or punctual interests.

Open networks bring together individuals who are isolated or who belong to different communities. Between them relationships are formed regulated by explicit contractual frameworks such as for commercial electronic data interchange (EDI) or for occasional transactions. Perritt also identifies another obstacle to the development of spontaneous rules among users. He writes that:

> "Participants in electronic network communities may have continuing relationships, but their relationships are unidimensional; they involve only a particular type of communication and no other important human activities. This unidimensionality greatly weakens the force of informal community. If a violator of network community norms gets expelled, he simply can connect to another network. (...)
>
> As the scope of networking increases, the likelihood that users will share values and feel membership to be essential decreases. This weakens the power of the social group to enforce its norms."[26]

This author notes that a network spreading over a municipality has greater difficulty developing and imposing a set of norms than a network uniting users who are part of a homogenous social group, like that of university researchers, where rules are easily generated which will be followed spontaneously by the participants without recourse to external forces.[27]

Thus, it is necessary to foresee the adaptation of rules regarding the relationships between the members of the communities in order to prevent or to resolve conflicts which may occur between users of open networks. In this respect, it is appropriate to situate the roles and responsibilities of those who take part in communication in open networks.

4. Roles and responsibilities

The identification of the roles assumed by the entities involved in open network communication permits a practical description of the legal situations in question. By identifying the roles played by the various actors,

25 Henry H. Perritt Jr., *op. cit.*
26 *Ibid.* at 360.
27 *Ibid.*

it is possible to better define their rights and responsibilities. At the same time, it becomes easier to determine or understand what they may and may not do.

Different types of deciding factors contribute to the production, processing and transportation of information. Depending on the diverse situations in which open-network communication occurs, these actors play different roles. Sometimes they even take on a number of roles. Thus, a user can become an information supplier or operate a public or semi-public forum for discussion. Such roles can occasionally be played by the system operator or even by the carrier.

In relation to present legislation on electronic media, such as television and radio, the open-network environment exhibits greater volatility of roles played by the main actors. In effect, the roles played in computer communications are highly interchangeable. It is no longer possible to formulate a set of rights and obligations for each role on the assumption that the roles played by the various participants in communication are always constant.

The goal and extent of the rights and responsibilities of the various actors in electronic communication does not depend so much on their official roles as on the degree of control and mastery they have or are thought to have over the information and communications taking place in the open networks or in the part of these networks over which they have some authority.[28] The degree of control exercised over what is transmitted over communications channels seems to be a main criterion for delimiting the rights and responsibilities of the actors.

In order to determine the extent of rights and to identify responsibilities in an environment like that of open networks, metaphors can be useful.[29] Using them helps to reveal the essence of the contexts in which communications occur and what actions agents perform in them. Metaphors allow us to situate the rights and obligations of actors by identifying their degree of control over messages and thus help us to determine the various levels of responsibility. The attribution of responsibility borrows a great deal from the regulations developed for situations analogous to open-network communications, such as railway transportation and the distribution of printed material. Three sorts of roles are played in an open-network environment, each of which has variants and can be combined with others,

---

28 Perritt Jr., Henry H., "Tort Liability, the First Amendment, and Equal Access to Electronic Network", (1992) 5 *Harvard Journal of Law & Technology* 65.

29 David R. Johnson & Kevin Marks, "Mapping Electronic Data Communications onto Existing Legal Metaphors: Should We Let our Conscience (and our Contracts) Be our Guide?" (1993) 38 *Villanova L. Rev.* 487; Henry H. Perritt, Jr., "Metaphors for Understanding Rights and Responsibilities in Networks Communities: Print Shops, Barons, Sheriffs, and Bureaucracies - Discussion Paper", Posted in "Information Law Papers", Villanova University Gopher Server, 24 p.

so that in certain situations a given entity may play more than one role. However, in open-network environments, there are invariably network operators, information suppliers, among which we find the users, and one or more information carriers. Let us examine, thus, the main facets of each of the principal roles.

4.1 CARRIERS

Carriers generally provide access to a telecommunications network which they sometimes control. Under present regulations, carriers provide access to the capacity to carry information under equitable conditions for all users in equivalent situations. In certain situations, the carrier may do more than simply provide access to a network. In fact, it often participates in billing and dividing the revenue generated: it then has a certain control over the contents transmitted.

Since the carrier sometimes uses some leadership when choosing the services distributed, we might ask about its responsibility regarding the contents carried, with respect to third parties and its service suppliers. It is precisely because the operation of certain networks gives carriers some say over the content carried that the issue of their responsibility in this respect sometimes comes up.[30]

It is well-known that telecommunications firms and cable television companies can act as carriers. Other companies can also play this role, particularly by renting certain facilities belonging to telecommunications or cable companies. The diversity of technological means reveals that information can be carried in many ways. Due to the multifariousness of telecommunications networks, electronic communication is only one of the types of communications made possible by the various networks.

In principle, telecommunications firms cannot regulate the content or influence the sense or goals of the telecommunications they carry for the public.[31] Most often, they limit themselves to providing transmission

---

30 Daniel Brenner, "Telephone Company Entry into Video Services: A First Amendment Analysis" (1991) 67 *Notre Dame L. Rev.* 97; Jerome A. Barron, "The Telco, the Common Carrier Model and the First Amendment - The "Dial-A-Porn" Precedent" (1993) 19 *Rutgers Computer & Technology Law Journal* 371; Patrick O'Neill, "Structural Implications of Telephone Content Regulation: Lessons from the Audiotex Controversy" (1991) 13 *Hastings Comm/Ent L. J.*. For French Law, see Jean Littingre, "La responsabilité de l'État français en qualité de transmetteur d'informations", in *La télématique, Actes du colloque organisé à Namur les 5 et 6 décembre 1983 par le Centre de Recherches Informatique et Droit des Facultés Notre-Dame de Namur* (Gand, Story Scientia, 1983) at 81-91. As for Québec law, not only must we deplore the rarity of work on law relating to telecommunications companies as such, we must also note the virtual non-existence of work on the responsibility of telecommunications companies for transmitted messages.

31 *Telecommunications Act*, L. C. 1993, c. 38, s. 36.

capacities in accordance with the conditions corresponding to requirements of equity and of being free of discriminatory practices.[32]

In contrast, the status of cable television companies is more ambiguous. In Canada, they are presently considered broadcast companies. Traditionally, they often had only a passive role as retransmitters of the signals of others. The capacities of today's coaxial cable networks have made it possible for cable companies to develop a number of services which are exclusively theirs, as well as to offer subscribers programming and other information services. They can also offer "interactive" services.

These multifaceted activities and services offered by cable television companies have earned them a hybrid status. For some of their activities, they are treated as broadcasters, with the consequences this implies. Most importantly, in this respect, they are responsible for the content they choose to carry. For other aspects of their activity, it could be judged more appropriate to treat cable companies in a way similar to telecommunications firms.

It is not inappropriate to liken the enterprise of carrying telematic communications to a newspaper or to consider it a telecommunicator. First, we ascribe a large degree of editorial freedom to them, leaving them complete liberty to choose the services they judge appropriate to transmit. However, if such companies are to be considered telecommunicators, they could be subject to stricter obligations regarding tariffs and access to their networks, such as the obligation to treat their subscribers and other clients in a non-discriminatory manner.[33] Clearly a whole range of intermediary positions can be imagined.

Thus, for the foreseeable future, the status of the carriers ranks high among the legal questions and uncertainties contributing to delaying the development of certain types of services.

4.2 NETWORK MANAGERS

Electronic communication is possible thanks to the establishment of connections between the various terminals of all those who wish to enter into communication: this is the idea of a network. Networks allow correspondents to be connected; these networks can themselves be

---

32 Michael H. Ryan, *Canadian Telecommunications Law and Regulation* (Toronto, Carswell, 1993) at 3-6 and ss.

33 Diane L. Hofbauer, ""Cableporn" and the First Amendment: Perspectives on Content Regulation of Cable Television", 35 Federal Communications Law Journal 139; Pierre Trudel and France Abran, *Un état des questions juridiques posées par l'avènement de la télématique grand public*, Report written for the Direction Générale des technologies de l'information, Ministère des communications du Québec, Montréal, Centre de recherche en droit public, July 1989, 70 p.

connected to other networks and give access to a great number of correspondents.

The network is the nerve centre of the virtual environment often called "cyberspace". It is both the entrance and the place where a certain form of control can be applied, which does not mean that such control is always practically possible or desirable. Network managers have thus a major role to play in regulating electronic communications.

Networks come in different sizes. For example, the Internet is composed of local networks (Local Area Networks (LAN)),[34] regional or metropolitan networks (Metropolitan Area Networks (MAN)) and wide area networks[35] on the scale of whole countries. The interconnection of all these networks creates a planet-wide virtual space. Network managers have, however, a degree of control over access and what comes through their networks to or from the exterior.

Networks can adopt information policies. Generally, these policies, which are sometimes made explicit in official documents or membership contracts signed by members and clients, are used by network managers to make clear their rules of conduct regarding issues such as:

- the privacy of electronic mail;
- the conditions under which software available on the network may be used;
- the obligation to use one's real name;
- the right to engage in commercial advertising;
- the right to use network resources for personal affairs;
- the responsibility for subscriber and client behaviour.

Doug Schuler[36] identifies the following issues which can be considered when establishing policies on access, use and content carried in a network. He writes that:

> "An information policy must anticipate and address questions and issues such as the following:
>
> How private is my e-mail?

34 Diane W. Savage explains that: "A LAN is a data communications facility that interconnects a number of data transmitting devices, like computers and terminals (these transmitting devices are frequently referred to as "nodes" and allows for the exchange of data". See: Diane W. Savage, "Law of the LAN" (1993) 9 *Computer & High Technology Journal* 193, 194.

35 Tracy Laquey, *The Internet Companion - A Beginner's Guide to Global Networking* (Reading Mass., Addison Wesley, 1993) at 21.

36 Doug Schuler, "Community Networks: Building a New Participatory Medium," (1994) 37/1 *Communications of the ACM* at 39.

Can you deny me access to the community network?

Can I post "adult material"?

Do I have to use my real name?

How can I register a complaint against a moderator?

I'm receiving abusive email. Can you put an end to it?

I'd like to use the network to advertise my product. Is that OK?

I have a commercial database service. Can you let people login to it?

The doctor in your question and answer forum gave you bad advice. I'm suing you!

Someone reprinted my posting in a magazine without my permission!

Somebody on your network posted stolen credit card numbers. We're confiscating your equipment!"

Schuler adds that these and many other questions reflect the various kinds of conflicts which can appear in a network, be it a community network, or a network dedicated to more specific ends. He notes that many of these questions have not yet found generally acceptable answers. Thus, the network manager is burdened with much of the task of delimiting conditions for access to the network and the establishment of measures meant to prevent and eventually aid conflict resolution.

The size of the responsibilities incumbent on the network manager depends in large part on the vocation of the network. Certain networks are defined uniquely as information carrying channels. Others consider themselves responsible for the content found in them.

In order to make it easier to determine the nature and intensity of the obligations of networks, recourse can be had to metaphors which permit us to situate them using analogies with known situations.

A network can be seen as a communication channel. It then plays a role similar to that of a telecommunications carrier. It offers transmission possibilities to others but has no control over the content carried. Its responsibility for information circulating in the network is thus minor. This is the situation of a telephone company which provides a telephone line by which harmful information could pass.

On the other end of the continuum, a network manager may assume responsibility for what is passing through the network it controls. This would be the situation of a network defining itself as a transmitter-editor: it behaves as if it had control over what is transmitted under its auspices.

For example, in October 1990, Prodigy announced new fees for messages sent by electronic mail through its network. A group of users posted a message on a network electronic bulletin board protesting these fees and calling for an advertiser boycott. Prodigy replied by prohibiting such messages on its network. It went so far as to interrupt the connection of protesters who had continued their campaign through other means.[37]

An intermediate metaphor is that of a library. Electronic networks are environments resembling libraries. A librarian might worry that certain books in the collection could be harmful, but he or she does not assume responsibility for the content of everything under his or her care. Yet the librarian's duty is to diligently remove all information designated harmful or in violation of the established rules when such information comes to his or her attention. This is the approach which was accepted in *Cubby v. Compuserve*.

In *Cubby v. Compuserve*,[38] the Compuserve network was sued as co-defendant in a libel action. This action resulted from information published in a electronic information letter titled "Rumorville USA". This information letter was published by a network subscriber who was in no other way linked with Compuserve. Judge Leisure exonerated Compuserve by noting that in this case,

> "Compuserve has no opportunity to review Rumorville's contents before DFA uploads it into Compuserve's computer banks, from which it is immediately available to approved CIS subscribers. Compuserve receives no part of any fees that DFA charges for access to Rumorville, nor does Compuserve compensate DFA for providing Rumorville to the Journalism Forum; the compensation Compuserve receives for making Rumorville available to its subscribers is the standard on-line time usage and membership fees charged to all CIS subscribers, regardless of the information services they use."[39]

In so far as Compuserve could have no knowledge of the harmful character of the information transmitted, it assumes no responsibility. However, when the network becomes aware of the damaging information it carries, it is incumbent on it to do what is necessary so that the information is removed. As Di Lello explains,

---

37 Edward V. Di Lello, "Functional Equivalency and Its Application to Freedom of Speech on Computer Bulletin Boards" (1993) 26 *Columbia Journal of Law and Social Problems* 199 at 207.

38 *Cubby Inc. v. Compuserve Inc.*, (1991) 776 *F. Supp.*, 135. See also: SASSAN, Anthony J., "Comparing Apples to Oranges: The Need for a New Media Classification (case note) *Cubby v. Compuserve Inc.*, 776 F. Supp 135 (S.D.N.Y. 1991)", (1992) 5 *Software Law Journal* 821.

39 *Ibid.* at 137.

> "Judge Peter K. Leisure applied the technique of "functional equivalency" to categorize an on-line information service and thus determine the legal standard applicable to it. The plaintiff in Cubby advanced a theory that Compuserve, an on-line information service that permits subscribers to access hundreds of different specialized databases, was a publisher rather than a distributor and therefore liable for any defamatory statements published. Judge Leisure determined, however, that defendant Compuserve is functionally equivalent to a news distributor, such as a bookstore, library or newsstand. Once that functional equivalency was established, relevant precedent led the court to the inevitable conclusion that Compuserve was not liable for defamatory statements that appeared in a database it offered to subscribers."[40]

Such an approach leads to the conclusion that the network manager's degree of responsibility is closely linked to the degree of control he has or is thought to have over the information transmitted or otherwise available on his network. This explains the crucial importance of the description of the role played by information suppliers.

4.3 INFORMATION SUPPLIERS

There are a number of types of information suppliers. Indeed, in open networks, everyone can become an information supplier. An individual with a computer and the appropriate software can send electronic mail to many people or set up an electronic bulletin board. It then becomes difficult to distinguish mass transmission from private correspondence.

Users as such are also information suppliers. Sometimes they undertake information transmission using lists or electronic mail. This is known as voluntary information supply. However in certain circumstances, users are involuntary information suppliers. Computer communication leaves traces. In effect, it is possible to keep and compile a journal of the connections and transactions performed by each user. In this sense, users, through their activity in the network, provide useful information for various ends pertaining to canvassing, monitoring, consumer profiling, etc.[41] A host of

---

40 Di Lello, *Loc. Cit.* at 210-211.

41 Flaherty, David H., *Telecommunications Privacy: A Report to the Canadian Radio-Television and Telecommunications Commission*, London, 1992, 140 p.; Cruse Jr., Rubin E., "Invasion of Privacy and Computer Matching Programs: A Different Perspective" (1992) 11 *Computer/Law Journal* 461; Kaplan, Marilyn R., "Commercial Speech and the Right to Privacy: Constitutional Implications of Regulating Unsolicited Telephone Calls" (1980) 15 *Columbia Journal of Law and Social Problems* 277; Groupe de recherche informatique et droit, *L'identité piratée* (Montréal, La Société québécoise d'information juridique, 1986).

points of information transmission and exchange are found in computer networks. Their designation as electronic bulletin boards provides an accurate description of their nature. Users connected to a network write information on them which then becomes available to all other users. Electronic bulletin boards, also called lists, are either open, accessible to all network users, or closed, with access available on invitation or under certain conditions.

In order to define the status of an electronic bulletin board, we must ask how closely the list operator supervises the information in the list. Referring to the criteria set out in the *Cubby* decision, the level of control or supervision used by those controlling the electronic bulletin board would be determining. In truth, it is difficult to exclude the responsibility of the electronic bulletin board operator when he has decisive power over the posting of messages. This approach allows the level of responsibility to be determined for those in charge of open lists, closed lists and other electronic bulletin boards. Their responsibility is closely linked to the degree of control they have over the information posted.

The way the law views communication situations depends on whether the message is transmitted to the general public or only exchanged between two interlocutors. The law treats private conversation differently from transmission of information to the public. Depending on the problems which arise, communicating messages by computer networks is compared to either telephone conversations, television services, or journals or magazines.

Written media, electronic media or private conversations?

There are major differences in the way the law views conversations, written publications, the use of radio frequencies, and communication over networks. This is why it is so important to determine the rules applicable to electronic bulletin boards. For the delimitation of their responsibilities, should information transmitters which are electronic bulletin boards be regulated by the principles applicable to printed media, electronic media, private conversation, or are they not in a category different from these three?

Common Law regulation: written media

Distributed written media are subject to the rules of editorial freedom. Printed matter may be published freely, constrained only as judged reasonable in democratic society. Editorial freedom is the form freedom of expression takes when it is applied to media as entities. The courts protect the editor's power to decide what to publish without state intervention.[42] *Gay Alliance Toward Equality v. Vancouver Sun*[43] is one of the few

---

42 *Reference re* Alberta Statutes (1938) R.C.S. 100.

43 (1979) 2 R.C.S. 435.

decisions which has dealt with editorial freedom in Canada. Martland J., writing for the majority, takes up a passage from the American decision in *Miami Herald Publishing Company v. Tornillo*,[44] which he considers useful in examining the essential elements of freedom of the press. From this he concludes that "The law has recognized the freedom of the press to propagate its views and ideas on any issue and to select the material which it publishes".

The status of written media is structured around principles of law applicable to all the other activities (common law): in principle, pre-publication censorship and authorization systems are excluded. The general principles of civil and criminal liability govern the activities of written media. These principles determine a set of prohibitions and prepare the rules of responsibility for distributed information.

If information suppliers were considered written media, their responsibility would be that implied by the principles applicable to written media. The general rules generated by civil and criminal law apply, or are intended to apply, to communications in the electronic networks. Legislation in most western countries evaluates messages by placing them in categories according to the context in which they are transmitted. For example, a pornographic message exchanged privately will not receive the same treatment as one shown on television at prime time.[45] These categories are often based on the interests and values which must be protected during information circulation: the law interprets messages depending on the interests and rights they are likely to affect.

The main rules of law relating to messages likely to be transmitted in open spaces such as networks have to do with:

- The integrity of the judicial process, in camera rules and bans on publication;
- Attacks on reputation (defamation);
- Threats to privacy;
- Contempt of court;
- General laws prohibiting the distribution of certain types of information: these laws vary in number depending on the country and may deal with extremely diverse matters;

---

44 418 U.S. 241 (1974).

45 Beall, Robert, "Developing a Coherent Approach to the Regulation of Computer Bulletin Boards" (1987) 7 *Computer/Law Journal* 499; Faucher, John D., "Let the Chips Fall Where They May: Choice of Law in Computer Bulletin Board Defamation Cases" (1993) 26 *U.C. Davis Law Review* 1045; GILBERT, Jonathan, "Computer Bulletin Board Operator Liability for User Misuse" (1985) 54 *Fordham Law Review* 439; Jassem, Harvey C., "Scrambling the Telephone: The FCC's Dial-A-Porn Regulations" (1988) *Communications and the Law* 3; Johnson, Deborah G., "The Public-Private Status of Transactions in Computer Networks" in *The Information Web: Ethical and Social Implications of Computer Networking*, Gould, Carol C. (Ed.) (Boulder CO, Westview Press, 1989) at 37-55.

- Obscenity;
- Hate propaganda;
- Distribution of discriminatory signs and symbols;
- Harassment;
- Unauthorized reproduction of copyrighted works.

These are only the principal domains in which there is law concerning the circulation of information possibly appearing in electronic sites. It goes without saying that there is not yet any systematic analysis of the way in which these sets of legal rules can or cannot be applied in environments like open networks.[46] The principle of liability implies that the person in control of the content always answers for what could be harmful or unlawful. In written media, the editor shoulders this responsibility. In exchange, he or she possesses editorial freedom: there is no obligation to publish what is submitted and no constraints can be applied in this sense.

Radio and television regulations

If we choose to classify electronic transmission sites as electronic media like radio and television, they would certainly be subject to obligations implied by common law, but also to certain more restrictive rules.

For example, radio companies are monitored and must conform to various principles and goals set out in the *Broadcasting Act*. These principles are added to the rules generated by common law. Among these principles is the principle of balance which has effects on many aspects of the activity of radio broadcasters. In particular, it is referred to in the rules on the treatment of debates on radio and television.[47]

The rarity of radio frequencies used for radio and television has traditionally justified the special treatment the law gives electronic media.[48] In Canada, the public nature of frequencies is invoked to justify stricter limits on freedom of expression in electronic media. International publications advocating freedom of expression recognize the possibility of different treatment for electronic media and the right of governments to subject access to radio frequency use to a system of prior authorization. Thus, the European Rights Agreement states that affirming freedom of

46 Many of the questions relating to media liability, especially criminal liability, are treated in: Robert Martin and G. Stuart Adam, *A Sourcebook of Canadian Media Law* (Ottawa, Carleton University Press, 1989); Nicole Vallieres and Florian Sauvageau, *Droit et journalisme au Québec* (Montréal, Édi-GRIC-FPJQ, 1981); Clare F. Beckton, *The Law and the Media in Canada* (Toronto, Carswell, 1982); Michael G. Crawford, *The Journalist's Legal Guide*, (Toronto, Carswell, 1986); Pierre Trudel, *Droit de l'information et de la communication, Notes et documents* (Montréal, Éditions Thémis, 1984).

47 Trudel and Abran, Droit de la radio et de la télévision, supra, c. 9.

48 Pierre Trudel and France ABRAN, "Le caractère public des fréquences comme limite à la liberté d'expression", forthcoming in (1994) *Media and Communications L. R.*, May 1994.

expression does not prevent a state from subjecting radio broadcasting companies to a system of authorization. The system established must, however, respect freedom of expression.[49]

In the United States, it is accepted that radio and television media, due to their special natures, can be considered differently from the other media regarding constitutional guarantees of freedom of expression.[50] The rarity of radio broadcasting frequencies has been the main subject of judicial reasoning which has concluded that the regulation of radio broadcasting was in accordance with the guarantees of the First Amendment. In Canada, this argument is sometimes used, even though the courts have never had the occasion to examine it. However, the history of Canadian radio broadcasting regulation is such that its justification is not rooted merely in the rarity of frequencies: the need to ensure the protection of national sovereignty has been identified as the principal motive for state intervention in this matter.[51] In any case, the status of electronic media is noticeably different from that of written media. We must ask ourselves whether electronic information transmission sites should be classified with radio broadcasting media or made subject to law governing written publications. To answer this question,

---

49 François Jongen, "La liberté d'expression dans l'audiovisuel: liberté limitée, organisée et surveillée" [1993] *Rev. trim.dr.h.* 95-117; Maguelonne DEJEANT-PONS, "La jurisprudence en matière de liberté d'expression audiovisuelle dans le cadre de la Convention européenne des droits de l'homme" in Charles DEBBASCH and Claude Gueydan, *La régulation de la liberté de la communication audiovisuelle*, (Paris, Économica, Presses universitaires d'Aix-Marseille, 1991) 285-328; Albert Namurois, "Aspects du droit de la radio et de la télévision dans le monde, en rapport avec la liberté d'expression" (May 1980) 27 *Études de radio télévision* 1-12; Marc Fallon, "La radio et la télévision face au juge européen" (1987) 47 *Annales de droit de Louvain* 153; Sydney W. Head, *World Broadcasting Systems - A Comparative Analysis* (Belmont, Wadsworth, 1985) at 377 and ss.; Donald R. Browne, *Comparing Broadcast Systems* (Ames, Iowa State University Press, 1989).

50 In order to better distinguish the nature and scope of certain rights henceforth guaranteed in constitutional texts, recourse to American analyses and precedents can prove very useful. It is clear these precedents have no binding value in Canadian law; American legislation is often noticeably different from that in Canada. Thus, these precedents are never used to prescribe what is or what should be. They are mainly used as indications of the way in which fundamental rights with a supra-legal value are defined. In *R. v. Keegstra*, (1990) 3 R.C.S. 697, the Supreme Court indicates the degree to which it is sound to have recourse to American precedents. Dickson C. J. (such was his office at the time) notes that:
In the United States, a collection of fundamental rights has been constitutionally protected for over two hundred years. The resulting practical and theoretical experience is immense, and should not be overlooked by Canadian courts. On the other hand, we must examine American constitutional law with a critical eye,...
Madam Justice L'Heureux-Dubé, in the *Comité pour la République du Canada v. Canada* decision (1991) 1 R.C.S. 139, writes that "it may be helpful here to look at the American experience, not with a view to applying their decisions blindly but rather to learn from the process through which they were derived".

51 Trudel and Abran, "Le caractère public des fréquences comme limite à la liberté d'expression", *supra.*

we must analyze the characteristics of these environments and determine the degree to which the traditional justifications for radio and television regulation hold for these new media.

Private conversations

Conversation essentially supposes a private relationship desired by all participants. It almost completely escapes the law. Except for rules of etiquette which almost always escape the control of state laws, there is not really any specific legal supervision of conversation. When it takes place over telecommunications networks, conversation is even protected from certain kinds of intrusion.

The study of the legal status of conversation and, by extension, correspondence, supposes special attention be paid to the notion of privacy.[52] There is, in effect, a set of information which, in given circumstances, is included in the protected domain of private life. This set is delimited by the requirements imposed on it by the exercise of other rights and freedoms, such as freedom of expression. These requirements result in limitations on the right to privacy.[53]

In private correspondence, it appears normal to accept *a priori* that the principle of the right to respect for privacy is opposed to intrusions and monitoring practices. Article 36 of the Québec Civil Code states moreover that:

> "36. The following acts, in particular, can be considered as invasions of the privacy of a person:
>
> [...]
>
> (2) intentionally intercepting or using his private communications;

52 Steven Winters, "The New Privacy Interest: Electronic Mail in the Workplace" (1993) 8 *High Technology L.J.* 197.

53 Patrick A. Molinari and Pierre Trudel, "Le droit au respect de l'honneur, de la réputation et de la vie privée: Aspects généraux et applications", in: Formation permanente, Barreau du Québec, *Application des chartes des droits et libertés en matière civile* (Cowansville, Yvon Blais, 1988) at 197-231. Pierre Trudel and France Abran (eds.), *Droit du public à l'information et vie privée: deux droits irréconciliables?* (Montréal, Éditions Thémis) 208 p.; Pierre Trudel, "La protection de la vie privée et de l'image aux États-Unis" in Institut de Formation Continue du Barreau de Paris, *Liberté de presse, respect de la vie privée et de l'image en droit comparé*, Supplement to the *Gazette du palais*, (1992) at 14-24; Pierre Trudel, "Des données informatiques personnelles aux données informatiques génétiques" in B. Knoppers, L. Cadiet, C. M. Laberge, *La génétique humaine: de l'information à l'informatisation* (Paris, Litec, 1992) at 355-366. Undoubtably *R. v. Dyment* (1988) 2 R.C.S. 417 provides the most detailed statement of the degree of protection privacy has under our constitutional law. In this case, La Forest J. asserts the existence of the right to privacy concerning information, not only regarding a citizen's right to oppose physical intrusion into his or her domicile or physical attacks on his or her person, but also the right to protect his or her dignity.

(3) appropriating or using his image or voice while he is in private premises;

(4) keeping his private life under observation by any means;

[...]

(6) using his correspondence, manuscripts or other personal documents."

In compensation, the carrier or network operator shall not be held responsible for harm which could eventually result from the circulation of information in private conversations. Responsibility for this information logically falls only on those who decide to transmit it. Yet, not all network operators follow the practices implied by this point of view. For example, in the United States employers are accorded certain rights to search the personal effects of employees, including electronic mail.[54]

Thus network operators who consider they need no defined grounds to have the authority to search the electronic mail of anyone linked to their network make themselves subject to a more rigorous standard of responsibility: they could logically be held liable for harm caused by information they have given themselves the right to monitor. Harassment is another issue related to the right to privacy. Given the approaches developed regarding unsolicited telephone calls, we can see that using electronic mail to harass people, to send them offensive or aggressive messages, makes liable the person responsible for such actions.

A mixture of written media, electronic media and conversation

The law relating to information circulation has traditionally given distinct treatment to situations of public distribution and situations similar to private conversations. General public computer network communication generates situations which belong to conversation and distribution. To varying degrees, they possess characteristics found in many legal situations. When we look over the standards from which the responsibility of information suppliers can be determined, we quickly see the mixed nature of their status in relation to traditional legal categories. Is their activity conversation or mass distribution?

In an environment of open networks, roles are less clearly defined: carriers, network controllers and information suppliers can all play, under specific circumstances, different roles from those they normally play.

All participants in information exchanges in open networks play different roles depending on the circumstances. In order to determine the roles and responsibilities of these actors, we must determine what they do.

54 Winters, *loc. cit.*

The greater their degree of control over the information, the greater their responsibility for harmful information or information with criminal implications. Thus we have the question of whether the information supplier's liability is strict. What control can this supplier exercise, what control did he or she usually exercise and what control would a reasonable person consider appropriate?

Given this model for determining the responsibility of the actors, we must now determine what sorts of obligations must be imposed on them and, most importantly, how. Finally, the appropriate conflict-resolution techniques must be identified.

5. Conclusion

The need to protect fundamental rights and the essential values of respect for human dignity does not disappear with the coming of open information networks. This also applies to the reasons whiy is judged necessary to regulate behaviour. Thus, we must leave behind the simple view that only market forces can provide regulation in this virtual universe. Since these environments are by nature world-wide, they cannot be mastered using reflexes derived from traditional legal approaches. Even less effective is an examination using only an approach strictly describing the rules of law.

The protection of rights and values in open environments requires a systematic analysis of the reasons for controlling the circulation of certain information and a rigorous examination of possible or foreseeable protection techniques.

Beyond the difficulties in conceiving mechanisms for prevention and conflict arbitration, it must be recognized that in some circumstances the circulation of information can cause harm and conflict. Conflicts can be resolved by following three models of rule design and application which Perritt identifies in the following way:

- an authoritarian model, in which a supplier of network services, like a corporate employer, Compuserve or WESTLAW, sets rules for access and use unilaterally;
- a democratic model, in which a voluntary association of networks users, bulletin board operators or trade association members sets rules through informal social norms or more formally through multiparty agreements; and
- a formal legal model, in which contract offers and acceptances, tort law duties, legislative statutes and administrative agency regulations define acceptable conduct.[55]

---

55 Henry H. Perritt Jr., "Dispute Resolution in Electronic Networks Communities" (1993) 38 *Villanova L.R.* 349 at 354.

Of course, these different models are inter-related. They never exist in pure form. Rules defined by private bodies and groups are themselves ultimately subject to the relevant law of the state.

The imputation of liability for the consequences of transmitting harmful information will continue to be the principal regulating mechanism. However, in order to ascribe responsibility to a body, one must be able to identify the actors controlling the information in the various places in this virtual environment. Certainly, it is impossible to completely suppress information circulation, and those participating in open networks can always look elsewhere for information with restricted or prohibited circulation. However, they assume responsibility for the distribution of such information within national boundaries.

In the name of this responsibility, network operators and other actors with some control over information will no doubt find it useful to adopt rules of conduct which they will attempt to impose on their partners. It is high time we began analyzing the processes of emergence and application of these self-generated norms of conduct, rather than continuing to repeat that non-government norms have no legal force. We cannot both note the relative inability of state regulation to achieve the balances necessary in open environments and refuse to better understand the alternative regulatory mechanisms, mechanisms which cannot be confounded with simple codes of accommodation or an "ethic" of respectability.